THE MAKERS OF CHRISTENDOM
General Editor: CHRISTOPHER DAWSON

THE LIVES OF ANGE DE JOYEUSE
AND BENET CANFIELD

THE MAKERS OF CHRISTENDOM

General Editor: CHRISTOPHER DAWSON

The
Lives of Ange de Joyeuse and Benet Canfield

by

JACQUES BROUSSE

*Edited from Robert Rookwood's
translation of* 1623

by

T. A. BIRRELL

SHEED AND WARD

LONDON AND NEW YORK

FIRST PUBLISHED 1959
BY SHEED AND WARD LTD.
33 MAIDEN LANE
LONDON, W.C.2
AND
SHEED AND WARD INC.
840 BROADWAY
NEW YORK, 3

Made and printed in
Great Britain by
FLETCHER AND SON LTD NORWICH AND
THE LEIGHTON-STRAKER BOOKBINDING CO LTD LONDON

CONTENTS

	Page
INTRODUCTION	vii
BIBLIOGRAPHICAL NOTES	xxxii
THE LIFE OF THE REVEREND FATHER ANGEL . .	1
THE MIRACULOUS LIFE, CONVERSION AND CONVERSATION OF THE REVEREND FATHER BENET OF CANFIELD .	87
INDEX	177

INTRODUCTION

THE QUALITY OF THE TWO BIOGRAPHIES

IN 1621 Jacques Brousse[1] published at Paris *La Vie du Révérend Père Angel de Joyeuse, Prédicateur Capucin, autrefois Duc, Pair, et Maréchal de France, et Gouverneur pour le Roi en Languedoc, Ensemble les Vies des RR.PP.P. Benoist et P. Archange Escossois, du même Ordre*; and in 1623 a translation was published by an English secular priest, Robert Rookwood.[2] Brousse in fact wrote only two of the lives himself, those of Angel de Joyeuse and Benet of Canfield, and it is those two which are reprinted here.

They certainly suffer considerably from the common failings of Baroque hagiography. Edification comes before information, and sighs and tears and pious ejaculations occur with rather monotonous regularity. The life of Fr. Angel suffers particularly in this respect; Brousse omits a great deal of important biographical

[1] Jacques Brousse (1590-1673) was a Doctor of Theology at Paris and canon of S. Honoré (the connexion with S. Honoré perhaps explains his interest in the Capuchins). He seems to have been involved in the Jansenist troubles and was suspended for some time on account of a sermon on Grace. In 1651 he went to Rome with Saint Amour and Lalane as a deputy of Arnauld in the case of the condemnation of the celebrated "Five Propositions" of Jansenius. Brousse did not, however, display the intransigence of his two companions and returned from Rome on the plea of ill-health in March 1652, without having played any large part in the negotiations. He seems to have been really far more of a Gallican than a Jansenist. (*Journal of Monsr. de Saint Amour*, trans. G. Havers, London, 1664, pp. 141-5, 167; *Dict. de Biog. Française*, Paris, 1954, fasc. xxxviii, p. 451.)

[2] Robert Rookwood (1588-1668), son of Edward Rookwood of Euston, Co. Suffolk, Esq., by Elizabeth, daughter of William Brown of Elsing, Co. Norfolk, Esq., younger brother of Antony, first Viscount Montagu. At the age of twenty-eight he decided to go to the Continent to study for the priesthood. On attempting to leave the country he was captured and imprisoned, but eventually escaped and made his way to St. Omers, where he studied for three years. He went from thence to the English College, Rome, where he was admitted on 3 October 1620. He was ordained a year later and remained at the College till 1626, when he left to become chaplain to the English nuns at Gravelines (where his sister Elizabeth was professed). In 1648 a group of the nuns left Gravelines to make a new foundation at Rouen, and Rookwood went with them as their chaplain and remained at Rouen till his death. (Cf. A. F. Allison, "Franciscan Books in English 1559-1640", *Biographical Studies*, iii, i (1955), p. 49; *Catholic Record Society*, vol. xiv (1914), p. 167; H. Foley, *Records of the English Province S.J.*, vol. i, p. 198; vol. iii, pp. 785-8; vol. vi, p. 294.)

information, glosses over awkward details,[1] and substitutes lengthy extracts from Fr. Angel's unpublished sermons, to which he evidently had access. Brousse may be excused for omitting a great deal of historical background that is essential for the modern reader, since the readers of his own time scarcely needed reminding of the Wars of the League; but it is unfortunate that he has neglected to give any precise and detailed account of Fr. Angel's activities after his return to the cloister. But so far as it goes, Brousse's life of Fr. Angel is considerably more reliable, at least, than J. de Caillère's *vie romancée* published in 1668 as *Le Courtisan prédestiné* and frequently reprinted and translated in various forms right down to the present century.

Brousse's life of Fr. Benet of Canfield will be found more satisfying, however, by the modern reader. It has the advantage, in the first place, of containing Fr. Benet's own account of his conversion. But in the rest of the narrative there is an amount of first-hand detail that is lacking in the life of Fr. Angel. Brousse tells us that he owes a great deal to the recollections of an Irish Capuchin, Peter Edwards, who knew Fr. Benet personally.[2]

A modern translation of Brousse would only make more awkward the discrepancy between the modern and Baroque biographical styles. It has therefore been thought better to reproduce in this volume the English translation of 1623 to give the modern reader something of the full and undiluted flavour of the original.[3] To appreciate fully the glamour of the French Capuchins in the seventeenth century needs not a little of the Baroque spirit; and besides conveying something of that, Fr. Rookwood's translation is a useful reminder that the English Recusants of the seventeenth century were not unaware of the main spiritual currents of the age. Mr. Aldous Huxley's *Grey Eminence* was the rediscovery of a

---

[1] Especially the question of exclaustration: see p. xiv.

[2] But certain dates and details are clearly wrong (see pp. 147, 150); nor are they corrected in the English translation.

[3] The translation is on the whole very free. It is clear that the translator had no special knowledge either of Fr. Angel or of Fr. Benet, for he takes over the errors of the original. There is one considerable omission, viz. pp. 596-7 of the French text, which refers to attacks on Fr. Benet's mystical teaching after his death. In the text reproduced in this volume we have modernized spelling and punctuation throughout, and in one or two places straightened out obvious muddles.

spiritual atmosphere that had been forgotten, but not unknown, in England.

The Capuchins and the National Background

In the brief editorial introductions which follow, there has been a conscious and constant compromise between too little and too much of the historical background. The establishment of the Capuchins in France in 1574 is inseparably bound up with the history of the last Wars of the League; the early French Capuchins had to establish themselves against a national background of political and social chaos.

Any generalizations concerning what the Wars of the League were about are certain to be untrue. But by the time Henri III ascended the throne in 1574 the conflict was far from being a clear-cut issue between Catholics and Protestants. It is not even wholly accurate to speak of three parties: (1) the League = the Guises = pro-Spanish policy = Catholicism; (2) Henry of Navarre = Huguenots = anti-Spanish policy; (3) the *politiques* or royalists = anti-Spanish policy = legitimism = peace and toleration. In fact, the League and its opponents stood for different things at different times and in different places. Personal, dynastic, regional and international rivalries all played their parts in the so-called "Wars of Religion".

The Capuchins were established in France under the patronage of Catherine de Médicis (the mother of Henri III), of the Cardinal of Lorraine, and of the Cardinal Charles de Bourbon (who was to become the League candidate for the throne of France). In addition to this, King Henri III was not only a close friend of many of the first recruits to the new province and of the second Provincial, Bernard d'Osimo, but also himself received the Capuchin habit as a tertiary on 8 December 1585. Furthermore, since a great number of the recruits to the order at that period were men of outstanding political and social significance, it is hardly to be wondered at that the order found itself inevitably caught up in the progress of political events. What must be stressed, however, is that it is very misleading and inaccurate to speak as if there were one simple and single "Capuchin policy" throughout the period with which we are dealing. The tensions of the political world outside were in fact reflected within the order itself; and it was chiefly due to the prudence of the first provincials that there was no irrevocable split in the young French Capuchin Province in the early years of its existence.

FATHER ANGEL DE JOYEUSE

Henri de Joyeuse (later in religion to be Fr. Angel de Joyeuse) was born in 1563, the third son of William de Joyeuse (1520-92), Lieutenant-General for the King in Languedoc, and his wife Marie de Batarnay. The life of Henri de Joyeuse is to a great extent bound up with the position of his family. His eldest brother Anne, later Baron d'Arques, was a solid extrovert, enjoying equally the pleasures of the Court or the excitements of the battlefield. The second brother, François, later Cardinal Protector of France, was a talented, persistent and courageous ecclesiastical diplomat. The younger brothers, Antoine-Scipio and Claude, followed the military traditions of their father and elder brother. The family as a whole, "Les Messieurs de Joyeuse", represented something very precious to Henri III, the last of the Valois. They were loyal to the throne and to the legitimist principle, capable of military or civil command, staunch Catholics, and good courtiers without being involved in courtly intrigue. Such families were rare in France and their rise to power and influence was hardly surprising.

The family home was at Couiza, in Languedoc. The religious differences in the province were most acute and bitter. Toulouse, the capital, was fanatically Catholic, but the region contained some of the most important Huguenot strongholds, and throughout the period with which we are dealing there existed an almost constant state of civil war.

Little is known of the childhood of Henri, except that at one time he expressed a wish to join the house of the Conventual Franciscans at Toulouse. Then, in 1577, he went off to Paris to join his two elder brothers at the College of Navarre, the then fashionable college for the education of the ruling class. His mentor there, so Brousse tells us, was Jean Guyon, Doctor of the Sorbonne; but it must not be forgotten that there were also on the staff such men as John Hamilton, the emigré Scottish priest and fanatical Leaguer.[1]

From the College of Navarre the three brothers joined the circle of *mignons* of Henri III. In 1579 Henri de Joyeuse was appointed Grand Master of the Royal Wardrobe and the same year, at the age of sixteen and a half, commanded a troop of light horse at the siege of La Fère. The following years saw the rapid rise of the three brothers. In September 1581 Anne was married to Marguerite de Vaudément, half-sister of the Queen, and two months later Henri married Mlle. de Lavalette, sister of the Duke of Épernon. In 1582 François became Archbishop of Narbonne and the following year his brother Anne secured for him the cardinal's hat at Rome. In 1585 Henri, as Governor of Anjou, besieged the troops of Condé at Angers and took the town without a blow, a victory that brought with it further honours and responsibilities, including the governorship of Touraine, Maine and Perche.

When not engaged in his campaigns, Henri de Joyeuse lived with his wife in Paris in the Faubourg Saint-Honoré; the garden of their house adjoined the Capuchin convent, which in its turn adjoined the Tuileries.[2] A daughter, Henriette-Catherine, was born of the marriage. Unlike his brother Anne, it was quite clear that Henri did not take easily to the life of courtier, soldier and governor. Though he was a close friend of Henri III it was probably that very characteristic of unworldliness which so attracted the King to him. Be that as it may, after the death of his wife in August 1587, Henri de Joyeuse delayed only a month to arrange his affairs and provide for the care of his daughter before he took the step of entering the Capuchins on 10 September. The dramatic move certainly surprised and dismayed the King. After trying in vain to induce Henri (now Brother Angel) to alter his decision, the King succeeded in persuading the Capuchin Provincial to allow Angel

---

[1] See Francisque-Michel, *Les Ecossais en France*, London, 1862, vol. ii, p. 119; Sir David Dalrymple, *A Sketch of the Life of John Hamilton, a Secular Priest* (British Museum, G. 5399/5); and *DNB*.

[2] *Études franciscaines*, vol. 39 (1927), p. 420.

to do his novitiate at the Paris house. October brought a fresh blow for Henri III with the death of Anne and Claude de Joyeuse at the Battle of Coutras. It was left to the young Antoine-Scipio to uphold the military traditions of the family.

Br. Angel's novitiate was not to be a peaceful one. In the following year Henri of Guise entered Paris as head of the League; the mob was whipped up against the royal house and on 12 May, "the Day of the Barricades", the King said farewell to the Capuchins of the Rue Saint-Honoré and fled by night from his capital to Chartres. A week later a curious procession wound its way from Paris to the doorway of Chartres Cathedral, where Henri III was hearing Vespers. The procession was led by Angel de Joyeuse bearing on his back a large wooden cross. After him followed the Capuchins of the Rue Saint-Honoré and a body of other priests and laymen from the city, forming a tableau of the Passion. The aristocratic De Thou ridicules this episode and most other historians follow him; but none of them really explains what was its object. Though many in the procession may have been Leaguers, it can hardly have been an explicitly League move. Was it to induce the King to return to Paris, or at least to patch up things with the Guise? Was it an act of reparation to the King for the insult and indignity which he had suffered? Or was it perhaps a spontaneous gesture with no specific underlying purpose—simply a dramatic testimony to the sense of inexorable tragedy which had overtaken the country? Whatever the Paris mob might do, no one of any sense was deceived into thinking that Henri of Guise was acting out of anything but ambition for himself and his house; and the Committee of Sixteen, which welcomed him in, was a curious combination of religious fanaticism and *petit-bourgeois* rascality. It was difficult for men of good will to see what was best for the Church, for France, and for the monarchy.

Br. Angel had been a year in the Capuchin novitiate, and it was time for his profession. On 18 August 1588 he made his will at Chartres, where it was witnessed by the King himself.[1] On 14 September Br. Angel was professed. Three months later he found himself once more caught up in national affairs.

---

[1] *Études franciscaines*, vol. 6 (1901), pp. 630 sq.

Henri III had not returned to his capital, but had convened the Estates General at Blois. Proceedings became protracted and the King determined to put an end to the Estates by a *coup d'état*. On 23 December Henri of Guise was murdered in the corridors of the royal palace of Blois; his brother the Cardinal of Guise was imprisoned and murdered the following day; and the aged Cardinal de Bourbon, the Guise and League candidate for the throne, was imprisoned.

The loyalty of the Joyeuses was put to a severe test. At Rome the young Cardinal François did his best to defend the King in face of the anger of Pope Sixtus V; at Blois Br. Angel, together with the Capuchin Provincial Bernard d'Osimo, did their best to smooth things over with the Papal Nuncio Morosoni. But the situation was very difficult, since the King was *ipso facto* excommunicate for his part in the assassination of the Cardinal of Guise. Br. Angel must have been relieved when he was sent to Italy in March of 1589; he was in Venice when Henri III was himself assassinated on 1 August of the same year.

Before he died Henri III had nominated as his successor Henri of Navarre, who was still a Protestant. But though Henri of Navarre might now be Henri IV, he still had to fight for his kingdom. As for the League, its tone and *raison d'être* change. With the Guises out of the way, it could now be simply represented as a body which refused to recognize a Protestant monarch. It is really only from this period onwards that the Joyeuses can with truth be called "ardent Leaguers".

By 1591 Angel was ordained and back in France. His father died in January 1592 and the brunt of the fighting in Languedoc fell on his brother Antoine-Scipio. In October Angel was in Toulouse with his brother the Cardinal when, on the 19th, the news came of the disastrous Battle of Villemur and the death of Antoine-Scipio on the battlefield. The events of the next few days require detailed consideration.

The townspeople of Toulouse, by nature volatile and hysterical, were deeply shocked. The victorious Huguenot army was only twenty miles away, and the Toulousains had lost their chief military leader in the battle. They turned instinctively to the survivors of the family for help. At first they demanded that the Cardinal de Joyeuse should assume the marshalate and lieutenant-governorship, but he declined on grounds of inexperience. They next insisted on Fr. Angel—and with more reason, for he had had some experience of military and civil administration. At this point the pious hagiographers of the seventeenth century usually devote some space to the tears and protestations of Fr. Angel. A modern Capuchin historian however, Fr. Agathange de Paris,[1] who has studied this episode in detail, points out that the main issue of conscience for Fr. Angel was simply whether or not he could canonically do what the Toulousains asked of him; there is no reliable record of his refusal.

Things had to be done quickly, and it seems clear that Cardinal François was the guiding spirit in organizing the situation. On 21 October an ecclesiastical commission was formed of nineteen of the leading theologians and lawyers of Toulouse. After deliberating from 7 a.m. till 2 p.m. they decided that, in view of the exceptional circumstances, Fr. Angel might leave his convent to accept the governorship of Languedoc. After the decision was reached, the commission, together with the clergy, nobility and mayor and corporation of Toulouse, went to the Capuchin convent to ask Fr. Angel to accept. The crowd, with characteristic Toulousain Catholic zeal, threatened to burn down the convent if the Guardian did not allow Fr. Angel to accede to their wishes. The Guardian, who was sick at the time, consulted with the community and eventually agreed to allow Fr. Angel to go. As for Fr. Angel himself, he left the convent calmly and stated to the magistrates that "he was happy to devote his blood and his life for the preservation and defence of the Catholic religion". He made only one condition: that if the Pope did not agree, he would return at once to the religious life, whatever the cost.

Fr. Angel then put off the Capuchin habit and appeared at the Archbishop's Palace dressed in black in mourning for his brother Antoine-Scipio, and he was clothed with the sword of office in the Cathedral by his brother the Cardinal. On 23 October he took the

---

[1] This account is chiefly based on his book *Un Cas de Jurisprudence Pontificale*, Assisi, 1936.

oath as Governor of the province before the Parlement of Toulouse and in November he was confirmed in his appointment by the Duke of Mayenne, Lieutenant-General of the State and Crown of France.[1] Meanwhile the Capuchin Guardian at Toulouse had reported events to the Minister-General and the Commissary-Provincial of the order. The latter replied affirmatively from Carcassonne on 27 October, i.e., by return courier.

Reference to Rome on the question was not so speedy. On 15 November the then Pope, Clement VIII, sent Angel a brief of condolences on the death of his brother, but made no mention of Fr. Angel's new situation, about which he must surely have known. Eventually, in January 1593, the Estates of Toulouse decided to send to Rome William of Maran, Regent in Law and Rector of the University of Toulouse, to solicit the Pope's official sanction. On his journey by sea, however, Maran was captured by the Barbary corsairs and had to be ransomed by the Estates and compensated for the inconvenience which he had suffered. In the summer of the same year the Pope had taken more or less official notice of the situation via the Cardinal Nephew, Aldobrandini, and had given at least provisional and verbal assent. Then, in November, the Estates requested Cardinal François de Joyeuse to recommend someone to go with him to present the case at Rome; he chose the Bishop of Lavaur, and together they arrived in Rome on 25 January 1594. The following June the papal brief of Clement VIII was issued, *Perpetua Nobilis Familiae Vestrae*, which regularized Fr. Angel's position. By this he was exclaustrated and transferred to the company of the priest chaplains of the Order of Malta. In supplementary briefs of 5 May 1595 (*Superiori Anno*) and 18 September 1596 (*Iampridem*), the terms of his exclaustration were widened to cover the governorship and administration of any province whatsoever, and the acceptance and use of honours, titles and goods despite his vow of poverty.[2]

[1] See Agathange de Paris, *op. cit.*, ch. v. Mayenne's letter of appointment makes Fr. Angel share the governorship equally with Cardinal François. In fact, from January to November 1593 Angel managed the military and François the civil side, but after November 1593 François was at Rome. To make the situation even more complex, since his profession in September 1588 Angel was civilly dead, so that he could not really in law be appointed to anything.

[2] cf. *Bullarium Capuccinum*, vol. v, pp. 31-3.

To sum up this episode, it should be first of all pointed out that Fr. Angel was never dispensed from his vow of chastity. It is certainly probable that Cardinal François wished for such a dispensation for Angel since, with the deaths of the other brothers, there were no male heirs to the family. All that the people of Toulouse wanted was for Fr. Angel to command the armies of Languedoc, and they had no special wishes as to what form his exclaustration should assume. The Joyeuse family had previously received papal dispensation from vows, and quite recently at that: Fr. Angel's father had been Bishop of Alet, and his younger brother Antoine-Scipio had been Grand Prior of the Order of St. John of Jerusalem; the latter was permitted to be absolved from his vow of chastity but died before he had an heir. However, not only was Fr. Angel, throughout this whole period, never absolved from his vow of chastity, he was moreover never strictly speaking secularized; his transference to the Order of Malta clearly indicates that. He was exclaustrated from the Capuchins to meet a particular and almost unique situation, but he remained always a religious.

The thread of national events must now be resumed. In October 1592, Henri IV sent a mission to Rome under Cardinal Gondi to treat with the Pope for a possible reconciliation. The mission was badly received and it was clear that the Pope still had hopes of the League. In May 1593, despite the previous papal rebuff, the King announced his desire to return to the Catholic Church, and on 25 July made his canonical abjuration at Saint-Denis. Once more, in November, he sent an embassy to Rome but it returned again in January of the following year without the papal absolution; the Pope was still playing a waiting game. Again the King tried to force the Pope's hand, and had himself crowned at Chartres on 27 February 1594. The move was a sound one, for it appealed to the inborn Gallicanism of every French Catholic. Moreover, the moderate Leaguers were becoming more and more uneasy at the prospect of increased Spanish interference and the possibility of the Infanta on the French throne. The League under Mayenne was becoming a Rump. In March the King entered Paris; it was now no longer a question *if* the League would capitulate, but when, and on what terms. The object was now to make it quite clear to Henri IV that he must honour his promises to the Catholics.

The game was therefore one of *finesse*; this must be realized if Angel's subsequent actions are to be understood. At the end of December 1594 Angel began negotiations with De Vic, the King's representative, and a truce in Languedoc was agreed upon. The negotiations dragged on, however, and it seemed clear that Angel's demand for a Catholic preponderance in Languedoc would not be granted. He then took a course of action that has been much discussed. On 11 April 1595 he broke the truce (unilaterally, as we should say), seized the Capitol at Toulouse and, embarking on a lightning military campaign, retook a number of important towns evacuated by the King's troops. Ventadour, the king's general, commenced counter-operations. Then, on 17 September, Clement VIII issued his absolution of Henri IV. On 23 September Angel asked the King for a three months' truce; on 4 December he was reconciled to the King. Early the following year, on 22 January 1596, by the Treaty of Folembray, the King appointed Fr. Angel de Joyeuse Lieutenant-Governor of Languedoc and Marshal of France and commenced to shower compliments, honours and riches on his erstwhile troublesome subject.

Why did Fr. Angel break the truce with De Vic? Was it aristocratic bad temper or a desire for personal aggrandisement?—he certainly got a lot out of Henri IV. A consideration of the sequence of events makes it seem much more likely that the whole thing was a put-up job. Fr. Angel must surely have known from his brother François at Rome that the papal absolution for the King would not be long forthcoming. When he broke the truce and took the offensive in April it was not in the expectation of a long campaign; and he sued for a resumption of the truce only a week after the papal absolution. As for the gifts and the honours, there can have been few illusions on either side about that. The King was not dealing with Angel as an individual, but as the representative of Catholic Languedoc; and each of them well knew that the more Angel could squeeze out of the King in the way of general political concessions and personal honours, the easier would it be to win over the more extremist Leaguers among Angel's people.

On 15 May 1597 Henriette-Catherine de Joyeuse was married to Henri de Bourbon, Duke of Montpensier, one of the richest men in France. His daughter now provided for, Fr. Angel took steps for his return to the Capuchins. Eventually, in October 1598, the necessary permission for his transfer from the Order of Malta and reception into the Capuchins arrived from Rome, and he began to arrange for the handing over of his civil responsibilities. On 8 March 1599 he re-entered the Capuchins at the Paris convent in the Rue Saint-Honoré, and the following day one of his confrères, Fr. Archange Dupuis of Lyons, the Lenten preacher at Saint-Germain-l'Auxerrois, announced the fact publicly from the pulpit. Henri IV called to visit Fr. Angel in the convent shortly afterwards.[1]

If Fr. Angel thought that he might now at last sink into obscurity he was to be disappointed. Within less than a month the convent at the Rue Saint-Honoré was to be once more in the news. The immediate cause of this was the affair of Marthe Brossier. This girl was a suspected case of diabolical possession and she had been brought to Paris on 30 March to be examined by an ecclesiastical tribunal. Among those examining her were two Capuchins, Fr. Seraphin and Fr. Benet of Canfield (the latter had been called in, it would seem, to substantiate whether the spirit that possessed the girl could speak English). There was a considerable conflict between the ecclesiastical and the medical viewpoints and the whole affair created a considerable public stir in the capital, especially because some of the girl's "diabolical" revelations were of a political and anti-Huguenot character. In order to prevent civil disturbances, the girl was taken out of the hands of the ecclesiastical authorities and placed under civil arrest by a decree of the Parlement on 13 April. On the Sunday following, Fr. Archange Dupuis of Lyons, well known for the vehemence of his anti-Huguenot sermons,[2] preached in the convent in the Rue Saint-Honoré against the order of the Parlement, as being an unwarrantable invasion by the civil authorities of the Church's rights and prerogatives. Dr. André

---

[1] cf. *Journal de l'Estoile*, ed. L.-R. Lefèvre, Paris, 1948, vol. i, pp. 565 sq.

[2] On 10 March previously there had been protests against the extremity of his attack on the book on the Mass by the celebrated Huguenot Duplessis-Mornay. Owing to the ambiguity of the French relative pronoun, Fr. Archange had left his hearers in doubt as to whether he advocated the burning of the book or of its author.

Duval of the Sorbonne preached to the same effect in the church
of St. Benoît—for once the Sorbonne and the regulars were in
agreement. On 20 April the Parlement ordered the immediate
appearance before them of the two preachers. Duval submitted but
the Capuchin did not. The following day an official called at the
Capuchin convent and ordered the surrender of Fr. Archange.
This was refused; eventually, the officer was handed a written
protest signed by the guardian (Fr. Jean Brûlart de Sillery) and the
definitor (Fr. Benet of Canfield), claiming ecclesiastical exemption
in virtue of the papal bull *Quoniam Nostro* of 5 April 1575. The
Parlement, on hearing of the reception of their officer, ordered to
appear before them Fr. Jean Brûlart and Fr. Benet of Canfield (as
signatories of the protest), Fr. Archange of Lyons, and Fr.
Alphonse, the unfortunate vicar of the convent.

Fr. Angel de Joyeuse now tried to use his personal influence to
intervene, and he went to the King at Saint-Germain-en-Laye.
The King received him kindly but refused to interfere with the
order of the Parlement. On 4 May the four Capuchins appeared
before the Parlement to hear the judgement delivered against them.
Two days later, by order of the Parlement, the judgement was
solemnly read again to the entire community assembled at the
Rue Saint-Honoré. Fr. Archange of Lyons was suspended from
preaching for six months and the protest of Fr. Jean Brûlart and
Fr. Benet of Canfield was there and then torn up in front of them
and of the whole community. Fr. Angel de Joyeuse remained un-
impressed by the proceedings; he afterwards observed that "the
wrong done to religion and the Church by the Edict of Nantes was
an injury which would take a long time to heal".

What was the significance of this seeming storm in a teacup?
The first thing to be remembered is that the Edict of Nantes,
though proclaimed in April 1598, had only been registered by the
Parlement of Paris in the February of 1599. This gave the Huguenots complete liberty of conscience, complete equality before the
law, and liberal, though restricted, liberty of worship. By its legal
recognition of two religions within one kingdom, the Edict of
Nantes was something unique in its time.[1] Nevertheless, it was an

---

[1] In German history, the Treaty of Passau of 1552 is hardly really comparable.

expedient, dependent on the word of the King, and by no means enthusiastically received by either side. It still remained to be seen what the edict would mean in reality. The second element in the case was that the religious orders closely associated with the popular support for the League were the Dominicans, the Jesuits and the Capuchins. After the assassination attempt by Jean Chastel in 1594, the Jesuits had been banished; on 3 April 1599, at the very height of the Brossier affair, the mysterious Fr. Langlois (or Langlais), a Capuchin of English origin belonging to the Lorraine Province, was broken on the wheel in Paris for his part in an alleged plot against the King.

It would seem, therefore, that the Capuchins were skating on very thin ice, and that they might well suffer the fate of the Jesuits. But they had one valuable card up their sleeve. In order to obtain an heir, the King wished to annul his marriage with Marguerite de Valois and to marry the niece of the Pope, Marie de Médicis. To negotiate this, he had that year despatched to Rome as ambassador a capable lawyer, Nicolas Brûlart de Sillery, none other than the father of the Capuchin Fr. Jean Brûlart.[1] It looks very much as though the whole episode of Marthe Brossier and the Capuchins was in the nature of a test case, to see how far the King would go on three issues: (1) the protection of the Huguenots from attacks in the pulpit, (2) the banishment of religious orders other than the Jesuits, and (3) the maintenance of ecclesiastical immunities against the Parlement. Henri IV was a realist. As far as theological controversy was concerned he was prepared to admit a free-for-all; the Capuchins were far too influential for any such drastic action as banishment to be taken against them; but on the question of ecclesiastical immunities the Parlement was to have the last word. It was a drawn battle.

After this Fr. Angel disappears from the political arena. From now till his death he occupied various offices within the order. He was twice elected Provincial; in 1602, when he attended the General Chapter in Rome, and again in 1607. In 1608 he went again to Rome for the General Chapter at Pentecost, and on the

---

[1] See *Études franciscaines*, vol. 9 (1903), pp. 607-12, "Le Parlement et les immunités religieuses en 1599—le P. Brûlart", by Ubald d'Alençon.

return journey he died at Rivoli, near Turin, on 28 September 1608, the Vigil of the Stigmata of St Francis.

The part that Fr. Angel played in French political life tends to overshadow his spiritual work. But the last nine years of his life saw him active in all parts of France. He helped to build new Capuchin convents at Alençon, Montfort l'Amaury, Le Mans, Pontoise, Beauvais, Joigny, and even at Saumur, the Huguenot stronghold. He also, after considerable preparation, succeeded in establishing at Paris a convent of Clarisses, or Daughters of the Passion as they were there called. Fr. Angel is to be found, moreover, as spiritual adviser to many of the saintly women concerned with the reform of the then existing female religious orders in France. It was, however, as a preacher that he was most widely known. Unfortunately the *corpus* of his sermons has not survived; Brousse, his biographer, certainly must have seen the material and tried to work part of it into his biography. What we have, therefore, is not a *corpus* but *disjecta membra*, and certainly not enough to form an adequate basis for a discussion of Fr. Angel's spiritual teaching. It is clear enough from other sources, however, that Fr. Angel was well in the current of the mystical revival of the period and that, like Fr. Joseph of Paris somewhat later, he is to be associated with the spiritual teaching of Fr. Benet of Canfield.

The life of a man like Angel de Joyeuse can never be understood if it is approached in the conviction that it is wrong for the Church, or for churchmen, to meddle—the word is always "meddle"—in politics. No one in the France of Henri III and Henri IV would have understood such a standpoint. It is the liberal practitioners of the last hundred and fifty years who have always demanded that Christians should maintain a lofty and disdainful indifference to political life and events. The life of Fr. Angel is a most dramatic illustration of the fact that renunciation of the "world" does not imply renunciation of social responsibility. His part in the making of Christendom was in the remaking of Christian France.

FATHER BENET OF CANFIELD [1]

William Fitch (hereafter we shall call him by his religious name) was born in 1562, the third son of William Fitch, Lord of the Manor of Little Canfield and Allyns in Essex, and his wife Anne, née Wiseman. The family background was Protestant—puritanly-inclined well-to-do landed gentry. But his aunt Jane Wiseman, née Vaughan, was a staunch Catholic. She was the "good widow" Wiseman, mother of the William Wiseman who assisted Fr. John Gerard, S.J. She was imprisoned in the Gatehouse, condemned in 1598 to the *peine forte et dure* through a trick of Topcliffe's, but released on the accession of James I and died in 1610. Her four daughters were nuns: Anne and Barbara were Bridgettines of Sion, and Jane and Bridget were Canonesses of St. Augustine at Louvain.[2]

Little is known of Fr. Benet's youth. In 1579 he went to London to read law and was admitted to the Middle Temple on 3 November 1580. Fr. Benet tells the story of his religious crisis and conversion in his *Autobiography*. During his years of study in London he had become more and more dissatisfied with the worldly atmosphere in which he was living. The crisis was precipitated on Saturday 23 July 1585 when there came into his hands "a book that I had heard much recommended, treating of a resolution to live well". This was a version of Fr. Parsons's *The First Book of Christian Exercise appertayning to Resolution* (Rouen, 1582), adapted for Protestant use by Edward Bunny of Merton College, Oxford, as *A Book of Christian Exercise appertaining to Resolution ...* (London, 1584). After some days of spiritual crisis which he describes in detail, Fr. Benet determined on a total reform of his life. The decision being made, it remained to decide what form of religion he should now adopt. He returned home in considerable confusion of mind. Then he unburdened himself to an intimate friend living in the house, who was a Catholic (though presumably

---

[1] The principal modern source for the life of Fr. Benet is the invaluable work of Fr. Optatus van Veghel, O.F.M. Cap., *Benoît de Canfield (1562-1610), sa vie, sa doctrine et son influence*, Rome, 1949.

[2] cf. *John Gerard* ... trans. P. Caraman, London, 1951, pp. 30-1, 50-3.

a lapsed one). Together they decided to go to London, and by enquiries among Catholic priests and Protestant ministers, to satisfy themselves as to the true religion. Fr. Benet at first planned to ascertain the Protestant and Catholic teaching on the subject of the Real Presence, which seemed to him to be the point of cardinal importance. However, before this could be arranged, he became convinced, he tells us, by a sudden revelation, of the truth of the Catholic faith. Together with his companion he was received into the Church on Sunday 1 August 1585 by an old Catholic priest imprisoned in the Gatehouse, probably Fr. Robert Darbyshire the Carthusian. In February of the following year, having first put his affairs in order and taken leave of his family, he left England for France and arrived at Douai. At first he thought of entering the Order of Conventual Franciscans, but then changed his mind, and received the habit at the Capuchin house of S. Honoré in Paris, together with two fellow countrymen.[1]

It may be fitting at this point to offer some comments on Fr. Benet's *Autobiography*. It is of course a purely spiritual autobiography written as a religious exercise. Three stages stand out clearly: the general moral conversion, the religious conversion to Catholicism, and the entry into the Capuchins. The subjective element in the autobiography is Fr. Benet's emotions and prayers in relation to those three stages—both as and when they occurred, and as he came to write them down.

This is not the sort of reading to which the modern reader of self-revelatory autobiography is accustomed. Fr. Benet's *Autobiography* comes into perspective if we compare it with a famous literary autobiography written nearly three-quarters of a century later—*Grace Abounding to the Chief of Sinners; or, A Brief Relation of the Exceeding Mercy of God in Christ, to His Poor Servant, John Bunyan*. Bunyan's background is Calvinist lower-middle-class; Fr. Benet's is Calvinist very-much-upper-middle-class. But for

---

[1] One was Fr. Archangel of Pembroke, later to be known for his relations with Mère Angélique of Port-Royal. The other may have been Fr. Francis Fitzherbert, fourth son of Sir John Fitzherbert of Padly Hall, Derbyshire (at whose house Bl. Nicholas Garlick and Bl. Robert Ludlam were arrested), and grandson of Sir Anthony Fitzherbert, Judge of the Common Pleas. See Fr. Benedict of Bolton in *Franciscan Annals*, lix (1935), pp. 303, 363, and R. Challoner, *Memoirs* . . . ed. J. H. Pollen, London, 1924, p. 130.

both men the central drama has many similarities. The writing of the conversion is in itself a religious act; the external world, persons, places, things, dates, are only relevant in so far as they are connected with the central spiritual crisis. Indeed, the more one compares it with Bunyan, or indeed with any of the other numerous spiritual autobiographies of the seventeenth century, the more one sees that the fulcrum in Fr. Benet's *Autobiography* is a typical Calvinist conversion. Fr. Benet's conversion to Catholicism and entry into the Capuchins are both dependent on the initial and decisive moral conversion. That accomplished, Fr. Benet begins to examine the rival claims of Catholicism and Puritanism. Note that he speaks constantly of Puritanism, not of Protestantism, as a religion; Anglicanism, as we understand and admire it, did not exist for men like him. The *via media*, the theological structure of the Anglican Church, was a seventeenth-century creation. Richard Hooker did more than any other to give the State Church a more than merely social or political dimension. In Fr. Benet's last year at the Middle Temple he might have heard Hooker preach, but it was not till more than a decade later that the first five books of the *Ecclesiastical Polity* were published.

Concerning Fr. Benet's conversion to Catholicism two things should be borne in mind. Firstly, that the key to the position was the doctrine of the Real Presence. Not that he had any doubt in his mind that the Real Presence was a tenable doctrine; but only that he wished to satisfy himself that the Puritans did *not* believe it— which wasn't very difficult to do. Had Fr. Benet's search for the true religion taken place in the age of the Caroline Divines, his quest might have been longer and more arduous. Secondly, we must not forget the close physical proximity of Catholicism in Fr. Benet's days. He knew Catholics as members of his family, as neighbours and as friends; the Inns of Court were at that time notorious for the numbers of Catholics—overt, covert or lapsed— among their members. There was not, as yet, something "foreign" about English Catholics; they were not yet a strange sect totally "cut off from the populous world around them, and dimly seen, as if through a mist, or in twilight, as ghosts flitting to and fro."[1]

[1] J. H. Newman, *The Second Spring*, London, 1852.

And when Fr. Benet wanted a priest, he knew where to find one—albeit in the nearest prison.

There is no special evidence to explain why Fr. Benet chose to join the Capuchin Order. But it may not be too fanciful to suggest that in the Rule of St. Francis he found an ideal most clearly akin to the gospel "primitivism" of the Puritan environment. And in the comparatively recently founded Capuchins he found the Franciscan rule in its most primitive and literal form.

Fr. Benet's fellow novices at the Paris convent of S. Honoré included some distinguished figures; apart from Angel de Joyeuse and Archangel of Pembroke, the group included Léonard de Paris (1566-1641), later to be one of Henrietta Maria's chaplains in England, and Honoré de Paris, of the distinguished family of Bochart de Champigny, who was later to be a celebrated preacher and champion of the Forty Hours' Devotion, and whose beatification process was opened in 1870.

After completing his noviciate at Paris, Fr. Benet made his profession in March 1588. He then went with Angel and Honoré to Venice to complete his philosophical and theological studies, as there was as yet no house of studies in the French Province. We find him back in France again in 1592 as novice-master at Orleans, where he remained till 1597, having been appointed guardian of the convent in 1594. In 1597 he moved to Paris, having been appointed Definitor, where he remained till his departure for England in 1599. During this period Fr. Benet developed in at least verbal, if not manuscript, form the spiritual teaching that was later to be published as the *Rule of Perfection*. Besides his influence on the members of his own order, he is also met with as the spiritual adviser of two of the leading reformers of the female religious orders in France, Mme. Acarie and Marie de Beauvilliers—though these two ladies received so much good advice from various sources that it is difficult, and not particularly profitable, to attempt to establish Fr. Benet's precise contribution.[1]

In the spring of 1599 Fr. Benet became involved in the affair of the exorcism of Marthe Brossier, which developed into a struggle

[1] L. C. Sheppard in *Barbe Acarie, Wife and Mystic*, London, 1953, points out the special significance of Fr. Benet's teaching for Mme. Acarie, whose vocation was to combine the mystical life with the duties of a wife and a mother.

for power between the civil and the ecclesiastical authorities. (There is no need to go into details here as the matter has been discussed more fully above, in relation to Fr. Angel de Joyeuse.)[1] A desire to return as a missionary to England would be natural in any exiled priest; Fr. Benet's withdrawal from Paris after the Brossier affair would be prudent, to say the least. Perhaps it was a combination of these two factors which caused his departure for England on 31 July in company with a Scots Capuchin, Fr. John Chrysostom Campbell. They arrived the following day on the coast between Dover and Sandwich and were almost immediately arrested. The Mayor of Sandwich sent them up to London to Baron Henry Cobham, Lord Warden of the Cinque Ports, under whose jurisdiction the matter lay. He in turn, after examining them, passed them on to Robert Cecil, Secretary of State, at that time at Nonsuch. Through the English Ambassador at Paris, Cecil knew that the two Capuchins were highly placed in French affairs, and presumably he anticipated that they were on some diplomatic mission. After examining them, however, and discovering that they had nothing to reveal to him, he had them committed to prison, Fr. John Chrysostom to the Marshalsea (from whence he was banished, 18 March 1600), and Fr. Benet probably to the Tower.

From the Tower Fr. Benet was soon moved to the Clink, and from thence, on 19 January 1600, in company with fifteen priests and four laymen from the various London prisons, he was transferred to Wisbech Castle. Since 1585 the Government had astutely used Wisbech Castle for the isolation of the leading recusant priest prisoners in a confinement well away from London. So long as they were in the London gaols the priests would always be, to some extent, in touch with the Recusant "underworld"; and although their apostolic work was drastically curtailed, they were still able, with a bit of bribery, to perform some of their spiritual functions— Fr. Benet's own conversion by Fr. Darbyshire in the Gatehouse is a case in point. The removal of the priests from the London gaols to Wisbech served the purpose of cutting them off from their London contacts and forcing them into each other's unavoidable company. Perhaps the authorities had planted one or two renegade

[1] See above, p. xviii-xx.

informers amongst them, hoping for some sensational revelations or, at least, for some grounds for what we should nowadays call a "smear-campaign". Be that as it may, all-too-human psychology certainly played a hand in the game. The prisoners inevitably got on each other's nerves, and in the claustrophobic atmosphere small differences began to take on sensational proportions. The tale of the "Wisbech stirs" has been already told—not without a somewhat repellent *Schadenfreude*—by T. G. Law in his *Conflicts between Jesuits and Seculars in the Reign of Queen Elizabeth* (1889).[1] The troubles at Wisbech did not create a schism among the Recusant clergy, but they certainly engendered the elements of mutual suspicion and mistrust that were to last for well-nigh two and a half centuries.

From the evidence at present available, it would seem that Fr. Benet did not take an active part on either side in the dispute, but maintained a reputation for being *au-dessus de la mêlée*.[2] On 26 December 1600 he was transferred to Framlingham Castle (when Wisbech Castle returned to the use of its owner, the Bishop of Ely), and early in 1603 he was banished to France.

Precise details of the latter period of his life are scarce. He undertook various official duties within the order and was stationed in several of the convents of the French Province. He was connected with the reform of the Abbey of Saint-Paul-lès-Beauvais under the Mother Abbess Madeleine de Sourdis, and was noted for his apostolic work among the Huguenots. He died at Paris on 21 November 1610.

These last years saw the publication of his two books, *Le Chevalier Chrestien* and the *Rule of Perfection*. *Le Chevalier Chrestien* appeared at Paris and Rouen in 1609. In his dedication to Henri IV, Fr. Benet tells that it was composed while in prison in England. The work is in the form of a dialogue between a Christian knight and a pagan, and consists of a detailed exposition on Christ-

---

[1] This has now been superseded by Miss P. Renold's excellent study, *The Wisbech Stirs (1595-1598)*, Catholic Record Society, London, 1958.

[2] However, it may be worth noting that when the Archpriest of the English secular clergy, George Birkhead, sent Dr. Richard Smith and Thomas More to Rome in April 1609 to appeal against the Jesuits, he also sent an emissary to Rouen to get the support of Fr. Benet (cf. *Dodd's Church History of England*, ed. M. A. Tierney, London, 1841, p. ccxix).

ian doctrine in the guise of an allegory—the Kingdom is Christianity, the King is Jesus Christ, the Queen the Catholic Church, and so on. The allegorical method is driven absolutely as far as it will go; even every little piece of the knight's equipment has an allegorical significance. This use of allegory for religious instruction and edification has, of course, many European analogues.[1] It is sufficient to call to mind the English tradition of this sort of thing, from Langland to, significantly, Bunyan. Fr. Benet was writing within a well-worn convention of popular exposition; if his book seems far-fetched and tedious to us now, it may be salutary to reflect on the effect of a book like *The Screwtape Letters* three hundred years from to-day.

But Fr. Benet's fame rests on the *Rule of Perfection*; it is that which has attracted such writers as Bremond and Huxley and thus brought him to the attention of the present century. The book seems to have been composed, in some form at least, as early as 1592, when Fr. Benet was in Italy. The first two parts were twice printed in English while he was in prison in England, but both impressions were seized and destroyed. After his return to France, the book gained an even wider circulation in manuscript, and a garbled form was even pirated in print (this included the third part, which, since it dealt with the highest stages of the mystical life, Fr. Benet always preferred not to publish, but to communicate by oral teaching). To prevent further piracies, Fr. Benet was forced into print. In 1609 an English edition appeared at Rouen and in the same year a French edition at Paris and Arras; all these contained only the first two parts. The third part was added in the French and Latin editions printed at Paris in 1610. Thereafter the book ran through over fifty editions, covering all the principal European languages. In 1689 it was put on the Index[2] at the time of the Quietist controversy, but there can be little doubt that the main reason for this was the contents of the third book, concerning the publication of which Fr. Benet himself was always very hesitant.

[1] For a full discussion see the article by A. Rebelliau in *Mélanges offerts à M. Émile Picot*, Paris, 1913.

[2] Where it still remains. See *Index Librorum Prohibitorum*, Rome, 1940, p. 45 (which gives the French title); also F. H. Reusch *Der Index der verbotenen Bücher*, Bonn, 1885, vol. ii, p. 621 (which gives the Italian, as in the original decree).

It is not the purpose of the present study to discuss in any detail the contents of *The Rule of Perfection*, but the fame of the book is inseparable from the life of its author. Like most seventeenth century books, the title-page serves the purpose which to-day would be performed by the publishers' "blurb". Let it speak for itself: *The Rule of Perfection contayning a Brief and Perspicuous Abridgement of all the wholle spirituall Life, reduced to this only point of the (Will of God). Divided into three Partes. The First treating of the Exteriour Will of God, contayning the Active Life. The Second of the Interiour Will contayning the Contemplative Life. The Third of the Essentiall Will concerning the Life Supereminent. Composed by the Ven. Br. (Benet) Heertofore (William Fitche) Englishman; Preacher, of the holie Order of the Capuchins of Saint Francis. Vita in voluntate eius. Psal.* 29. So the essence of Fr. Benet's teaching is that it *has* an essence. It is important to stress that he has tried to arrive at a *rule* of perfection, a sort of spiritual H.C.F., for all walks of life—and that rule is the surrender of the human will to the will of God. Fr. Benet is in the true Franciscan tradition when he insists upon the significance of the supreme act of surrender of a human will to the will of God: the passion of Our Lord Jesus Christ. The reason for the tremendous popularity of *The Rule of Perfection* was because it was not written for any one particular section of society[1]—it had a message for the courtier, or for the rather *mondaine* nun, as well as for those who were well advanced in the mystical life. And it appeared at a moment when a fresh breath of spiritual vitality was blowing through the whole of French life and culture after the Wars of Religion. What Sully did for the French economy, Fr. Benet did for the mystical life.

The sources and analogues of *The Rule of Perfection* are manifold, and have been discussed at length elsewhere; attention naturally concentrates on the Netherlandish and Rhineland mystics. But one point is worth making here. The impartial reader of *The Rule of Perfection* will surely concede that the book lacks that joyous, indeed poetic, delight in the created universe which is to be found in the Catholic neo-Platonic and Baroque devotional

[1] La Belle Acarie is a case in point. See above, p. xxv, *n* 1.

literature of two or three decades later. Fr. Benet has the Puritan tinge. Now, he certainly owned a copy of the *Cloud of Unknowing*,[1] but his threefold division into the Active Life, the Contemplative Life, and the Life Supereminent reminds us most of all of Dowel, Dobet and Dobest in Langland's *Piers Plowman*; and of all the medieval writers Langland was the most sympathetic to the Puritan mind: Langland's first publisher, Robert Crowley, was an Elizabethan Puritan.[2] Granted that this connection may be somewhat tenuous; nevertheless, what cannot be overstressed is the fact that one part of the English medieval tradition did become, as it were, channelled off into the Puritan and Nonconformist tradition.[3] Now in his exhaustive study of the editions of *The Rule of Perfection* there is one that Fr. Optatus has overlooked.[4] The third part of *The Rule of Perfection* was translated and published in England in 1646 as *A Bright-Starre leading to and containing in Christ our Perfection*, by Giles Randall the Antinomian;[5] and a copy of it was to be found in the library of the sophisticated English Quaker merchant, Benjamin Furly of Rotterdam, in the early eighteenth century.[6]

A convert to Catholicism from an English Puritan background; a convert Englishman taking a leading part in the French religious revival; the writer of a spiritual classic which came back

[1] Cf. *The Cloud of Unknowing*, ed. J. McCann, London, 1947, p. 152.

[2] J. M. Cowper gives a sketch of his life in the introduction to *The Select Works of Robert Crowley* (*EETS*), London, 1872.

[3] G. R. Owst's chapter on Bunyan in *Literature and Pulpit in Mediaeval England* (Cambridge, 1933) is especially valuable on this.

[4] But Mr. E. I. Watkin has not; see his *Poets and Mystics*, London, 1953, p. 58.

[5] Randall in his preface says that the book is "high and hard and almost unheard of amongst us", yet he hopes it will have "good success amongst the *Children of the Light*, who are taught of God and who run and read the hidden and deep things of God". (The "Children of the Light" was a current term for the Quakers.) An account of Randall and of this book is given by Rufus M. Jones in *Spiritual Reformers in the Sixteenth and Seventeenth Centuries*, London, 1928, pp. 253 sq. Jones refers to the unique copy of *A Bright Starre* in Lambeth Palace. A recent enquiry has revealed that the library is in process of cataloguing and the volume has not yet reappeared to date.

[6] Furly's library included a Dutch version of the whole *Rule of Perfection* (Antwerp, 1659), Fr. Parsons's *Christian Directory* (1585), to say nothing of Dom Serenius Cressy's editions of Walter Hilton's *Scale of Perfection* (1659 and 1672) and the *Revelations* of Dame Juliana of Norwich (1670). See *Bibliotheca Furliana* ... Rotterdam, 1714, pp. 116, 147, 151, 152, 158.

later to England under Quaker auspices[1]—the wheel has come full
circle on an extraordinary career.

[1] It was probably through Furly's influence that his neighbour at Rijnsburg,
the French Protestant mystic Pierre Poiret included Canfield's *Rule of Perfection*
in his *Bibliotheca Mysticorum Selecta*, Amsterdam, 1708 (p. 149). Poiret's
bibliography of mystical writers had a great European influence in the eighteenth
and early nineteenth centuries—among, for instance, Scots clergymen who felt
oppressed by the rigours of Calvinism and German romanticists who were tired
of the aridities of the Age of Reason. In the nineteenth century, the wealthy
Wesleyan goldsmith Christopher Walton (1809-77) used Poiret's bibliography
in building up his "Theosophian Library" at 8 Ludgate Hill. Walton gives
prominence to Poiret's mention of Canfield in his *Notes and Materials*... 1854,
and among his manuscripts there is a transcript of a considerable part of an
English translation of Book III of Canfield's *Rule of Perfection* (Dr. Williams's
Library, MS. Walton 1107/3; presumably this was from Giles Randall's translation mentioned above, p. xxx, *n* 5).

BIBLIOGRAPHICAL NOTES

IT would be pointless and tedious to give here a complete and detailed list of the books consulted for this present edition. But it may be useful to point out some of the principal modern works on the subject for those interested in further study.

The best life of Fr. Angel is that by Fr. Louis de Gonzague, O.F.M. Cap., *Le Père Ange de Joyeuse, frère mineur Capucin, Maréchal de France, 1563-1608*, Paris, 1928. It covers most of the ground conscientiously. P. de la Vaissière gives a useful study of the Joyeuse family as a whole in *Les Messieurs de Joyeuse*, Paris, 1926. Jean Cruppi's *Le Père Ange, Duc de Joyeuse, Maréchal de France et Capucin*, Paris, 1928, is a careless and impressionistic piece of book-making. An admirably detached and critical study of Fr. Angel's exclaustration is *Un Cas de Jurisprudence Pontificale* ... Assisi, 1936, by Fr. Agathange de Paris, O.F.M. Cap.; it contains a valuable appendix of documents.

Fr. Benet of Canfield has been handsomely served in Fr. Optatus van Veghel's *Benoît de Canfield (1562-1610) sa vie, sa doctrine et son influence*, Rome, 1949; a useful review-article on this by L. C. Sheppard is in *The Downside Review*, lxix (1951). Fr. Cassian J. Reel, O.F.M. Cap., has written a life of Fr. Benet in English as an Oxford B.Litt. thesis; it is unfortunately as yet unpublished, but a typescript copy reposes in the library of the Historical Faculty at Oxford.

On the general Capuchin background *Les Frères Mineurs Capucins en France*, Paris 1937-9, by Fr. Godefroy de Paris, O.F.M. Cap., is admirably detailed and frank. Fr. Cuthbert's *The Capuchins*, 2 vols., London, 1928, is a most useful and pleasantly written study. Short biographies and detailed bibliographies will be found in *Lexicon Capuccinum*, Rome, 1951, an invaluable piece of international co-operation.

OF THE REVEREND

FA. ANGEL

OF JOYEUSE

CAPUCHIN PREACHER.

*Sometimes Duke, Peer and Marshal of France
and Governor for the King in Languedoc.*

*Together with the lives of the Reverend Fathers,
Father Benet, Englishman and Father Archangel,
Scotchman, of the same Order.*

*Written first in the French tongue and now trans-
lated into English by R.R., Catholic Priest.*

I H S

AT DOUAY.

For John Heigham.   With permission of Superiors, Anno 1623.

THE LIFE OF
THE REVEREND FATHER ANGEL
OF JOYEUSE

a Capuchin and preacher:
before his entry into religion
Duke, Peer and Marshal of France and Governor
deputed by the King in Languedoc.[1]

Of his descent and nobility

THE FIRST CHAPTER

IT is no small honour among men, to be nobly born, but yet it is
far more eminent in the presence of God when it is accompanied
with true virtue. Many there are who shine in the one, not without
great glory and applause: but few of them attain to the perfection
of the other. And yet, notwithstanding, this worldly and transitory
glory, in comparison of immortal (wherewith the blessed souls are
glorified) deserveth rather to be reputed a dream or a shadow than
any real quality. For it dependeth merely upon the opinion of
mortal men and so consequently quickly dieth and fadeth; whereas
solid virtue, whose perfection (if it could be seen with corporal
eyes) would ravish men with its eminent beauty, doth indeed
crown them that embrace her with immortal laurels, who live and
flourish for all eternity in Paradise. For God (who of His infinite
goodness hath made us heirs of this kingdom, yet so that we make
purchase of it by our works, as Our Blessed Saviour hath bought it
with the price of His blood) doth not regard bare titles without
effects. For indeed the more eminent men are, and mounted above
the common and ordinary rank, so much the more are they bound
to excel others, and to maintain their dignities by the extraordinary
practice of the heroical virtues of the Cross. So that their examples

---

[1] We have omitted the Epistle Dedicatory, the Preface, and Twelve Points in
commendation of the Franciscan Rule.

may serve to guide and conduct others over whom they are set (for that is God's holy ordinance); and so discharging their duty, they may avoid the dangers of those dreadful threats which God denounces to the great ones of this world: *The mighty shall suffer mighty torments.* The blessed Father Angel of Joyeuse, as admirable in the one as imitable in the other, both in the world and in religion, knew so well to join virtue with nobility and so to bear himself that he ennobled himself with maintaining this happy match of the one with the other. Touching his noble descent, it is well known that the most honourable and noble family of Joyeuse (from which he descended) hath been and is one of the most ancient and most illustrious families, not only of Languedoc, but of all France; out of which are come many noble and worthy persons, whose virtues and memorable exploits are eternized by happy demonstrance of the effects and witnessed by monuments to the view of the world. The hydras or water-adders which they bear for their arms, subdued by their first progenitors, have served to incite their posterity to brave adventures, when they were to be undertaken for the defence of the Church or the State. And for evident proof hereof the Most Christian Kings (whom God hath honoured with the title and graces of the eldest and firstborn sons of the Church) have given testimony of their valour and worth by conferring unto them titles and honours due only to eminent virtues. For out of this house are descended masters of the camp, marshals, admirals, dukes and peers of France. So that it may be rightly called a temple of honour, built upon a firm foundation of virtue and prowess. Which consideration hath moved the princes of blood in France and the most princely family of Lorraine, to search after this family and honour it with their alliance.

During the reign of Louis the Eleventh, Louis Joyeuse married Jane de Bourbon, which marriage caused great public joy; which it pleased God also to bless with happy and fruitful issue, of the Counts of Chartres and Bonneval (who sprung from them). Afterwards Anne Joyeuse, admiral, duke and peer of France, married Margaret of Lorraine (sister of Louis of Lorraine, wife of Henry the Third). And in our time Henriette Joyeuse, daughter of Henry Joyeuse, Count of Bouchage (who was the blessed Father Angel of

whom we treat) was married to Henry of Bourbon, Duke of
Montpensier (one of the most noble grafts that ever came from
that royal family of S. Louis). And after his death (for he died in
the very flower of his age) she was married to Charles of Lorraine,
Duke of Guise, who had by her a noble and happy issue of such
towardness[1] that they do now, in the blade of their tender infancy,
give great hope of extraordinary virtue in more perfect age, when
they shall know how much it importeth them to follow the
example of their grandfather (this blessed Father Angel) and not
to degenerate from that noble stock of Guise, from whence they
are come; which hath been renowned for many noble triumphs
had over the Saracens for the honour of the Cross of Christ: and
hath been since for many ages as it were the sword and buckler of
the Catholic faith, in subduing rebellious and revolted miscreants,
and reducing them to the obedience of their holy mother the
Catholic, Apostolic, Roman Church, out of which there is no faith,
no piety, no religion, no charity, no grace, no merit and consequently no salvation. It being therefore evident that this family is
singularly adorned with these great alliances, yet notwithstanding
it is made more famous by the actions of heroical virtues which, as
little bright fires affixed to a heavenly globe, have so beautified the
soul of blessed Father Angel that his life hath been as a wonder of
rare perfection, even in the judgement of most wise and judicious
beholders thereof.

He was the son of William Joyeuse, a man of singular piety and
great courage: who was honoured by Henry the Second in admitting him to his order of knighthood; and established him Lieutenant in Languedoc, where he executed that charge with so great
prudence and moderation for the space of five-and-thirty years,
that for acknowledgement of his merits he was made Marshal of
France by Henry the Third.

His mother was Marie of Batarnay, a woman of so rare piety and
example of good life, that it may well be thought that God (who
doth often bless the children for their parents' sake) did pour the
torrent of His benedictions upon her children for her sake. And
albeit there have been many excellent and most virtuous dames

---

[1] aptitude

which have either descended of this house or been allied to it, yet she was as it were a mirror in representing them all and had none of those good qualities wanting which any in particular or all in general had in them of worthy remark.

She was called the mother of the poor, having merited really that happy title. She did often visit prisons and hospitals and was extraordinarily charitable to those shamefast poor who were in great necessity and yet did not publicly beg relief; of which sort of poor there is great quantity.

Her affections were wholly bent to devotion and her thoughts were not fastened to any earthly things, but always raised towards heaven. She was free from all spot of ambition, having an aversion from the Court, living with all contentment in Languedoc with her husband, not without singular edification of the whole province by the lustre of her example.

And for the Court, she had wholly abandoned all memory, as she did all affection of it, had she not been forced to live some years there, partly to satisfy the desires of that pious and religious queen, Louise of Lorraine, and partly to take charge of her children, who, living then in great honour and esteem, were to be governed and guided by her presence, lest the fervour of their age might transport them to do otherwise than was hopefully conceived of them in their infancy. For her husband was fain to continue in his government to remedy those evils which threatened the whole estate and to quench the fire of infinite troubles which sprang from dissension in matters of religion, the devil playing the busy seedsman in sowing the cockle of errors and heresy among the pure wheat of true religion.

This devout and honourable dame, being thus enforced to endure the absence of her husband (whom next to God she loved and honoured most dearly), making her profit of this loss, augmented daily the practice of her devotions and mortifications and gave herself to all sweet entertainment in her frequent and fervent prayers and soliloquies; and not contenting herself with spending the day therein, she made the night serve for this entertainment, as a more proper time, even for the inward ears of the soul, to receive in true silence what God also would speak unto her. The long nights passed in this manner often seemed to her but short, and when sleep seized upon her (which is necessary for sustaining the frail body) she took it in a chair, not in a bed: so as after she had slumbered a while, she returned to her holy and pious meditation till the breaking of the day. And then she accustomed herself to make her first visit to the church, where she poured out her soul in such ardour of devotion that the effects do witness it by the heavenly benediction wherewith God did reward her, in that her example kindled devotion in other noble dames and obtained many graces of God for herself, her children, and indeed the whole realm. And hereof this is no small testimony that upon the day of the marriage of her son the admiral, when the King and the whole Court were occupied in banqueting, tilting and courtly triumphs of joy to show how they rejoiced in this marriage, she retired herself and shut up herself in her oratory, praying with many tears and inward groans that their excesses and superfluities might not provoke God to punish her children.

This devout lady, having spent all the forenoon in the church (where we are principally to lift up our hearts and hands to God), she disposed of herself in the afternoon to attend in the Court, employing herself wholly in good works conformable to her charity and humility and to make benefit of those occasions which might offer themselves to do good. After her travail (which was able to weary and wear out a strong body) her ordinary food was brown bread with beef or some other more gross and common meat; so that she was never seen to touch those meats which are more fine and delicate (although her table, according to her quality, was ever furnished with the best); refusing those meats by extraordinary abstinence and mortification, which she (being vehemently amorous of God) did charitably distribute to the poor, who are His members. She fasted all Fridays throughout the year and kept precisely the fast of Lent. And likewise from All-Hallowtide to Christmas she fasted with extraordinary austerity. And among her virtuous actions one is very remarkable, that on that day that she was by her friends promised in marriage, as soon as she heard of it, she prostrated herself before her parents and not without shedding many tears besought them to give her leave to enter into religion, (such love and affection had she to serve God in the state of virginal purity). I will not dilate myself by speaking of the noble progeny of this family of Batarnay; it shall suffice to know that it is a most ancient and noble house, of great renown and esteem in Touraine and Anjou, whence are come the Counts of Bouchage.

The noble person William of Joyeuse, having espoused Madame Marie of Batarnay, had by her seven children (whereof some came to perfect age and made their nobility and valour appear to the view of the world and so won the hearts of many by their worthy and amiable conversation, that their sovereign prince, valuing them among the best and noblest persons, gave them titles, dignities and charges answerable to their perfection). The eldest brother was called Anne de Joyeuse, who when he was at ripe age, was made Admiral, Duke and Peer of France, Governor and Lieutenant-General for the King in Normandy. These honours engaged him to do noble services, so that serving his prince and country in the siege of Fère, he was wounded in the mouth by a harquebus and lost two of his teeth. He took many towns with his forces, which he commanded, in Auvergne, where he had so happy success that for his valour and prudence Henry the Third made choice of him to stand in the breach against Henry the Fourth, then King of Navarre (who made all Guyenne to tremble for fear of so potent an enemy, as after he made himself redoubted through the world, having put himself into the bosom of the Church and acknowledged her for his mother). So there was no other thing but the cause of religion and the service of his king which pushed him against so mighty an enemy. Wherein, if the success was not answerable to the desire and hope of the State (God in His providence having otherwise disposed of it, for secret causes unknown to us), yet was there wanting no courage or valour of his part, as his exploits manifested in that battle principally at Moth S. Eloy, where so many enemies were defeated. Though irreparable disaster followed shortly after in the Battle of Coutras, where a sudden fear surprising his army, they broke their order; and while his soldiers were preparing themselves to flight, he cast himself into the midst of his enemies, thinking thereby to oblige them to follow him. And there sacrificed his life with many other gallant gentlemen, for the service of his prince and the defence of the Catholic, Apostolic and Roman Church.

The second brother was Francis Joyeuse,[1] the most illustrious Cardinal, whose noble and pious actions would deserve a volume apart, both for the number and excellence of them. He was so wise and prudent that the great monarch Henry the Fourth committed to his charge the most important affairs of Christendom, which he managed wisely and happily, with general applause, yet without charging the King or State or clergy with the expenses of the dispatch of them, supporting it wholly by his own revenues and patrimony. He was protector of France and of the Capuchins, but more particularly of the poor, to whom the greatest part of his patrimony was distributed. He was always occupied in augmenting the Church, either by building of new monasteries or giving great sums of money to those which were already begun. And whereas the foundation of the Church consisteth in the knowledge of the truth, which cannot be gotten ordinarily but by solid studies, he provided means for erecting a seminary before he died; where there are thirty young men to be maintained and instructed for the public benefit of the Church and of his country. He committed the charge of it to the fathers of the Society of Jesus, whose ordinary profession is to instruct youth and make them perfect and accomplished in all sort of good sciences. This was at Pontoise, where he thought to have built a college for them, where his body lieth, which he required should be carried from Avignon, where his library also is (one of the best in France) which he gave unto the fathers, with his chapel. But for divers considerations it hath been transported to Rouen as a place more fit and proper for so good a work. I let pass six thousand crowns which he gave to the church of Our Lady of Loreto, for the maintenance of three French priests and the reception of poor pilgrims; with many legacies given by his last will and testament and faithfully accomplished by his niece Madame de Guise (besides, those of Madame de Vidame his aunt, which came to more than two hundred thousand crowns), which serveth to show the piety of so great a prelate and hers also which so faithfully hath executed his will.

[1] His life was written by Antoine Aubery and published at Paris in 1654.

The third brother was called Henri Joyeuse, who in the height of prosperous fortune and in the midst of such honours and graces as his prince and the Court could yield him, abandoned and renounced all worldly contentments and put himself into the poor habit of a Capuchin. Which heroical and pious act was so powerful that he drew instantly by his example a great number of gentlemen who were tainted with the malice of the corruptions of the world, to make the same holy change of life and to bear the cross of Our Blessed Saviour in this holy seraphical order. After his entry into religion, he took the name of Father Angel Joyeuse, whose life and actions I have undertaken to write in this treatise; and to expose it as a burning light, both for religious and for seculars, who certainly conformed his life according to his name and was an angel in his discourse, in his zeal, in his exhortation and in his conversation, for the greater edification of many others.

The fourth son or branch of this noble stock was Scipio Joyeuse, who after the decease of his father was a lively and true image of him in valour and courage, which he showed for the defence of the Church and State; and succeeded him in his charge of the lieutenantship of Languedoc. He had many noble conquests and palms of victories in divers battles; and in the end at the siege of Villemur, where great forces coming for rescue of the besieged and forcing him to raise his siege, he himself broke the bridge of barques and boats which were made by the enemies, to cut off all means for the enemy to recoil; and put himself in vanguard of his infantry with his pike in his hand, till he received two wounds in this noble attempt and so fell into the river and yielded up his life. Whose body was not recovered from the enemies till the year following, when they began to treat a truce.

The fifth of the sons was Claude Joyeuse, who was Marquess of S. Sauveur, who at the age of fifteen years lost his life with his eldest brother at the Battle of Coutras. Thus we see the nobility and eminence of the family, whence he descended who was as a phoenix dead to the world, burnt in the odoriferous spices of his holy vows and hiding his life with Jesus Christ, within a little cell of retreat and a lodging-place peculiar to God (for so he was wont to say to his brethren to sweeten the yoke of religion); deserving eternal honour and renown, in that he made so happy a marriage and true concord between two things which seem so contrary (although indeed one dependeth upon the other), that is, between the excellence of nobility and the poverty of religion.

Of his birth and education

THE SECOND CHAPTER

THE blessed person was born in the year of Our Lord 1563. Who afterward had his holy birth in baptism and was presented to the holy font by Monseigneur de Montmorency, Constable of France, and there took the name of Henri, which he changed for the name of Angel when he became religious. As soon as he came into the world and was but a tender sucking infant he gave hopeful signs of those heavenly graces which appeared afterward in his youth. When he grew to that age that he was somewhat capable of the seed of virtue and knowledge, his father, being wise and prudent, had great care to provide for him a virtuous and learned master, that his children might be trained and seasoned well, both in virtue and good learning. Their master's name was Monsieur Martin, a man of eminent knowledge and exemplary life, whose labours were approved by the good fruits of those seeds he sowed. Nature is powerful in working of great effects, but yet education prevails more, having force often to change and correct natural imperfections and vices, and engraft sweet fruit in a crab stock. But when education does only help goodness of nature, there follow then miraculous effects. Among the rest (being all of great towardness) this Father Angel, though the youngest, was most forward; who began presently to comport himself far above his childish age, as if he would then begin to lay the foundation of those solid virtues which shined in him afterward. Wherefore his master, admiring his forwardness, took some more particular care of him than of the rest, as in proposing more questions to him and more particular instructions now and then apart. And God who in His eternal providence and love does design some to a more happy end for His glory and their salvation, does give means and graces most fit for that end. Which often causes that we, not easily comprehending the reason of it, can hardly be induced to believe that there are such extraordinary actions proceeding from those graces, if we were not eyewitnesses of them ourselves.

No man beheld and saw him, being yet but young, who did not think that his countenance promised some great matter. The inward beauty of his soul streamed forth beams outwardly. He was never wearied in praying and serving God; he frequented the church very devoutly and heard Mass with an extraordinary feeling. In hearing of sermons he was diligent to treasure up the principal points which were of most fruit and edification. When he was but a child of seven years of age he went often to confession and had so great grief for his little faults and imperfections, as if they had been great enormities. In discerning of which faults he showed that he had much understanding. He chose for his confessor the Reverend Father Robert de la Hosque,[1] Guardian of the Observant Franciscans, whose piety and knowledge was of great remark. His parents took great contentment in their son's devotion and thanked God for pouring these blessings on him, and requested his master to foster and encourage him in all acts of piety and devotion. Herein they were unlike to many parents who seek to divert their children from any such actions as though they foreshowed some ill fortune to them, and herein become murderers of their children's souls, in loosing the reins to them of licentiousness, debauchedness and disorders.

It happened in the year of jubilee[2] that many young men born of noble parents, wearied with the world and reflecting seriously upon true and eternal contentments, moved by good and holy inspirations, took resolution to retire themselves into the desert of religion and to serve God more fervently and with more quiet and repose. They put their resolution in practice instantly, not suffering those good inspirations (after they were examined and found such)

---

[1] The text reads "De Rocqua", but see Louis de Gonzague, *Le Père Ange de Joyeuse*, p. 17.
[2] The Jubilee of Pius V was published at Toulouse in May 1571 (*Études Franciscaines*, xxxix (1927), p. 253).

to cool and so took the habit of the Cordeliers at Toulouse. These examples were great motives to Father Angel, so that even then (being but nine years old) he showed an extraordinary desire and affection to follow their steps. He revealed it to his confessor, who (as he was prudent in his actions) sought to divert him from these thoughts, lest his parents might suspect him for infusing them into his tender soul. But yet was he inflamed so with this fire that his confessor could not quench it. Oh how powerful and charming are the sweet baits whereby God does draw our hearts unto Him!

The first desires of religion took hold of this tender young imp by the means of these examples, and were strengthened in him by reflecting upon those heavenly recompenses which Christ promises to those who follow His steps. But they were brought to perfection by occasion of a miraculous and very remarkable action. He being one day in the library of the Cordeliers at Toulouse (which library is esteemed one of the best in France) and taking a book at hazard into his hands to occupy his spirit in reading somewhat, he suddenly felt an inward motion in his soul, which seemed to be expressed with a voice saying to him: "See if you find yourself disposed to observe willingly that which is in this book." Hearkening to this voice, he opened the book and the first words he found written were: *The Rule and Life of the Friars Minors.* Whereupon his soul melted as it were with the sweet delights of so particular a vocation and his face was dyed presently with a vermilion colour in token of this extraordinary motion and heavenly grace, whereof he esteemed himself unworthy.

Having now so inwardly taken and laid up in his heart this manner of God's holy calling him, he used all possible care and caution to hide this from his brethren who were in company with him, and therefore gave over to look more in the book for the present, lest the reading of it might give occasion of some suspicion to them. But they were no sooner out of the library and gone home but he seeks out his confessor and imparts this matter to him and presently renewing his former importune request, humbly beseeches him that he might be admitted into their religion, since it was the will of God that he should profess that life.

Father de la Hosque was much perplexed hereat and hardly knew which way to turn himself. Therefore after he had dispatched him for the present with hope of enjoying these contentments which he sought, he enters into further consideration of so weighty a matter and resolves to advertise[1] his friends and parents of it, assuring them that if it were the will of God, no attempts and practices of theirs would prevail against it. Upon knowledge of it by Fr. de la Hosque they thought it expedient to divert him from these thoughts by sending him from Toulouse and they showed him what difficulties he was to undergo: as, that he must rise at midnight, go bare-footed, lie very hard (without putting off his clothes), that he must wear no linen and be obliged to strict obedience, contrary to his own will. And they told him he was too delicate and too weak to support this yoke and that he should live with far more contentment in the world. They added besides that, having one brother already dedicated to the Church, there were none left for the support of their family but his eldest brother and he. And to conclude, in their exhortations they signified to him that he was yet too young to determine of any such course and that hereafter upon riper age and better judgement (if he were so minded) that they would permit him to satisfy himself. His parents were troubled hereat by reason they apprehended some secret instigation of him to this, rather than a true vocation; which was to their great comfort, as his mother did witness afterward, persuading him to persevere constantly in religion, when the devil set his strongest batteries against him to draw him back to the world which he had so nobly and piously abandoned that the memory of that act will never die. But in vain were all the persuasions of his friends till they removed him from Toulouse and sent him with his brother to Paris, hoping that the change of place and conversation would also change his affection. For it is a thing almost impossible that a young tenderling should continue his good desire when the object is taken from him which first occasioned it.

Paris is one of the most famous and flourishing universities in the world for all sort of good arts and sciences, renowned also for persons of excellent wits and rare perfections. In this university

---

[1] notify

the College of Navarre is eminent and most famous for the education of kings, princes and cardinals and the greatest part of the bishops of France, who are examples of piety and great ornaments of the Church. In this college was this young plant set, as in a good and fertile soil.

Monsieur Guyon, Doctor in Divinity and a student of this college, was chosen to be master to him and his brethren. He was a man of great note for learning, piety and his diligence in framing and beautifying these young noble wits over which he was set. In so much that this blessed father, being but thirteen years of age, by his pains and the happiness of his own wit did compose so well, both in verse and prose, that many would not believe it to be possible that he could do it in such manner, till they were eye-witnesses of it themselves.

This young noble imp would never be idle, but spent even those times which were allowed for his recreation in some particular good studies. It was held half a miracle to see him without a book in his hand. His companions, moved by his example, did set him before their eyes as a pattern of virtue, sweetness and diligence. He would let no day pass without hearing Mass and that with extraordinary devotion. He communicated every month and with such feeling that his soul was a fiery furnace of true devotion and fervour, witnessed by those exhalations of sighs and aspirations which he had; and this was the main and principal study to which he bent himself. Having laid all good foundation for more high and subtle speculations, he began at thirteen years of age to enter into his course of philosophy. In which knowledge, though there be many difficulties by reason of the obscurity of the terms and conceptions, that it requires strength of understanding and imagination to comprehend it, yet by the benefit of his clear natural understanding he waded easily into it and quite through it. By this means he was formed and framed in his understanding to the right conceiving of the most secret and hidden mysteries of our belief and in his will better prepared by the knowledge of moral virtues to the practice of them. For it is certain, as we must know that which is good before we love it, so the greater knowledge we have of it, the more fervent we are in the search of it. After he had ended his studies with great

commendation and evident proof of the excellence of his wit,[1] he
was driven from his college to the Court, by the order and appointment of his parents, where, although in outward appearance he
forsook his studies, yet he did not so leave them but that he retained a true affection to them, having nothing more often in his
discourse than learning and in heart nothing more engraven than
true religion. And yet, not without great admiration he joined and
leagued three things together, which seem to be mainly opposite,
to wit: religion, good literature and the Court. For even in those
court actions which have in them ordinarily much vanity he
showed example of true piety and devotion without any affectation,
but a most gracious decency. He was adorned with all good parts
which are most amiable. He was courteous and affable to the
meanest sort; sweet and gracious in his outward carriage; modest
and grave in his actions; serious and prudent in his discourses;
valiant and courageous in matters of execution; a sworn enemy of
vanity; a scourge of revelling and railing; a perfect hater of flattery
and ambition. To conclude, he was a mirror of all Christian and
moral virtues, faithful was he always to God and his king, full of
hope for heavenly joys, charitable towards God and his neighbour,
temperate and very sober in his diet, a passionate friend of justice,
labouring with might and main that it might be rightly executed.
His virtues and perfections won him the grace of Henry the Third,
who in witness of his affection made him presently Master of his
Wardrobe.[2] The prince's favour, which makes men of young years
more vain and glorious, made him more humble, seeking rather
daily to grow more in virtue than greatness of fortune. He would
refuse no man that sought access to him, but when men's suits
were just and full of equity, he would himself present their peti-
tions to the King. Religious men had a great support of him and he
reputed it a great honour to entertain them at his table. And his
esteem of them caused them oftentimes to acquaint him with their
necessities more freely, which he relieved with incredible charity.
And herein he was so much noted that the King himself styled
him "the advocate of religious persons". These were the disposi-
tions, which were like the steps of Jacob's ladder, upon which he

---

[1] intelligence   [2] In 1579

mounted with the Angels, till the King of Angels received him in his glory, which is the effect and fruit of God's grace and meritorious works.

Of his marriage and how he lived during the time thereof

THE THIRD CHAPTER

THE King in all occasions having abundantly witnessed his particular affection to this blessed person and desiring further to confirm him in a stable state of those honours and favours which he had conferred unto him (that he might not entertain any affection of leaving the world, as he had done before), persuaded him to marriage, which was to shut the door against all occasions or invitements to that end. God knows whether he were bent thereto in affection, but in the end, won by the counsel of his parents and commandment of the King he made choice by the advice of the King of Mademoiselle Catharine de la Valette, daughter to Monseigneur de la Valette, Colonel of the Light Horsemen, whose noble courage, well tried by many noble exploits, both within and without the realm remains as a heritage; and is daily augmented by worthy acts for the defence of the Church and the State in the person of Monseigneur d'Espernon, Duke and Peer of France and Colonel of the Infantry, his son and brother of this noble dame, whom nature and art did strive to adorn, even in her first birth, and her rare virtues and perfections far surpassing her age have made her a pearl of her time and a miracle of this age. It fell out by God's special providence that this happy marriage was made and accomplished; there was so incredible similitude of affections in this holy couple. For she was inflamed with the same love from heaven that he was, and no less enemy to vanity than he, reputing it the venom and poison of great dames. As he in a manly sort made no esteem of exterior beauty, so she contrary to the disposition of her sex detested all painting and farding[1] as a thing odious

---

[1] embellishment, make-up

in the sight of God. He was among young noble courtiers a man whom all beheld as an example to follow, and she was of no less eminence among noble dames. And now they being joined and tied one to the other by the bands of holy wedlock and knot of mutual love, seemed to have but one heart in two bodies, or one soul in two hearts, which caused the very same affection to all goodness and the like detestation and hate of vice. It is one of the wise man's sayings that riches and possessions are left in patrimony by the parents, but the gift of a modest and wise woman comes from God only. And when she is known for such in the state of her virginity he gives counsel to the parents to marry her with a man of the same perfection, to the end that God may be the better served by such a commixtion. But the virtues of them both did so shine in the Court that they were had in such admiration that the greatest enemies of virtue or lovers of vanity were forced to confess ingeniously that such a blessed couple could hardly be matched with their like. Such force has truth that it makes the professed enemies of virtue to confess and praise it.

Before they married together they practised great works of piety and did as it were redouble their good affections, each inciting the other by example. What should I speak of their particular devotions in their private cabinets? Hours seemed to them but moments when they entered into communing with their own hearts and reflecting upon their consciences; sometimes they were absorbed by profound meditation of the providence of God, which does powerfully and sweetly conduct all things by the diversity of so many wills to the exaltation of His Glory. Another while they turned their thoughts from the vanity of the world, where seeing nothing but wind and smoke, they beheld with astonishment the blindness of many souls which build towers of their hopes upon so weak a foundation. Among other things they were not unmindful of the shortness of this life and the divers accidents which as sworn enemies lie in wait to take it from us, and they discerned here clearly the infinite occasions of sin, more in the Court rather than in any place, and such as are able to make the most wary goer to slip. And lastly to control all charming temptations, they considered oft the assurance of death and the uncertainty of the time, with the account which must be rendered of our actions when we are to arrive at the port and be disembarked out of the rotten vessels of our feeble bodies. Out of these good meditations it grew that their communication and ordinary speech was of God, of virtue, of good works and of heaven. The sweetness thereof so seasoned their souls that they never had speech of the delights of this world, but showed great disgust and disdain of them. The sweetness of these heavenly meditations is such that none can value them in any sort, without feeling some foretaste of them here. These holy and blessed exercises caused them one time, after some good discourse, that they protested and plighted faith one to another solemnly, that the survivor would renounce the world and enter into a cloister, where passing the rest of the days in religious exercises he should offer also the sacrifice of holy vows to God and pray for the soul of the departed.

Can it easily be conceived what measure of graces their blessed souls received from heaven or how sweet these odours were wherewith they were (as it were) perfumed by the sweet ointments of heavenly unction? For what a miracle is it to see such aspirations sent up to heaven by a couple of such young noble persons, whereof the eldest was not yet twenty-two years of age. I know not whether from that time they made not a vow of chastity and did not live afterward in continence. God only, who saw their affections, knows it. For the more they endeavoured a spiritual advancement in piety in the presence of God, the more were they careful to hide it from the eyes of others, especially of courtiers, where devotion and piety are styled by the name of counterfeit devotion and hypocrisy. Their home was a holy temple and house of religion. They had a careful eye to the behaviour of their servants, that they might not give offence to any and that their talk should not be dissolute according to the common fashion of those that serve great persons.

Every morning after they had offered their hearts and souls to God and resigned to His holy will all the actions of the same day, then taking their Hours (that is, their books of prayers and devotion used by the Church) they said their Office together, so that they who heard them without and not seeing them would have said that they had been two religious persons shut up in their cells, offering up their prayers and praises according to the obligation of their vow; nor were they in their souls differing from them, but in habit and profession only. They could not endure any dishonest or wanton speech, neither such as was any way injurious to others; which sort of talk is but too rife in the Court. For such fruit does the perfect love of God produce that we will not only forbear to offend God ourselves, but also procure as much as lies in us that He be not offended by others.

At this time the Order of the Capuchins began to be in great reputation (as it is at this present) for the integrity of the rule of S. Francis, which they do observe according to the rigour of the letter, even as Our Saviour declared to S. Francis, when the religious on the mountain of S. Columbe thought it to be austere and rigid, heard a voice from heaven which said that it was from God and that His will was that it should be observed according to the letter without any gloss. This order was much reverenced for the austerity and for the novelty of the religious which were but freshly come into France at the instance of the great Cardinal of Lorraine,[1] whose virtues and great sufficiency were well known by that authority which he bore in the Council of Trent, presiding there; who having first obtained licence of our Holy Father Gregory the Thirteenth in the year of Our Lord 1573, presented them to the Most Christian King Charles the Ninth and to the Queen his mother, who gave them a place for their convent near the Tuileries (which are His Majesty's gardens of pleasure) in the suburbs of S. Honoré, where the bones of this blessed father rest; the same illustrious Cardinal having given to the Capuchins before a place for a convent, at Meudon, near to his castle. After this by the conduct of God's Holy Spirit (who has a particular care of His Church and of religious) they so multiplied in France that they are spread almost through all places thereof; and yet they would be more if they builded convents in all places where they are earnestly

---

[1] The Cardinal of Lorraine died in 1578 and the French Capuchins then came under the aegis of the Cardinal Charles de Bourbon. For the history of relations between the Cardinal of Lorraine and the early French Capuchins, see Godefroy de Paris, *Les Frères mineurs Capucins en France*, Paris, 1937, vol. i, fasc. 1, pp. 17-66.

sought for and indifferently received all those who present themselves to live in observance of their rule.

Now it happened that one day, as the Count de Bouchage, coming from the town, being in a coach with the King (for the King
seldom went without him), he saw by chance or rather by divine
providence two Capuchins who passed by with their wallets upon
their backs; he fixed his eyes a long time upon them and in the
view of them felt extraordinary inward motions of his soul and
seemed to hear an inward voice saying: "These are they whom I do
cherish with all affection." The King, seeing him sad and pensive
suddenly and his eyes still fixed upon the religious, doubted lest he
might imprint them in his heart whom he beheld so intentively,
and said to him: "These are the true followers of S. Francis and do
observe his rule according to the first institution." "It is true,"
answered the Count, "and in this they are twice happy, for they do
not only avoid the enticing baits of the world and of ambition and
vanity, but they put themselves into a state of more assurance for
obtaining that glorious heavenly crown; for as much as mortifying
and crucifying their carnal appetites here on earth, they suffer with
their head Jesus Christ crucified, whose words are deeds and cannot fail." This unsought view of them with other few words did so
inflame his affection that he desired in his heart that he might
presently change his state of life and instead of his coach and rich
clothes, he could have been well content presently to have been on
foot with a wallet on his back. Upon this presently he called to
mind his first holy inspiration and how God had spoken to him,
when he was but young of age, in the library of Toulouse, as is
before mentioned.

Hence it fell out that he fell into some agonies of perplexity, not
knowing what to do in such straits as he was. For on the one side
he now resolves himself that this was the rule wherein he should
spend and end his life; and on the other side, the bands of marriage
with his dear spouse whom he loved most affectionately, could not
permit him to take this course of life so much wished for. But what
should he do in this case: for either he thought he must impart his
mind to his wife (whom he loved more dearly than himself) and so
invite her to shut herself up in a cloister; or else he must forsake

her without taking his leave and communicating his intention. But this he could not do; for the same day he proposed it to a Capuchin under another name, and it was told him that no man could leave his wife and become a religious man, unless she likewise entered into religion. Whereupon he determined to attend the holy will of God.

In the meantime he daily augmented his works of piety; gave himself to mental prayer with more fervour, frequented the sacraments more often than he did before. And for the better effecting of this he quitted his own lodging and bought one near to the Capuchins, to the end he might better practise his good intentions and enjoy the conversation of these good religious fathers whom he respected and cherished as angels sent from heaven, and had them as directors of his actions. Insomuch that he did often assist them at midnight, while they sang their Matins, and obtained by special privilege to have one of them for his ghostly father, which was also granted to his wife. And who would have thought that this virtuous course of life should not have been to his full contentment, keeping no doubt most religiously God's commandments and doing so much good by his rare example. But God, whose secrets far surpass the weakness of our understanding, would accomplish a greater work by him, as we shall see in the sequel of this narration.

While he gave himself to this virtuous and holy course of life, it pleased God to take from him his dearest spouse, whose decease so struck his heart that he grew dying to the world, as though he would also die with her. She died being but twenty-two years of age, in the spring of her virtues, whom God took to Him to make her partaker of a more excellent and permanent glory; leaving her friends much sorrowful, but that they were comforted by the fruits of her former piety. She left one only daughter, eighteen months old, a true heir of her virtues, who is now Madame the Duchess of Guise, whose prudence in worldly affairs and singular piety and fervour in the true service of God is well-known and much renowned through all France.

Of his entrance into religion and farewell to the world

THE FOURTH CHAPTER

THE Count of Bouchage, after the death of his dearest spouse, languished with sorrow, that his eyes could find no kind of worldly delight, neither would his heart affect or love anything. His loss was so great that he would not entertain any earthly hopes to build on, which are as movable as quicksands, but at the length recollecting himself he considered that all such strokes come from the hand of God, though we know not the cause of it and the will of God therein. And therefore as the sun when it appears, scatters the thick foggy clouds which darkened the air; so did he chase the clouds of this affliction and cheered himself by taking holy resolution worthy of his noble spirit and gave the cartel of defiance[1] to fortune and all the misty brouillerie[2] of the world which deprive men of beholding the true light of the true sun of eternal glory. He discerned those things truly in their nakedness and bareness which worldlings beholding with a fair glass do so much desire and admire. Insomuch that oftentimes he compared the world with the great priest Eli, who sent back Samuel, when as he, being called by the voice of God, ran to Eli. And it will not be amiss to set down his very words as they were written with his own hand, that it may appear that this my discourse is so founded upon the truth.

"The world," says he, "as another Eli drives us from it when we are put back of these very creatures which we tender and which we love, finding in them a thousand disgusts, infidelities, instabilities and defects. Our friends forsake us, our servants mock us, our companions betray us, and in the midst of all pleasures and delights we find infinite sorrows and bitter gripings. What is this else but to make us know that the world to which we run does reject us and give us many scorns and sharp blows? And what does it say but: 'Get thee gone, I am not thy God; get thee gone, the good and the contentment thou seekest is not to be found in me'." He spoke herein as a man of great experience and wisdom to those

---

[1] a written challenge   [2] deceits

who, being transported with the dalliances of the smiling fortunes of the world, have sworn a league and alliance with the grandeurs and prosperities of it.

This contempt of the world grew daily in him, as no doubt the light of grace did grow, yet could he not execute it, by reason of many encumbrances which followed the death of his dear spouse. I mean the discharge of her last will, which he did very faithfully; and the fear which he had of occasioning great discontentment to his friends, and incurring the King's displeasure, knowing how dear and inward he was esteemed by him. These considerations and many others hindered him that he did not so speedily accomplish his holy purpose as he would. But God, who laughs at the counsels and designs of men and turns them as it seems best to His holy wisdom, had compassion of him in the end and by the sweet gale of His Holy Spirit (which brings in perfect calm to afflicted and troubled souls) made him know His will by an action extraordinary and miraculous.

One day being occupied in holy exercise of piety and devotion according to his wont, falling into remembrance of his dear wife and her excellent virtues, he could not forbear deep groans which the anguish of his heart drew from him perforce; so that, seeking to appease these inward troubles, he took his Hours (which is his book of prayers, for so Catholics call them) into his hands. At the first opening of his book he fell upon this verse: *Dirupisti Domine vincula mea, tibi sacrificabi hostiam laudis; Thou hast broken my bonds, O Lord, I will sacrifice to Thee the sacrifice of praise.* Pausing a while upon the words (for so devout souls who are exercised in matters of devotion do frequently) he began to think that these words did touch him very nearly, as though God had expressly spoken to him and said: "God hath broken the bonds of thy marriage, which did hinder thee from following His steps; therefore is it most reasonable that I now obey the voice of His holy inspiration and offer up myself as a sacrifice to Him, which is the best manner of prayer which I can express." And as he was occupied in this holy thought his book fell out of his hand; he took it up again and the same words again were the first that offered them to his sight: *Thou hast broken my bonds, O Lord, etc.* "Assuredly", says he, "this is God who speaks." And again being elevated in mind and not heeding his book in his hands, he let it fall the third time and yet again fell upon the same words, whereupon being astonished he shut the book, fell on his knees and bathing his eyes with many tears and opening his heart to God, he used these amorous words full of devotion.

"O Almighty God, Saviour of the world and most bounteous lover of Thy creatures, I see well that Thou wilt have me and there is nothing that can serve me to resist Thy holy ordinance. Thou hast possessed all the power of my soul, so that the objects are removed which had fastened them to the earth and now they look upward upon Thee, who art the last End of all things. But alas (O most gracious and merciful Saviour) what is there in me which provoking Thy mercy hath caused Thee to turn the eyes of pity upon me? What is there in me which might in any sort be worthy of such a vocation? Nothing certainly, but great maims, corruptions and sins, which rather provoking Thy fury and indignation, should banish me from Thy presence and have caused dreadful punishment and eternal tortures. For it proceedeth from Thy love and mercy that I yet live in the desert of this world; Thy love hath been my buckler and my support and now by an infinite excess thereof Thou dost draw me from the world and settlest my feet in the right path and dost conduct me through a most perilous wilderness. Guide therefore, O Lord, Thy most wretched creature and impotent servant, do with me what shall seem best in Thy eyes. I resign myself wholly to Thee and cast myself into Thy arms; frame all my actions and conduct all my desires to the glory of Thy holy name."

Thus he put on a courageous resolution which he did not defer long after to execute and to become a noble soldier of Our Blessed Saviour and serve Him under the ensigns of seraphical S. Francis and so to make himself a pleasing holocaust before God, offering his body to Him by the vow of perpetual chastity, his soul and affections by holy obedience and his goods and whatsoever he most possessed by the vow of voluntary poverty. Many can be content sometimes to entertain good thoughts, which put them in mind of the vanities of the world, and discover them to be but less than the shadows of a dream. They will say that all that the world proposes resembles the apples of Gomorrha, which are fair without, but smoke and ashes within; yea, they will call the world cozener, traitor, disloyal, and yet suffer themselves to be transported with her enchantments and fair promises: but among a hundred thousand it is hard to find one which has the courage to take such a heroical resolution, but in the end they play the cravens and become slaves to the world and render it homage in most base and ignoble manner.

Having now resolved to put this in execution very speedily, he entered into deliberation, by what means he might effect his purpose with least difficulty. He durst not reveal his intention to any man, for if the King had had but the least notice of it, he would have interposed his authority to hinder it; and if his brethren had known it, they would immediately have acquainted the King with it. Therefore he without help of any secular person did set in order all his affairs of importance and disposed secretly of his house. He gave to the reverend fathers of the Order of Minims that house at Nijon[1] which he had bought, being near to the Capuchins, with twelve hundred French livres for yearly rent (which are paid to them still by Madame de Guise), obliging them to say two Masses for the intention of his mother and wife and to maintain a schoolmaster for the instruction of youth at the suburbs of S. Honoré; and he left to the Capuchins his gardens who would not accept the house. And in the end he managed this business so prudently and secretly that he took the habit before any of his friends suspected any such matter and so gave his farewell to the world in a most noble and pious manner, as it may appear by a lively description of it, made by Monseigneur the Cardinal Perron of late and happy memory:

The Farewell of Monsieur Joyeuse, Entering into Religion

"Since the happy day is come which has not only opened the eyes of my body, but has awakened my sleepy spirit and has light-

---

[1] i.e., Nigeon-lès-Chaillot, Paris. Brousse is not strictly accurate in all this, since Fr. Angel did not in fact make his will till his solemn profession the following year, 19 August 1588. (Cf. Gonzague, op. cit., p. 156-7.)

ened it with a pure and holy light in showing me the reposing place of my sovereign good and soul's health, I will first of all give thanks to Thee, O great God of mercy, from the bottom of my heart and soul that Thou hast vouchsafed me this day this unspeakable grace and favour in stretching forth Thy hand to draw me out of this world and the tough and deep mire thereof; and in putting me in the way of Thy holy will. Thou hast delivered me from obscure and dangerous darkness and placed me in the brightness of Thy grace and benediction. Thou hast plucked me from the thraldom of sin to set me at liberty under the sweet yoke of Thy holy obedience and comfortable expectation of eternal life. Therefore let all my senses in a perfect harmony and all the powers of my soul wholly bend to the serious consideration of so great a benefit, desire nothing, think of nothing but of Thy honour and glory, who hast been so gracious and so merciful to me; let all my cogitations be nothing but to meditate of Thy great power and might and let my sight have no other object but the contemplation of Thy meritorious works and let the hymns of Thy glory be the exercise of my voice. And as for thee (traitorous world) which hast withheld me till this day by thy alluring baits, I do now defy thee and abandon thee forever.

"Farewell then (O worldly vanity) for I go now to die for thee, O fair and pleasing place of retreat where I now make my entry. O what a goodly palace is this! The stately portal is enriched with a great cross, adorned with nails, whips and pincers. This frontispiece is beset with dead men's skulls and bones. O brave and victorious trophies which do represent that great victory of life over death, of heaven over hell, by which victory we were ransomed and drawn forth from the bottomless gulf of dreadful darkness, and death was subdued, which held us captives under the yoke of sin, and so restored to our first country and heavenly right. O heavenly seals of eternal bliss, ye are the due to us if we will seek you under these brave ensigns. O precious and rich ornament, what jasper, what polished porphyry stones, what pillars of choice marble, what costly pieces are to be compared with these riches? O Cross, let me embrace thee, the dear cloak of my soul's health; by thee I have entrance into the kingdom of heaven and mount above the high regions of the heavens; thou representest the whole world, for thy four points regard the four corners of the world which are not saved but by thee. O cross, which art the ladder which reachest from earth to heaven, from hell to paradise, O let me cleave fast to thee to the end that I may be raised up to the heavens with thee. O cross, image of pains and torments which my Saviour endured to overcome death, teach me to vanquish that which remains of death and lives yet in me by sin and teach me the patience, which it is behoveful to have to conquer myself. O nails all bloody, which have fastened the Redeemer of the world to the cross, fasten my affections upon His pains and settle my soul in that constant virtue which ought to tame my vicious designs. Press down my sinful hands with the fear of God, to the end that they stir not when temptations incite them to any evil act, and that innocence distilling down from all parts, may be the blood to nourish my soul. And O ye whips and scourges, besmeared with blood, make the feeling and colour of my mortified and benumbed body to quicken again. Drive from about me all sort of delights, which like pricking flies and hornets, do envenom and wound me, so that as ye have caused the blood to flow which hath cleansed our sins, so cause ye that to be spilt which hath polluted my conscience. Abate in my flesh all delight thereof, that I may be new born in purity and sincerity. And thou, O sponge, full of bitterness, distil into my heart one drop of this sharp liquor, but yet wholesome and quickening, which my Redeemer tasted of at His death. Give me a little taste of His languorous passion, for my soul as a sponge hath so drunk in the unsavoury and pestilent humours of the world that if it be not somewhat pressed and wrung by anguish and torment, it will corrupt and perish wholly. And thou, O spear, which opened the holy sides of my Saviour, open my sides and pierce my heart, that I may see what fond desires, what brutish concupiscences were there sealed: so that blood (which is the desire of the flesh) and water (which is the vanity and inconstancy of earth) may flow even to my fingers and mounting up to my eyes may restore to them the sight of heavenly and divine things, which my sins have covered with a thick skin and cloud. After this I will put on my head the crown of thorns as an evident sign that those who are crowned in this world with thorns, shall wear a crown of glory in another world. Let us then enter into His holy habitation which is a true inn set upon the highway to heaven. O what magnificence is there in this baseness, what richness in this poverty, what pleasure in this pain! O my soul, thou hast long languished in the furious concupiscences of the world, now art thou arrived at the heaven of health, where thou needest not covet anything, saving that thou hast. For thou hast all things, because all things are in God, who is all in all, and here He offereth himself to thee. Give me, O give me the weapons of this happy warfare, that I may fight while the day lasteth and that I may conquer myself and so triumph over the world. O fair and rich robe, thou shalt cover the infirmity of my members and hide the pride of my flesh. These pieces patched in shall be so many memorials to me of the weakness of my nature, which suffereth itself to be stained and pierced through on every side by the filth and corruption of the world, to the which I ought now to apply holy and religious meditations, and now to sow it and re-enter it into the divine nature by holy and virtuous actions. Welcome fair girdle, though thou art gross, yet too weak to keep down the garments to the body, that is, to subdue the flesh to the spirit and to restrain the disordered concupiscences, that they occupy not our thoughts but may be strangled in our bosom so soon as they are born. Courage then, O heart, I am now ready to enter the lists, God strengthen and fortify me, that I may get the conquest to God's glory. Farewell world, farewell."

He spoke not this by words of mouth but expressed it really and effectually in all his actions; not in an ordinary fashion, but with so much fervour and inward contentment of soul as that, the inward light sending forth evident beams outwardly, they that were most conversant in spiritual life were forced to say, *Haec mutatio dextra excelsi*, This change of the right hand of the Most High: for what more strange than to see a noble man of that quality and rank, raised on high with great honours, rich and great in place and authority, a favourite of a king, who seemed to hold fortune in his hands and to impart of it to others, at the age of four-and-twenty years, when he was now in the spring of his fortunes, suddenly so

changed that he would clothe himself with so vile and contemptible
a weed (I mean in the opinion of worldlings, who measure all
things by the ell of their vanity) and to become poor, naked, and in
necessities, so that he was not master of so much as the very cord
wherewith he was girt, and to abandon the Court, not by any
disaster (which often casteth many out to the disgrace of the world)
but by a holy violence of love, the most puissant passion of all
others?

At this time the reverend Father Bernard d'Osimo[1] was Provincial, a man of great reputation for the holiness of his life and
true sincerity of soul. In testimony of his sanctity God wrought
many miracles by him after his death. His body also was found a
long time after, uncorrupted, yielding a most sweet and fragrant
odour, which is not seen at any time, but accompanying the bodies
of holy men. This blessed father gave Father Angel Joyeuse the
habit, admitting him to it the Fourth of September in the year
1587, six-and-twenty days after the death of his wife; who at midnight went to the convent of the Capuchins, attended only with
two of the servants of his chamber and his chaplain, who not knowing whither he went, were much astonished when they saw him on
his knees before the altar in the presence of all the religious and
saw him cast off his cloak, strip himself of his doublet and shirt and
put on a rough habit and gird himself with a gross cord, which
manner of clothing seems to be irksome even to the strong lusty
labourer. O blessed soul truly guided and lightened by the Holy
Ghost, for it was not the Court, nor flesh and blood which has
taught thee this lesson, but the extraordinary grace of God, to
which thou, having opened entrance into thy soul without any
apprehension of a cold and sharp winter, hast undertaken so hard
and painful a voyage (to the eyes of the world) that the number is
very small of those who have the courage to trace the same steps.

These are such favours, which God does not to all, drawing men
in divers manners to Him as it seems best to His holy will and

---

[1] Fr. Bernard d'Osimo was elected Provincial for the period 1581-4 and then
again in 1585. (The year's break between the first and second period of office was
binding on all provincials in accordance with the statutes of the order.) Fr.
Bernard employed great tact in healing the rifts between the French and Italian
factions in the young French Province.

according to their manner of life. For although infirmity be a great means to make us turn to God, when we, forgetting His benefits, entertain ourselves with vanities and idle contentments (and even by this way the holy seraphic S. Francis was called), notwithstanding, honours are another means of vocation and very proper and effectual, but much differing from the former. For the first forces us by afflictions to lift up our eyes to heaven; and the other makes us to observe how all the pleasures and delights of the world must have a wormwood taste in the end and indeed breed sorrow and grief. And this vocation, as the more excellent, takes hold only of the most elevated spirits and the purest souls, who do clearly discern truth from falsehood and the substance from the shadow.

This it was that wrought with the Count Bouchage, that by reason of his fervour he was called Angel, and so commonly afterward had the name of Father Angel Joyeuse. An angel indeed, guardian of purity, and a glass of many noble good souls which followed his steps, as he had imitated many infinite others which went before him. For this holy religion of S. Francis has been professed of kings, princes and many honourable persons, and shall be till the end of the world, drawing men to it by splendour of purity and integrity, which as a bright sun, shining with great lustre makes the perfection of it in this life evident to the profane and irreligious persons and represents unto them the crowns which are received for it in the life to come.

John Brenne, Count of Vienne, of the race of the great Duke of Bouillon, first King of Jerusalem, after he was crowned king at Tyre in the year 1210 and made Emperor of Constantinople, after many tropies won from his enemies, forsaking the world, took the habit of S. Francis, of whom a poet wrote in this manner:

Brenna was mighty and great in kingly power
But yet by S. Francis' habit he climbed a higher tower.

Henry, King of Cyprus, after that he had a long time governed that island, betook himself to the religion of S. Francis and led a life renowned for sanctity, whereof the miracles give sufficient testimony, which it has pleased God to work by the invocation of him for an intercessor. And behold what is written of this:

He that was King of Cyprus and great in wealth
Maketh himself a Franciscan for his soul's health.

John, King of Armenia, the sovereign master of four-and-
twenty kings (who governed divers countries of this realm, a great
enemy and conqueror of the Saracens), did not make so much
account of his crown as of that of S. Francis, for he forsook the
one and bore and died with the other, as the poet witnesses:

Armenia wonders at their king of royal seed
Casting down his sceptre and clad with S. Francis' weed.

James, King of Majorca, chose rather to be a poor soldier under
S. Francis' standard, than to be a great king in his realm:

Majorca stood astonished to see their head
Abandoning all delight, eating poor S. Francis' bread.

Peter, son of John, King of Aragon, a professed Franciscan, was
a man of holy life, a great preacher; and preaching before Urban
the Fifth and the Emperor did so join eloquence with his virtue
that he drew many tears from his hearers. He kept the rule according to the rigour of the letter, if ever any did, as is expressed.

O happy and thrice noble Aragonia of spring
Who tookest the poor habit of religion and doffed a king.

I let pass Robert, King of Jerusalem and Sicily; Adolph, King
of Holsatia, and infinite others who moved by the secret gale of
God's spirit, turned the sails of their thoughts and designs to this
holy port of assurance. And not to go further, have we not this
present year, here in France, the noble design of the Count de
Voult, issued out of one of the most famous and most ancient
families of France, who in the height of his fortune, ready to marry
and at the age of four-and-twenty years, has given the defy to all
the pleasures of the world and now being clad in the poor habit of
a Capuchin is entered into his noviceship in this city of Paris.

Of his noviceship

THE FIFTH CHAPTER

THE Count of Bouchage, having made this great and pleasing sacrifice to God of himself, and having got and merited the name of Angel, the morning was no sooner come but the bruit[1] of this act, spreading itself through Paris, came to the King's ears as soon as he rose; who being astonished much at this report and struck with great sadness by reason of his great affection to him, took his coach instantly and went to the convent of the Capuchins, attended with the brethren of Father Angel, who besought him with all humble and earnest instance that he would not go out of that convent till he took their brother with him, persuading themselves that if they made not use of this opportunity by the King's authority, they should never enjoy the sweet conversation of their brother hereafter. Therefore the King sent for the Provincial and asked him how he durst admit him without his leave or without once advertising him of it, whereas he knew well what particular affection he bore him among all his nobles. Whereupon he commanded his clothes presently to be brought, for he said that his presence and service was necessary for him.

This good father, both wise and pious, made him no long reply, knowing that it was as hard to quiet a troubled spirit in the beginning of a passion as to stay the course of an impetuous torrent: and therefore said only this that he went not out of his convent, nor his chamber to seek him, nor to solicit him, and that he had not received him but upon his most earnest and importunate suit and prayers: so that he took heaven to witness and his soul for a caution and warrant of his, if he chanced to make shipwreck and loss of his soul in the world, yet notwithstanding the port was and should be open for him, when he would go forth, but he humbly besought His Majesty not to lay any such command upon him, as to put him out by force, having a great horror to commit such a mortal offence which he could not do, though he were to die for it.

[1] report

While he spoke these words, he gave charge to a brother to call him. Who entering into his chamber, found him on his knees and his eyes lifted up to heaven and melting into tears, praying heartily because he had heard the noise and the resolution of the King and his brethren, who were in the cloister. He came down immediately, but much against his mind. As soon as the King saw him in this habit, with his head shaven and barefooted, he fell almost into a trance with sudden astonishment and suddenly so changed his colour that he could not speak, he was so overwhelmed with sorrow. And in the depth of this passion of mind, tears as new witnesses of his singular affection towards him trickled down his cheeks; his brethren also transported with great anguish of mind, fell upon his neck groaning and lamenting, professing that they would rather die than to leave him in this manner. O what force grace has in a poor soul, it may appear by the sequel. This father saw them weep and lament with dry eyes and showed a smiling and cheerful countenance to them amidst their mournings, for in a grave, modest and religious manner he made them see that he had no cause of grief, but rather of great joy; but that only he could not but be moved somewhat that they were so affected.

The King at length recovering himself and fetching a deep sigh, asked him what moved him to choose that kind of life, so contrary to his tender and delicate constitution, which he thought could never support the yoke of such austerities? What discontentment he had received at the Court that he should forsake it and enter into such a course of life; if he doubted of any change of his affection towards him, he would give him as good assurance of it as ever any man had. As for devout serving of God, he told him, God is found everywhere and men may work their salvation in all places. That S. Louis and many other saints had lived in the Court and yet ceased not to lead a holy life. In fine, he told him he should do much wrong to his family, if he went on in this course of life and therefore prayed him by that love and affection which a subject owes to his prince, who tenders and loves him, that he would presently follow him and forsake this life. What could he say more to abate the courage of a man of great resolution? His brethren tendered the same request with all possible instance, but all in vain, for he had no ears to hearken to them in this request. To the King he made this answer:

"Sir, it is not any discontentment that has moved me to seek this retreat and incited me to the contempt of the world and the vanities thereof. It is the grace of God which in the plenty and variety of contentments has made me see they are nothing but smoke. It is not any doubt or fear of your princely affection, for you have always affected me far beyond my desert. It is rather a lesson which I have learned of you, which without my own knowledge and practice, I have also received from heaven. For how often have you told me when I was alone with you in your cabinet and entertained some thoughts of devotion, that this world was full of deceitful baits and that ambition (as a most cruel lioness) did devour the most zealous; and that it was fit to follow those vocations which we have from God; and as all things tend to their centre, so ought we to direct all our intentions to God. I have now made my benefit of these holy exhortations; permit me therefore, I humbly beseech you, if you will do me the honour still to love me, that I may stay here and so enjoy my contentment, for he that loves wishes always the contentment of him whom he loves."

He spoke moreover touching the vanity of the world, that it is a poison which infects in such a manner that the most experienced physicians in spiritual medicines can hardly avoid it; that it is the daughter of the first of the devils, sister to that enmity which he bears to man: for to follow it is to forsake God and to love God is to detest it. God will not dwell in hearts divided. Besides, this world is very transitory and heaven is not given but to those who take it by violence; that it is as hard to save our souls amidst the pomps and vanities of the Court as to live in the midst of a furnace and not to feel the heat of the flames. In fine, his words prevailed so much with them that they were well appeased and returned with contentment, admiring the goodness of God that had endued so noble a body with so noble and heroical a soul.

After he had passed this first brunt[1] so courageously to the glory of God and joy of His angels, he met with a more dangerous assault, which seized upon his powers and abilities, the first

---

[1] attack

encountering only his affection; for what avails it to will and desire anything which is beyond our reach and which we cannot put in execution; no man performs anything well to which he was not before inclined in will to do, but many love great desires which surmount their strength. For the space of three months, his body having been accustomed to fine and good feeding, he could not eat the ordinary meat of the religious; and the inconvenience was the greater that he, desiring much to mortify himself, would not eat any extraordinary. The brown and hard bread which was given in alms to the religious, took away his appetite at the very sight; neither could he drink of the claret wine, for besides that it was sour and sharp and mixed of divers kinds, it may be he never used to drink of that sort of wine. These were dangerous batteries, able to subdue a brave defender. The physicians concluded, whether for favour or for money, it is not known, that he must necessarily forsake his religion for to save his life. His brethren in the meantime used all solicitation they could for this end, hoping that by gaining of time he would change his purpose. But the religious helping him with their prayers, his charity triumphed over all these to God's glory and the increase of his merits. He cared not for death and was not unwilling to quit the tabernacle of his weak body; having already forsaken the world, he would inure his body to mortifications, for he said he was entered into religion for that end and resolved to support all pains and travail in that kind.

His blessed mother, Madame de Joyeuse, only among all his friends did passionately desire his perseverance, and to this purpose she visited him often and encouraged him as much as lay in her, being herself much advanced in the school of perfection, and as he witnessed himself, the sight only of her was in stead of strong refection and strengthened him much in this holy course of life, in despite all the brisk encounters of the world, the flesh and the devil. She sent him every day two loaves of bread with a little bottle of white wine, and God who never gives us good desires without force to perform them, did distil down such benediction upon this bread, that with very little or no other meat he passed the time of three months in that rigorous fast which the religious do exactly observe. So powerful is love that when it commands us actions, all the greatest contrarieties and gusts are made easy and sweet. During this time he accustomed himself by little and little to eat of the common meat and at length gained so much of himself that there was not any of the religious (who had been never so hardly bred) that could pass with this nourishment more easily than himself: insomuch that he contented himself with herbs, beans, peas, pulse and for the most part with bread and water, while others ate such meat as was brought home at the common alms: wherefore he was reputed one of the most austere of his profession.

The morrow after he took the habit, the religious fathers, without regard of his quality (for among them there is no distinction in persons for their birth, be they of noble, or of mean parentage), began to put him to all vile and base exercises, both bodily and spiritual, fit for the trial of those who enter into the school of mortification. And he without any disdain or any repining obeyed in all things with great promptness, so that he was the first in all these exercises, and served for an example to incite others. What a change is this that he which was yesterday clad richly like a prince, attended with many servants and obeyed as a great seigneur of his rank, the day following clothes himself with a coarse sack and is commanded to dig and labour in a poor manner? That he which was served with so much respect and honour, subjects himself to sweep chambers and wash others' poor dishes; that he who yesterday with Joseph bore the sway and rule in the greatest and weightiest affairs of the King, to-day with Mardochaeus, clad with sackcloth and ashes, is despised and put to do those base offices which are enjoined to novices for proof of their humility and to quell their proper will, the plague and bane of religious souls. What pleasure he took in these humiliations it is not easily expressed; God, which knows the heart, did recompense him accordingly and by the effects we may easily conclude his true sincerity and perfect humility.

It happened in the time of his noviceship that the Duke of Joyeuse (his eldest brother) and another of his brethren were slain at the Battle of Coutras[1] for the defence of the Catholic faith and

[1] 20 October 1587

the state of their country, whose death was a cause of great mourning to all France. Their bodies according to their quality were brought to Paris and received with as much honour, according to an ancient manner, as if they had returned in conquest and were laden with the spoils of their enemies. They were attended by a solemn procession unto the church of S. Jacques du Haulte, past where it pleased the King also to assist[1] them, giving an ample testimony of his affection towards those who had laid down their lives for his defence, and he did not leave them till he saw their funerals, ended according to their merit and valour. Here among the religious persons the Capuchins were present to say the Office of the Dead for their intention, among whom there was hardly found anyone which could recite the Office without interruption of tears and groans. Only this Father Angel (though yet but a novice) without any exterior sign of such sorrow continued the singing of the Office and kept in that great sorrow, which did more nearly press him than any other. This death of his brethren, besides the grief which he had thereby, was also a shrewd temptation to him, for he was partly moved by the blood which cannot but boil in such a case, and partly by divers of his friends, who under colour of consolation visited him often to take the revenge of his brethren's death. But his buckler to resist these darts was a verse of Solomon which he had learned by heart and had often in his mouth: *Son, when thou comest to serve God, stand in fear and prepare thy heart for temptation.*

There arrived yet to him a more dangerous temptation than any of these former. Whereas these came not but from the world and the flesh, which are to be subdued by reason; but this last came from God, whom it pleased to take from him that inward gift which he had; so that all things which seemed before sweet to him suddenly became sour and unpleasant, for the inward consolation which is as the breast which God makes his young ones to suck, so to make them find contentment amidst all austerities and irksomeness of flesh and blood, was taken from him, so that now he fell into a wonderful dryness and languour of spirit, not finding any gust in his prayers, meditations and holy exercises, which are as it

[1] accompany

were the aromatical perfumes of a devout soul. Notwithstanding all this he ceased not to frequent the same holy practice of his devotions, neither was God's grace impaired to him hereby. For the best spiritualists know well that there is a great difference between the practices of piety and devotion and feeling a pleasure and sweet gust therein: the one being a direct act which tends directly to God as to the utmost Object; the other is an action of our knowledge, which causing a reflection upon that which we have done, brings with it joy and contentment. The first is a pure act of virtue, the second the fruit which we gather thereof: God concurs with the first and so by it are the solicitous actions of virtue exercised; but He deprives us of the second, which is our knowledge, whence rises our contentment; whence darkness comes instead of clearness, and dryness of spirit in the place of affection, and heaviness instead of joy. For more familiar explication of this we know that he who being extremely thirsty, shall take any liquor into his stomach without tasting it, should certainly drink it though he should not believe it, because he finds no contentment in the drinking: so fares it, when God takes away his comforts, we do not cease to exercise virtuous actions, but yet the want of our knowledge and gust makes us to think that we do not these actions.

Being in this distress he discovered[1] his inward affection to his superior, which is the best armour of defence a novice can use against any such temptations. The religious fathers assisted him by their holy prayers, and his virtuous mother was not wanting to encourage him, assuring him that it was God who would prove him and that He did often treat in this manner His best favourites. And therefore He which does mortify and quicken again when it pleases Him, who brings us to the brink of hell and brings us back according to His holy will, after He had tried his resolution and made him triumph over all these batteries, recompensed him an hundredfold for these pains and anguishes which he sustained. It happened that one night after Matins, the religious being all retired into their cells, he continued in the church praying; and there prostrating himself before the altar, he forced himself to overcome this great desolation wherewhich he was afflicted. It is

---

[1] revealed

not possible to represent this grief, for as much as the soul is more noble than the body, so are the dolours greater and there is no martyrdom comparable to it, seeing that martyrs, inwardly lightened by the special grace of God, have found great comfort in their torments and roses among their thorns. Whereas this poor novice, afflicted in spirit and deprived of spiritual pleasure, received no consolation from above, from whence he expected his ease and deliverance.

Lying therefore flat before the altar, praying with all the powers of his soul, he felt suddenly an extraordinary motion within him, so that some spark of that heavenly fire which purifies the spirit kindled so great a flame in his heart, that he being not able to smother it cried out so loud that the religious who were at rest in their cells, were awaked with the noise. Oh holy soul, now is thy contentment come and the bitterness of the affliction past, yet not so that thou canst have any assurance from the like assaults, over which (if they fall out) thou shalt by God's holy grace triumph as thou hast already. For after all these incursions of temptation he had a violent combat in debating with himself, whether the life of Carthusians and their solitude were not more proper and fit for him. But recommending this to God in earnest prayer, he received inspiration from God that he should persevere in that course of life which he had now undertaken. Whereupon he came to the reverend Father Julien[1] (master of the novices) and said in his ear, to him: "My father, I have made a vow to God to live and die a Capuchin." From that time he enjoyed a sweet repose and calm of his soul. All his mortifications were pleasures to him, his shirts of hair were roses, his fastings were great banquets, his disciplines were delights and the grace which he received from above was so well entertained by his co-operation that he went on courageously in his intended course and was never after disquieted by any accident.

[1] Fr. Julian of Camerino, a convert Jew.

Of his profession and manner of life

THE SIXTH CHAPTER

FATHER Angel Joyeuse, having now passed the year of his novice-ship which is truly called the year of probation, because even as gold is tried in the furnace, so was he tried of God and man by all sorts of mortifications, and so by these actions augmented his grace and his merit. The time of his profession being come, that he was to enter into an obligation with God, by solemn vow to live the rest of his days in most simple poverty, most pure chastity and most perfect obedience, he humbly requested the reverend Father Bernard d'Osimo, who was to receive him in the presence of all the religious on God's part, that he would admit him among the professed religious, as he had done the year before among the novices. This good father, whose words were piercing even to the inward marrow of the conscience to make him apprehend the ugliness of vices and the beauty of virtue, with the different end of the one and the other, knowing of what great importance a vow of a religious is, by which he cannot do that under pain of damnation, which he might have done before without the least scruple of offending God, bent his persuasions with all fervour to let him see the sweetness of liberty (which was as yet in his power); that it was a small matter to forsake our ease and commodities, but to forsake our will, that this was a great enterprise. He told him that he might yet freely enjoy his contentments and the Court, that he might buy heaven better cheap, and that the King and his friends would receive infinite contentment thereat. In fine, he said, religion was so heavy a yoke that the most courageous did stoop to sustain it, that he had tasted somewhat this year past, but all that was but honey in comparison of that which he must suffer, as to pass mountains covered with snow barefooted; besides, that this was a marriage which cannot be broken, so that instead of commanding he must obey, abandon his own proper affections, die to his natural desires, despise worldly passions, make light of all revilings and appro-briums, embrace calumnies, love poverty, have no other riches but affliction and finally to nail himself to the Cross forever. And therefore that he should be well advised what he would do. Hereupon he asked him if he would go backward or forward. What courageous spirit would not have been daunted with this speech?

But this blessed novice, having well tasted of the sweet liquors which the world represents (which seem rather sweet than are truly), was so far from being diverted by this discourse that contrariwise like a palm tree, the more it is charged, the more it rises, so he became more courageous and resolute than before and besought him more instantly for his admission. Wherefore prostrating himself before the altar he solemnized this contract of his profession with unspeakable joy, putting himself into the hands of this blessed father, his superior. O mutation or rather resurrection, to give the last farewell to inclinations of sensuality and worldly delights in this manner! This food is too hard of digestion for a common and ordinary soul, it is such that God does not give but to His best favourites. His profession being made, it is almost incredible how he augmented his fervour in prayer, his austerity in fasting, his rigour in disciplines, blessing God from the bottom of his soul that He had called him to this kind of life, which comprised all his former benefits. These are his own words.

"O my soul, bless Our Lord and forget not His benefits; this", says he, "is an abridgement of all the rest, a new creation, a new justification, a new redemption, an earnest-penny and gage of glorification, in fine, a consummate heap of all the mercies of God. And by a long induction, repeating the mercies and benefits bestowed upon him, he puts first the plenary absolution which a religious man has, both from sin and the pain due to it. Secondly, that it cures all maladies contracted by sin, to wit, ignorance by an amorous knowledge of God which is called sapience or wisdom. It cures frailty by the superabundant grace. It heals concupiscence by love of God; and malice by the love of our neighbour. Thirdly, a religious person is exempt from many occasions of sin. Fourthly, God has singular care of them and protection. Fifthly, the perfection of spiritual consolations accompanies it insomuch that a religious person as an eagle renews and transforms himself into

Jesus Christ, by grace in this life to be wholly changed into Him, by glory in the life to come."

"To enjoy these benefits," he said, "I would (my brethren) we did bear a singular love to our rule and that every one of us did use diligence for the strict observation of it. The first thing that we should do were daily to remember the promise we made at our profession. The second is to take joy in that we have made this promise and vow, and daily to renew it. The third is to meditate every day in the week in this manner. On Sunday upon obedience; Monday on chastity; Tuesday on poverty; Wednesday on charity; Thursday on humility; Friday on penance and mortification, in our habit, in our sleep, in our meat; and Saturday on the peace which ought to be among us. The fourth is humbly to request our superior and brethren that they would advertise us and admonish us of our faults and defects in the observation of the rule and constitutions, to the end that we may amend them and receive willingly their reproofs for so good an end. The fifth is to take one day every month for a general and exact examination of all faults committed against the rule and to accustom himself to do some particular penance for the same fault"; and in this manner, said he, we might exercise ourselves to a true obedience of our rule which we have promised to keep. And lo, hear the frame and model of his life (expressed in his own words) which he did lead from the day of his profession, subduing still the desires of the flesh and making it obedient to the spirit by violence of austerities and mortification.

The first time that upon obedience he took any voyage afoot (as it is their custom never to ride without extreme necessity) the soles of his feet were so tender that before he had gone five leagues, he was fain to bind his handkerchief about them, least they might be sore hurt by the hardness of his sandals. And indeed the pain was so dolorous that he could not go, till his companion was forced to procure an ass to carry him to the place whither they went. But after this voyage his feet were so inured and hardened that he went twice to Rome, and being Provincial of the Order for six years together, he went every year three or four hundred leagues afoot in visiting the province. It is almost incredible what austerities he used, both at home and abroad. If as he was abroad there was much good meat presented to him, he would take the meanest sort, both to suppress the allurements of sensuality as also to give good example to secular persons, who scan narrowly all the actions of religious men. He avoided all occasions of meeting where he thought he might be known, lest he might be treated better than a poor Capuchin. Therefore he chose rather to retire himself to the cabinets of the poorest sort, than to great houses where he should be well entertained. He fasted all the eves of Our Saviour and Our B. Lady and disposed himself to receive new graces by extraordinary and fresh mortifications, disciplining himself with great rigour and contenting himself with bread and water, which he did eat on his knees as a man unworthy of so good refection. And his body, contrary to the ordinary manner, was nothing weakened by these penances, but did daily augment and renew its forces and continued them without any mitigation, even to the hour of his death.

One or two years after his profession the civil wars were so hot in France that there was nothing almost to be seen in all parts but the marks of fire and sword, as was evident by infinite churches ruinated and chapels spoiled and sacked, holy altars overthrown by the fury of a pretended religion. To avoid these cruelties and insolencies which such troubles bring with them, besides the great disquieting of good and peaceable spirits, the Father Provincial was constrained to send many religious to Rome among whom was this blessed Father Angel Joyeuse.[1] This long voyage weakened him much, together with the incommodities which they suffer who carry no money, as the poor Capuchins are fain to do, relying wholly on God's providence. When he was come to Florence, the Duke was desirous to see him, because he had heard much spoken of him worthy of admiration, and with the permission of the Guardian the Duke had long discourse with him, so that the Duke said openly that there was somewhat in him more than human, which commendation made him change his colour, so humble he was and loved rather contempt than praise.

[1] But see Introduction, p. xiii, for further reasons. On 5 March 1589 Fr. Angel received an obedience to go to Italy or to Lorraine. He met his brother Francis in Venice in June, and was ordained priest at Venice in 1591.

He was informed before he came out of France that the Religious Observants had a habit which S. Francis did wear (which they esteemed as a precious relic and make great daintiness to show it to any man, being locked up in a coffer with two keys, whereof the Duke keeps one and the convent another). Therefore the Duke making offer of any favour he might do him according to the manner of great princes, he humbly thanked him and told him the poor Capuchins stood in need of nothing, but yet being a child of S. Francis he should much oblige him if by his favour he might see the habit of this seraphical saint, which was in the custody of the Observants. His Highness granted him this request and required Father Guardian to show it to him. He had also this grace done to him that he was permitted to put it upon his own habit and seeing it was like to his in colour and roughness, in fashion and in the capuce or hood, lifting up his eyes to heaven and stretching out his arms (displayed in manner of a cross) he cried out with a most loud voice: "O God, what happiness is this, that I have obtained that which I so much desired: I am now fully content and my soul having abandoned all earthly affections does regard nothing (O my God) but Thee, who art my sovereign God and last Felicity."

Going from Florence he took his journey towards Rome, which journey he made with great pain and difficulty, being very sickly and ill-disposed in body, yet at length arriving there, not without suffering great incommodities, he sojourned there some time for the recovery of his health and restoring of his strength (much impaired by so long and painful a voyage). The reverend Father General sent him hence to Venice, to study divinity, where he passed his course in these studies with great admiration. This course of theology being finished and his dexterity and sufficiency well shown to the reverend Father General, both upon his own and other men's experience, he was sent to Lorraine and made guardian in a convent. To which charge he carried himself so prudently (as in all other business wherein he was to employ his authority) that he made it appear he was as fit to command as to obey, well experimented[1] for practice as for speculation; finally, as prudent and judicious as he was austere and sharp in mortifications.

[1] experienced

*How he forsook the habit of his religion and
upon what cause*

THE SEVENTH CHAPTER

THIS blessed Father Angel Joyeuse, having continued some years in Lorraine and edified all the country by his eminent example, the Reverend Father General, yielding to the instant prayers of the French fathers, sent him into Gascony; for they thought that his only presence (abstracting from his practice of regular virtue) was greatly necessary there, and that the whole order of religious men would have thereby matter of great consolation, for God divers times makes use of the motive of our own proper interest to put in execution the purposes of His eternal providence, whereof we cannot comprehend the cause, but the knowledge of the effects. All the orders of religion wished that he might be sent into Gascony, but they did not forsee that he should be taken out of his religion there and so incur the danger to lose him wholly. He was no sooner come hither, but he was made Guardian at Toulouse to the great contentment of all the religious and the chief men of the parliament in that city, thinking it a great comfort to have him for superior among good religious men, whose parents and brethren had obliged the whole country to them by their travails for the common good. But alas, all this joy was but a flash which presently was gone, and a great grief succeeding, made them lose all the comfort of their former joy. For Monseigneur Scipio de Joyeuse, Lieutenant-General for the King in Languedoc, having lost his life in a battle against the Huguenots in the siege at Villemur, five leagues from Toulouse, the country was much afflicted by his death for want of a governor and principal leader, the civil wars being there most hot. And the nobles and people of this country were so affected to this house and family of Joyeuse that they would not content themselves with any other (whereas France had many noble and worthy persons) but one of this house.

Hereupon all the flower of noble gentlemen of Languedoc who had followed his deceased brother, accompanied with the chief men of the Parliament, humbly besought Monseigneur Cardinal de Joyeuse to take compassion of their case and to accept this charge and become a governor and father to them in so urgent necessity. He desired them to excuse him as being very unfit for such a charge, in regard of his profession; and besides, he told them this were to bring in more confusion instead of setting better order and to ruinate the province in thinking to raise it and comfort it; whereas, he said, I have more need to be governed than I have experience to govern others. But his compassion and affection towards them made him think of his brother who was retired to a cloister life, having heretofore shown himself in the Court with great honour and credit. Oh blessed soul, thou art now in the paradise of such true repose as can be had on earth, and now they enter into counsel how they may put thee into the hell of trouble and unquietness.

This blessed father thought of nothing less than such a brunt,[1] though the devil danced for joy, thinking to have gained more by this market than he did; and gave manifest signs of it, which had been able to have frightened him if he had much reflected on them. For one night while he was taking his rest on his hard couch, he heard an extraordinary noise, that the devil made on the floor, beating the ground and the tables with his sandals. He wakens upon it and saw to his thinking a religious man full of heaviness and sorrow, set in a chair; whom this enemy of man had stripped of his habit violently and had put on him a fine shirt with other clothes, which might be fitting for a courtier. This vision did not much trouble him, because from the time of his noviceship he had had many such, thinking it was only some temptation to distract him and break his sleep, that he might be the more unable to perform the good religious exercises of the day following, little thinking that it touched him so near till he saw himself out of his habit and cloister.

At this time there lived [at Milan] a very virtuous and devout damoselle, whom the glorious Saint Charles Borromeus did much esteem for her virtuous life and particular revelations which made her famous through all Italy. This holy dame, having had a revelation hereof and having had communication with him formerly

---

[1] attack

when he came from Venice, knowing what a grief it is to a true religious devout soul to return to the world, after the true and sweet delights of religion, wrote to him a month before he left his cloister (although the letter came to him but five days after he had forsaken his habit) and exhorted him not to be dismayed and troubled in that he should be compelled to return to the world and follow the Court; for (says she) it is God's will it should be so. But she assured him that he should resume his habit again and end his days gloriously in that order of religion, and so consequently should increase his merit before God, more than if he had gone on still in his course without interruption. In the end of her letter she promised to remember him in her prayers as one that was particularly recommended to her in a second place, even by God's holy inspiration.

The nobles and parliament men, continuing their resolution taken, came the next morning to speak with him at the convent; who did conjure him by the affection which all his family had always witnessed towards their province and by the charity wherewith they doubted not but he was inflamed towards his neighbour, to take compassion of a million of souls which were in danger to be devoured of the roaring lion, and in most desperate case for want of a pastor; and therefore they besought him instantly to lay down his habit and take upon him the charge of his brother, and to stand in this breach for their defence against so dangerous enemies of the Church. This their request made his heart bleed for sorrow. For on the one side the great distress of God's Church moved him to the quick; on the other side he had a wonderful reluctation and strife within himself to quit his true contentment of his solitary and religious life. Wherefore he spoke to them in this manner: "My masters, your intention is very commendable and your design full of zeal for the common good. But I pray you remember that I am a religious man, that I have wholly abandoned the world, and that I have obliged myself under pain of eternal death, by a solemn vow in the presence of God and the Church, to live and die a follower of our seraphical father S. Francis. Judge ye therefore of how great a crime I shall be culpable if I break my vow and become a bankrupt to my religion which I have professed. God, who cannot be the author of sin and punishes often the sins of the parents in their children and of the pastors in smiting their flock, instead of defending this province from the hands of their enemies (as it is meet to think that this is God's hand which is upon us) may forsake it and leave it to the spoil of the enemy, for my fault. You have many noble and worthy men of great judgement and experience; make use of them who are able to steed you much more than a poor religious, who will be scorned of those enemies, rejoicing also to see monasteries and religious houses made empty by them, it being one of their main projects." This was all they could gain of him at this time; yet they set a watch upon him that he might not go into any other place, purposing to take him out by force if no other means would prevail.

In the meanwhile there was a solemn and public meeting of the nobles, the Parliament and religious men at Toulouse, in the hall of the Archbishop; who after they had debated this matter very seriously, concluded with one consent and voice that in such a public necessity he was bound in conscience (seeing that all the province also desired it) to quit his habit and to take a sword and serve the weal public, which was to be preferred, according to the rigour of divine and human laws, before his own particular good. They went therefore again the next morning to the convent with full resolution to take him forth, and there they enforced their requests with all vehemence and demanded his assistance and presence but for a time, promising it that they would advertise His Holiness of it and obtain his leave, as they did. For he sent his consent with the resolution of two cardinals, Bellarmine and Baronius, who were of opinion that this act was lawful and expedient.

This[1] was the last blow which made him yield, seeing also the cries and lamentation of the people, who had beset the convent on all sides and cried with a pitiful voice and able to move any man's heart: "We will have Father Angel for our Governor". And in case he would not condescend to their requests, they threatened to take him by force and burn the convent. How then was he able to resist this powerful call of the people, which may be well thought to be

[1] i.e., *not* the Pope's assent, but the promise to obtain it.

the voice of God? He replied only that his purpose of entering into religion and forsaking father and mother and his only daughter in the cradle (the greatest object of his earthly contentments), was to resign himself wholly into the hands of God and to avoid by all possible means the occasions of offending Him, which rather than he would do, he would undergo a thousand deaths. But since the learned clergymen were of that mind that he was to follow God's will therein, he protested that he did leave his cloister unwillingly, and that if there were any offence to God, that they should and must bear it and answer for him. So, weeping bitterly, after he had embraced all his religious brethren (who for sobbing and weeping were not able to speak to him) he forsook his habit and said (being drenched in the bitterness of sorrow), "Farewell, my repose and my comfort."

The next morning he came forth in a black suit to witness his inward mourning, and his brother Monseigneur the Cardinal, Archbishop of Toulouse, girt him with a sword. All the nobility, presidents and counsellors of the Parliament rejoiced exceedingly at this sight and persuaded themselves that having obtained his assistance, peace was already made and concluded. They came to him to congratulate him with all signs of great cheerfulness and thankfulness to him for this favour, making solemn protestation that they would die at his feet, whatsoever enterprise he should undertake. His answer was short but pithy and comfortable. "You know," says he, "to satisfy your importunate request that I have forsaken my earthly paradise to return again into Egypt and into the desert of troubles and unquietness, for the service of God and His Church and France in general and particularly your country; this action is sufficient to make you understand my hearty affection towards you. I hope the heavens will favour us so that the clouds and fogs which threaten a terrible storm and tempest of war shall be dispersed by the bright beams of the sun and spring of a holy and assured peace, to the end that I may return to my former repose and there end my days."

From thence he went to a great place in the city called S. Stephen's, where he was received of the people with great shows of joy and contentment. Among all his excellent perfections this was worthy of admiration that he had so universal a spirit and pliable to what he would bend it, that continually being united to God by love and by his inward thoughts, he gave satisfaction to everyone according to his demands, for he had no sooner taken his sword and fashioned the hair of his head and beard in another manner, but he gave infinite contentment to all the nobles who came to salute him and so behaved himself to every one of them according to their rank and quality in that grave and decent manner, as if he had never lived a cloister man. He showed also in his natural sweetness (which represented somewhat a religious person) a gait and port full of majesty (as the quality of a governor and captain requires to keep soldiers within the bounds of their duty), that following his guard among the nobles, many did observe something in him more than common and ordinary, which made him much admired and honoured of all.

Shortly after, seeking all means to reduce things into order, he assembled the states of that province at Carcassone, where he entered into treaty for a truce of three years[1] with Monsieur Maréchal Montmorency, his godfather and kinsman, one of the most brave and noble seigneurs of his time, who was afterwards for his merits honoured with the charge of Constable of France. This truce, bringing peace and quiet which had been so long wished, was so sweet and graceful to each party that they both did magnify the mediator of it, persuading themselves that God had sent him as an angel of peace and for their delivery. And indeed this particular truce in Languedoc drew on the like through all France and after the happy reduction of Henry the Fourth into the bosom of God's Holy Church, this truce grew to be a peace, so that there followed a perfect calm.

While these affairs were so prosperously managed by this blessed Father Angel, our Holy Father the Pope, being advertised of his prudence and dexterity in directing of affairs of importance and of what authority and credit he was and how necessary his presence was for the government of Languedoc, to the end that he might ease and clear him of any scruple which might haply rise in

---

[1] Initially the truce concluded with Montmorency on 14 December 1592 was for a year, from January to December 1593; it was subsequently extended.

his mind by reason of his first profession, he changed his vow of a Capuchin with that of the Order of S. John of Jerusalem and sent him upon his own proper motion an authentical bull, by which he did fully absolve him from the vow which he had made among the Capuchins, giving him power to succeed, sell, buy, possess and to perform other such actions as if he had never been religious, only marriage excepted, which is forbidden by the vow of the Knights of Malta. This bull was executed by Monsieur the Bishop of Lodève,[1] Bishop of Carcassone, who is lately deceased; who at that time, being assisted by a Commander of Malta, gave him the white cross, to the great desire and contentment of the whole order.

All this could not alter his purpose of resuming the habit; those spiritual comforts which he had tasted in that life were still imprinted in his heart and although he was out of his cloister and absolved from the observing of his vow, yet did he practise the most principal actions of that life, when he could have fit opportunity; to wit, the fastings, disciplines and other mortifications, by which he conserved his true devotion and affection to this life. He had besides his usual fervour a double rampart which was able to resist the assaults of the world. For his blessed mother, as long as she lived, ceased not, as a holy S. Monica, to shed many tears for him and to offer up her prayers daily to God for his return to religion. Besides a learned and virtuous father of this order, exciting him often by lively and pressing remonstrances and pious exhortations, kept him waking that he fell not into any profound lethargy, into which the world casts her best favourites.

About the end of the troubles of France, his mother, Madame Maréchale, departed this life at Toulouse, the mirror of all virtue and piety; who making an end conformable to her life left great occasion of mourning to all France for her death. He assisted her always in her last sickness with great edification and took her blessing and her speeches even to the last gasp; which were as goads to him, to stir him up to the love of God, and living flames of that inward holy fire which consumed her soul and most certain pledges of the glory which she was to receive after her decease.

After this he went often to Paris (the troubles now being happily

---

[1] Christophe de Lestang, Bishop of Lodève and Lavaur.

ended) where he was entertained of Henry the Fourth, as the perfections and qualities of so worthy a prince did merit, who confirmed him in all his charges and dignities of Duke, Peer and
Maréchal of France, Lieutenant-General in Languedoc; and he
caused him to take again the Order of the Holy Ghost, which he
had received before of Henry the Third in the institution which he
had when he forsook the world. In these journeys to Paris he
treated with the King's consent and favour the marriage of
Madame Henriette de Joyeuse, his only daughter, with the most
illustrious prince Henry de Bourbon, Duke of Montpensier, which
marriage afterward being accomplished, by heavenly benediction
brought forth a most noble plant, Marie de Bourbon, Mademoiselle de Montpensier, a princess of our time and a true image of the
perfections of her father and mother.

How he took again the habit of a Capuchin

THE EIGHTH CHAPTER

Now whenas all things went on so prosperously with this blessed
father, no man thought that he would once have dreamed of
returning to his former life, and the rather because he seemed in
outward appearance to court these favours of his prosperous
success in the world. But even at this time had he a perfect
remembrance and memory of his true contentment past, which as
a waking ghost seized his imagination and hindered entrance for
any other thoughts which savoured of the world or of ambition. He
was so wise that he knew well the inconstancy of all worldly things,
and how weak the foundation is when we build our hopes upon
them. And therefore, howsoever he might in outward show
prudently seem to look cheerfully upon the world, it was for no
other reason but to carry his purpose as secretly as he could,
neither was it the scruple of his vow which caused him to retire
himself, for he was well assured of the sufficiency of his dispensation even in the judgement of the most learned. So that it was only

the love of God with a desire of true conformity with Him, which caused him to be nailed again to the cross of austerities and to undergo his first mortifications and to make his return more honourable than his first entry, by how much he did forsake greater dignities and honourable charges.

He revealed his intention to a father of the same order[1] who, preaching in Advent and the whole Lent at S. Stephen's (the metropolitan church of Toulouse), stirred up many to devotion by his learned discourses and fervour. This father missed none of his sermons, what business soever he had, and he heard him oftentimes with tears. After his sermon he took occasion to see him and conferred with him about some points which he had more particularly noted. He congratulated him of his manner of preaching, saying that he preached as a true apostle, reproving vice and exhorting to virtue, without those curiosities which many affect, which indeed are rather beseeming a theatre than a pulpit. In the end, after many visits he opened his heart to him and communicated to him his firm resolution to resume the habit. To that end he required the aid of his good prayers and of his counsels, because he saw many blocks in his way, which were hardly to be removed.

This father knowing well the course of the whole business, dealt with him wisely and deliberately and would not approve this motion, doubting as he told him, lest his retreat to religious life might prejudice the public peace. He said that God had drawn him once out of the world to make him understand better the vanities of the world, to the end that returning again into the world he might stand more warily on his guard and not be so easily surprised of those enemies which captivate the greatest part of noble persons. He told him also that heaven was not only for religious men, that he might very well save his soul in the world and with as much merit in the vocation and profession in this noble and illustrious Order of Malta; and to conclude, he persuaded him that he might receive more clear direction from God in a business of so great import, which did concern his salvation and the conservation of a state, to frequent the Sacrament often to this end, and then no doubt but God would concur extraordinarily with

---

[1] Fr. Archange Dupuy de Lyons.

those actions of piety and lighten him so by increase of new graces that he should perfectly understand His holy will.

Shortly after he chose Father Ignace, an Italian of the Company of Jesus, a man of singular learning and prudence, for his confessor, to whom after his confession he revealed this his intention. This father, who had very little knowledge of him before, thought that this was such a desire as would lose the edge upon any occasion of a little opposition and that he might as easily be diverted from this purpose, because his friends had power over him to cause his coming forth of the cloister. But afterward he was of another mind and wondered at his strong resolution and saw that his constancy was much to be honoured and admired. Some months passed on, that he used to communicate all feasts and Sundays, commending this affair to God. And he found that the violence of this affection grew daily more and more insomuch that he fell to importune that reverend father, returning this answer (as admirable as remarkable) to his oppositions: "Father, I do believe that many work their salvation in the world, but God will not save me but in religion", always setting before his eyes that dreadful sentence of holy scripture: *What profiteth it a man if he gains the whole world and lose his soul?*

After he had deposed his habit he kept dearly three things which he held very precious: the rule of S. Francis and a discipline, which are inseparable companions to all Capuchins: the one is to have always in memory what they have promised, the other to mortify their fleshly appetites; the one and the other that they may be conform and like to their father. The third thing was a book of spiritual exercises, very proper to the most perfect spirits. He began from this time to make these things more familiar and ordinary than before, whereupon his nearest friends and people of his own house, seeing him to withdraw himself often to solitary retreats and to avoid all occasion of keeping company and to pass most part of the night in his private cabinet, they began to doubt lest he was projecting with himself a second retreat to religious life. Moreover he contented not himself with this, but laboured to store himself with some books of sermons and others of devotion, which he could not read in the daytime, by reason that he was very wary to conceal his purpose, and therefore he spent that time of the night in reading those good books, which was ordained for his repose.

It happened one night, after his servants were retired from his chamber, he attempted that which he had done when he was but nine years of age, to wit, to take it as from the mouth of God and to know perfectly His will by the first words which he read in the opening of the book. O good God, how admirable are Thy secrets! At the first opening and view he happened upon the words of the Revelation which were in the sermons of the subtle and learned preacher Bitonte:[1] *Be mindful whence thou art fallen, and do penance and do thy first works.* He needed no exposition to apply this to himself. The next morning he told the father Capuchin (coming from his sermon): "My father, God hath given me better inspirations than ever I deserved, but He never spoke so clearly to me as this night past. I must be very deaf if I hear not His voice and very ignorant if I do not understand." And so he told him what had passed. And certainly there is no man but will judge there was something extraordinary.

This was at the beginning of Lent, during which time he daily augmented his devotions. He understood shortly after that the R. Father Jerome of Sorbo, General of the Capuchins,[2] was to come this year to make his visit in France, which gave him great consolation, conceiving that by speaking with him he should easily obtain his request without danger of any voice to hinder it. But the good father went not beyond the convent of Carcassone in the province of Toulouse, whereupon he wrote to him and acquainted him with his purpose, and earnestly requested the father to whom he had opened his heart, to carry his letters to him, being now to go to the General Chapter. In these letters he besought him with all the powers of his soul and by the vow which he had made to S. Francis, that he would receive him again to their order and sent

---

[1] Antonius de Bitonto, the fifteenth-century Franciscan preacher, and not Cornelio Musso, Bishop of Bitonto, a noted sixteenth-century preacher.

[2] On his election as General at the twenty-second General Chapter on 31 May 1596, Fr. Jerome of Sorbo had promised to make a visitation of the French Province. He began the visitation in the first quarter of 1598; the chief purpose of his visit was to insist on ecclesiastical immunities for the Capuchins. He received Fr. Angel's letter on 23 March 1598 at Castelnaudary.

him his obedience to take the habit in that province which he should judge the most commodious for avoiding of diversion and of trouble.

The reverend Father General received his letters very lovingly, and wondering at his zealous manner of writing, said that he was conducted and guided infallibly by God's holy spirit; yet he did not give him but one half of that contentment which he hoped for. He made him this answer that he was very desirous to gratify him for the honour and the benefit which would redound thereby to the order, but because he had been dispensed withall by our Holy Father (who did not give such dispensation but for a greater good) he could not receive him till he had advertised the Pope thereof and received his consent. This answer perplexed him much, for he was afraid lest His Holiness would not yield this consent without communicating the matter to the King, and he had no hope to procure the King's consent. He notwithstanding determined to send one of his own servants,[1] who carried letters from him to our Holy Father Clement the Eighth and to the protector of the order, who was the Cardinal of Saint Severin. In these letters he declared his design and his humble suit, showing them that he might put it in execution without any prejudice to the State. He conjured them with all earnest submissions that a child owes to his father, or an inferior to his superior, that they would permit him to follow those good inspirations which God had given him, and that he could not defer it any longer without eminent peril of his life, so great was his disgust and irksomeness which he had of the world. These are the holy violences of pure love, not to find any contentment but in the possession of the object loved, whose absence is insupportable because it carries with our heart all our affection, the strongest passion of the soul.

His Holiness was much astonished at this devotion, and after he had well considered this affair, with all the circumstances, perceiving that he was certainly moved by God's holy spirit to this act, he commanded the protector to signify to him that if he did judge in his conscience that his assistance was no longer necessary for the

[1] The Sieur de la Terrasse, Fr. Angel's envoy to Rome, returned at the end of June 1598 with a brief from Clement VIII permitting him to return to the Capuchins.

country of Languedoc, he was well content that he should resume the habit; but he exhorted him that as yet he proceed very advisedly, lest his permission being obtained under a false pretext of saving his life, might occasion eternal death; urging him moreover to persevere in this holy purpose, which God does not recompense but in the end and upshot of the work; that he was like to be an adamant to draw many affections after him; and, to conclude, that God and His Holy Church should be exalted by this work and to this end gave him his holy benediction.

This being so, the R. Father General sent him his obedience to take the habit in that province where he was most inclined in his devotion; and the years which he had passed in the world with the Pope's dispensation, for the defence of the Church and the State, were allowed to him as if he had spent them in religion, for he went not out but by violence and against his will; and he confirmed to him the title and office of a preacher, which the reverend Father Policius,[1] General had given him before he left the habit. These letters revived him, who was half dead before by apprehending that he should be refused. He had no sooner received them, which was in the month of June, but he presently prepared himself to go to Paris and to set in order all his affairs; and likewise, that seeing Monsieur de Montpensier and Madame (his daughter) he might take his last farewell of them, yet so that they should not know he took his farewell.

It fell out in the meantime by God's providence that this good father to whom he had revealed his purpose at Toulouse,[2] was sent by Father General to preach at Paris at S. Germain of Auxerrois, which was much to this good father's comfort and joy. He took this for a certain presage that it was God's will that the good father should assist him to the end, whom he had used in the beginning. And so he had cause to think, for after he had long considered what province should be most convenient for him to make his new retreat, and after many conflicts between the flesh and reason (whereof one required a place somewhat remote, the other counselled him to choose a place near his home, because he might not be deprived of his dearest friends by distance of place), at last

---

[1] Fr. Jerome de Polizzi   [2] Fr. Archange Dupuy de Lyons

he concluded to go to Switzerland to take the habit, that so by distance of place he might not be troubled with ordinary visits which often occasion other dangerous distractions to religious men. This consideration therefore moved him to incline to go to Switzerland, but he was dissuaded by this good man, who showed unto him effectually that his retreat in the face of the Court would be much more edifying and exemplary, and that his absenting of himself would argue pusillanimity and want of courage; that he need not have any other visits but such as he would, and that such a spirit as his was did not incur danger to be diverted by any persuasion. And besides all this, that his presence would be very necessary for the consolation of Monsieur de Montpensier and Madam his daughter, who without doubt would be far more afflicted, if they were not only deprived of his conversation but also of the fruit of his virtuous counsels. Whereupon resting upon the advice of this good father, he wholly submitted himself to the disposition of the fathers of the convent of Paris.

This consultation for choice of the most expedient place for his reception continued from S. Francis' day[1] to the first week of Lent, during which space of time he disposed of his worldly business, and in the end it was concluded that he should take again his habit in the convent of Paris, for the reasons above specified. And although he was a little otherwise inclined in his own judgement, foreseeing extraordinary importunity of his friends in this case, yet to show himself truly obedient, as well out of religion as in the same, he resolved to follow their advice, and he put this in execution so dexterously that his own family understood rather his retiring from that course than any will and affection to return. For the second Monday in Lent, *anno* 1599, the King being at Monceaux, he accompanied in the morning Monsieur de Espernon, his brother-in-law, who went to the King and brought him on his way a league from Paris and sent with him one of his officers, who carried a packet of letters from him to his son Monsieur de Montpensier, where among other letters of compliment or consolation there was one for the King, to whom he gave to understand that it was God's will (all things being settled in good peace) that he

---

[1] i.e., from 4 October 1598 to March 1599

should return to the centre of his repose, from whence he was taken by the violence of afflicted people. Wherefore he humbly besought His Majesty that he would be pleased to approve the same, giving him most humble and infinite thanks for those offices and dignities which he had bestowed upon him, all which he now right humbly resigned again unto him, protesting to be perpetually mindful of him in his prayers and sacrifices.

It is needless to ask whether the King and the whole Court were astonished at this news, for the better to conceal his holy design, he seemed for a while to love the world with as much passion as others did. In the meanwhile, the same evening after he had made an inventory of his goods with Monsieur de Marnef and ordered the private affairs of his house, he retired himself to the convent all alone about seven of the clock, giving charge to two of his servants that they should not open the door to any, whosoever came to knock thereat, and to answer them that he did retire and rest himself, and that the next morning after the sermon they should know the cause of his retirement. O blessed rest, the earnest of eternal life, far different from that of the most part of worldly men, where the images of desired objects trouble the imagination and cause dreams which under the pretext of procuring a happy rest produce eternal misery to their conceivers!

After some hours spent in prayer, solacing himself with the angels, about eleven of the clock before midnight he took again the habit before the high altar with unspeakable joy, and melting with inward contentment of heart he renewed his profession and his vows in the presence of all his brethren, protesting that he would die in the practice of them. And as they would have had him to stay until the morning for the making of his crown and razing of his hair conform to the rule, he most earnestly requested Father Alphonsus, vicar and superior in the absence of the Guardian, that he might be dispatched out of hand, so that he might see nothing about him in the morning that should savour of the world. So desirous was he to make this external change, being already quite changed and inwardly transformed in his soul. His crown being made he went to the quire to sing Matins with the others (their custom being to rise at midnight to render praises unto God, whilst peradventure other worldlings employ that time in works of darkness), where he observed that decency and reverence as if he had made no interruption at all from this holy exercise; which many of the religious did much wonder at.

The next morning, this his change of life, being published by the preacher of S. Germain,[1] was quickly known both in Court and city. For this father having assisted him a year and a half, made (in form of a funeral sermon) the end of his sermon upon this subject with words so lively and so full of fire that he himself first breaking into tears, made his auditors also weep, where this duke's own gentlemen, pages and other servants were spectators, all struck with great amazement upon such tidings, thinking that their master reposed in his bed even then when he was become a Capuchin. All the princes and ladies of honour, hearing this, came likewise to see him at the convent, who when they saw him in the church among other religious, they could not forbear to tears and sobs in such doleful manner that they could hardly salute him. There was not one amongst them all but Madame de Belisle, the sister of Madame de Longueville (who was then treating to become a religious woman and since both lived and died most blessedly in the Monastery of the Encloistre) who had the courage to speak unto him. She rejoiced with him for this happy change, esteeming him most wise and happy to make this choice and to despise and abandon all worldly things, which have but vanity for their being and instability for their foundation, and so to possess God more certainly, whose rewards fleet not with the world but last forever. He received these ladies with a smiling countenance and made them a short spiritual discourse of the grace he had received from Almighty God and that this grace was of much more value than the world could imagine, adding that if men in the world should but taste of the sweet delights of a religious life, that private houses would be changed into monasteries. But because they regard not but the external face of things, which seems to be full of rigour, they bemoan them which are in this manner sweetly drawn unto God from the wicked world, as if they had lost their wits and judgements and cast themselves into a sea of misery.

[1] Fr. Archange Dupuy de Lyons

Wherefore he told them that if they had done him the honour to love him, as he always believed unto that present, that they ought to rejoice with him for this his change, because this was the more safe and secure way to come to God, the final End of all things created.

This second conquest, being so gloriously gotten against the enemies of man, the world, the flesh and the devil, who had laboured to allure him by the charming baits of honours, riches and sensual pleasures, got him so much honour in the world and so excited all France in the admiration of his virtues that as a courageous captain he drew out of captivity and (that I may so speak) led in triumph a great number of gentlemen and courtiers, who following his steps, sounded a retreat to all vanities, withdrew themselves from the billows and waves of a courtly life (where the best experienced pilots are often drowned), to live in sweet repose under the shelter of the Cross, within the cloister of the Capuchins.

Of his doctrine and manner of preaching

THE NINTH CHAPTER

ALTHOUGH a good natural inclination gives a man a great advantage to make him excellent in the profession which he pretends to undertake and although this be a true axiom, that nature surpasses art and that art prevails little or nothing where nature is not capable; yet nature alone is not capable of itself to put in practice all that which art can do, and sciences being certain habitudes which produce themselves by the actions, it suffices not to have a nature well disposed, but labour must be annexed thereto; which serves as the last disposition to a quality so perfect and so eminent.

The blessed Father Angel of Joyeuse seemed always to have an excellent natural inclination unto learning and for pains in his studies he went beyond all others of his age and profession. He observed also an excellent method in his study (which may serve for a rule to those who follow the same course) to attain to perfection: first he never opened books without before having invoked the assistance of God's holy spirit, knowing that all science and understanding is the gift of Almighty God, and that knowledge which is not accompanied with charity (the fire whereof is kindled by the spirit of love) does but puff up and does not edify. Neither did he content himself only with lifting up his heart to God, as many do before they undertake their studies, but always before study spent some time in prayer, offering his affection unto God, praying that if it were for His glory, the good of his neighbour and his own, that He would illuminate the darkness of his understanding to conceive the depths of His secrets, stir up his will to labour therein with fervour, quicken his memory and make it capable to give a good account of that which he should judge fit for his vocation and rule; but if on the contrary part, either the health of his soul or the purity of his vows were to suffer thereby any detriment whatsoever, that perpetual ignorance might be the recompense of all his labours and his travails. It is hardly credible how great progress he made in his studies, being moved thereto by so holy and so glorious an end.

His hours designed to his studies were those as when he had no other exercise in the convent, for as touching his Office he never failed. And albeit the students among the Capuchins are not dispensed withal for saying their Hours in the choir, yet notwithstanding, as though he had nothing else to do, he was always there one of the first, and withdrew himself thence as late as possibly he might; whence he received such extraordinary light, that in one hour he conceived and retained more than many others did in a whole day.

He heard every day one Mass before the conventual, which all the religious were to hear, and oftentimes he served another, thinking no time so well bestowed, and exciting others to devotion by his profound humility in his manner of serving Mass. The father which was reader, and his fellow students, wondering at the little time he had for study and of the progress which he made, asked of him, what the rule and order was which he observed? But he was so far from thinking well of himself that he judged himself to be one of the most ignorant and not worthy to wear St. Francis's habit.

After his course in philosophy, the reverend Father General made him a preacher, in which charge he discovered[1] that zeal that his words enkindled the fire of devotion in the frozen and hard hearts of many persons that were enemies of piety. He preached not long, or rather, not at all during his first abode in religion, because immediately after his permission he was constrained to go forth. But after his return, having taken some time to make a perfect recollection of himself and a true atonement between God and his own soul, he began to labour with such courage in so holy a mission that, forgetting the feeding of his own body, he showed himself infatigable to serve to his neighbours the food of their souls.

His first public assays were in Paris in the church of the Capuchins and after at S. Medericus, S. Germain of Auxerre, S. Andrew of Arques and through all the best cities of the kingdom of France, where his auditors did always depart from him with great applause and admiration. He had a particular grace of God to move men's hearts to a true feeling of their sins, which they did witness by their bitter tears and change of life. God Himself only knows how many sinful souls he converted to the true path of their salvation and what a number, intimidated with the apprehension of God's severe judgements, left their debauchedness and are covered with sackcloth in holy cloisters.

There are some of his exhortations yet extant under his own hand, wherein are to be seen so goodly discourses, so elevated conceptions and so lively characters of a seraphical zeal, that even the most judicious spirits cannot read his words without a great impression of virtue: what then were they able to do, being quickened with his own spirit and coming from his own mouth? Surely they were as so many piercing arrows which did heal in wounding and wound in healing; killing to the world and quickening unto Jesus Christ. Those who hearing them gave them entry into their souls. "O my brethren," said he (explicating these words of the Apostle S. Paul to the Colossians 3, *Despoiling yourselves of the old man with his acts*), "what mean we that we do not despoil ourselves and put off our old garments, if we will be clothed with

[1] revealed

royal garments? If a king should make this offer to a poor man, put off thy vile and base apparel and put on mine, were not such a one a fool who would not part with his apparel to put on such as were so noble? So fares it with us who are clothed with the old man and yet see that God will clothe us with His divine will, we, wretches that we are, do not contradict Him; if at the hour of our death He find us clothed with other rags, woe be unto us." These words, are they not so many sparkles of holy fire? which how powerful and fruitful they were, the very effects themselves do sufficiently testify. For there were certain persons at this sermon whom an irreconcilable enmity held so divided to the detriment of their own soul and notable scandal of their neighbour, that no sort of consideration could reconcile them, who at the departure from one of his sermons embraced one another and swore each to other perpetual amity.

Furthermore, where he understood of any quarrels and factions between persons of quality, he was very diligent to quench those flames and making them to know the heinousness of their dis-ordered passions, reduced them to reason; whereby God was glorified and the State received benefit by the union of peace which ensued thereon, whereupon depends its whole preservation. In this point he was a true follower of S. Francis, for an author of his time who assures to have heard him preach at Bologna on the day of the Assumption of Our Blessed Lady, *anno* 1620, says that in all his sermons he principally aimed at this mark, to wit, to extinguish the fires of dissensions and to renew the alliances of happy peace, adding that God gave so great efficacy unto his words that he appeased such a tempest of quarrels and factions amongst the nobles, as was sufficient to have set the whole commonwealth all on fire, if the effects had accompanied their designs.

And to the end that God might concur with his labours in preaching, he had always in his mind the wholesome speeches of S. Francis, who said that that preacher is much to be lamented who destroys and corrupts by his bad life that which himself built and founded by the truth of his doctrine. Wherefore he began first with himself, and redoubling his own mortifications never went up into the pulpit, but first disciplining himself with extraordinary violence, whereof the blood which dropped down was a faithful witness; knowing well that it avails little or nothing to teach others and not to put in practice the points themselves. Not content to chastise himself thus severely, he shut the windows of his chamber and speaking to God from the depth of his heart in this obscurity, he spent an hour in meditation upon the point he was to speak, humbly beseeching the assistance of heavenly grace for the performance of that work to God's glory and to the profit of his hearers' soul.

This holy custom of meditation, besides the power which it had to stir up men's hearts, produced yet another fruit, which cannot be valued by any but by those who make profession thereof: for by this means he got a great facility to be able to speak of any matter that occasion might present, if he were advertised thereof but one hour before. And although this might in part be attributed to the excellence of his wit, yet doubtless it proceeded principally from his holy meditations, as water purified within a holy limbeck and dropping sweetly down from the fountainhead of so pure a soul to which the Holy Ghost communicated Itself after a manner known only to those who are partakers of the same.

This, notwithstanding, did not hinder him that he applied himself unto his studies, as often as his other occupations did permit him, but the great desire he had to co-operate to the health of souls did much rob him of the particular colloquies,[1] but God Himself, for whom only he laboured with such affection, rendered him the recompense by giving him the knowledge of sundry things in a short time. For amongst the things which he hated most it showed that ignorance was one of the chiefest, taking his motive from the threatening of God, thundered out in the Prophet Isaiah against his people, saying: *The cause why My people are led away prisoners is for that they had not knowledge*. Mark, I pray you, how he discourses upon this point.

"He does not say for having robbed or committed adultery or idolatry, but he goes to the fountain and first cause of all evil, *for that they had not knowledge*. This truly is a terrible sentence, but reason confirms it; for a man is a reasonable creature, as you know,

---

[1] i.e., time for private study

and capable of reason and discourse, different in this from beasts; who, deprived of reason, are guided only by the instinct of nature, which is the cause that what they do, they do by necessity and natural inclination; but man being reasonable, instinct alone does not suffice him, but he must have reason and discourse to conduct him; for which cause it is that he goes discoursing from principles to conclusions, and says as follows: All things that are good are to be done: this is good, it is therefore to be done. Again, all evil is to be fled; this is evil, this therefore is to be eschewed. The will (as you know) is a power which of itself is blind, which knows nothing, but as it receives light from the understanding, therefore, *non fertur nisi in praecognitum*; it cannot love good, nor hate evil, unless it know it; it cannot work this, nor avoid that, unless it first love or hate it when it comes to pass; that if it be bound to work that which is good, it cannot work it, unless it first love it; it cannot love it, unless it know it; and it cannot know it without science. Therefore by this connection *a primo ad ultimum*, from the first to the last, knowledge is necessary to do good and to fly evil. And for as much as our end is supernatural, it suffices not a Christian to have some science or natural knowledge such as the philosophers had, but there is a far more eminent knowledge required of him, which is that of faith and of the Holy Scriptures."

And then endeavouring to show what this knowledge ought to be, without the which we are not in the true path that tends to salvation, he spoke in this manner: "A man may be considered in four estates. The first is, as only a natural man. The second, as a Christian. The third, as a religious man. The fourth as such a religious man, to wit, clerk, lay, simple priest or preacher. In all these estates a man has need of knowledge, but with this diversity, for in the first, as man, it suffices that he knows what natural reason does dictate to him, good and evil, to embrace the one and to fly the other. In the second degree, as a Christian, he is bound to know the law of God, His commandments and those also of His Church, the articles of faith, with other ordinary points of Christian doctrine. In the third degree, as a religious man, he ought to know all things aforesaid, and moreover he ought to know the obligations and precepts of his rule, with other things appertaining to a true spiritual life, other prayers or devotions. In the fourth degree, as such a religious man, he ought to know the things which appertain unto his office: if he be a lay brother, the Christian doctrine, the precepts, the equipollences[1] of his rule, things spiritual, and those in particular which appertain unto a lay brother. If a clerk, he ought to know both all this, and moreover to say his Office. If a simple priest he ought to know cases of conscience, understand the Summists[2] and the matter of the sacraments. If a preacher, he ought to understand and know how to explicate the Holy Scripture and to have skill in divinity. Briefly, everyone ought to render an account of those things which do belong unto his office, and consequently everyone ought to acquit himself of the obligation of his charge, according to the degree of his estate. If he be but a man, to be good morally. If a Christian, to be a good one. If a religious, to be a good religious and so of others: for of ignorance it comes that a man is not a man, but a beast: nor the Christian, nor religious, such indeed and in effect. Finally, let us conclude that from the ignorance of things necessary, follows the ruin of cities, realms, commonwealths, religious and of the whole world."

And a little after, speaking of S. Francis, who says in the beginning of his rule that the brethren of that order ought to desire above all things to have the spirit of God and His holy operation in their souls, he exclaims, saying: "O words of wonderful importance and worthy to be written in letters of gold, even in the midst of our hearts. S. Francis says as much in those few words as all the spiritual books can say in the whole world. For in these words are contained and comprehended all the perfection of the spiritual virtues which may be desired in a passenger of this life, to have the spirit of Our Lord, that is to say, to be made one in spirit and in will, together with His holy operation, to wit, His love: for as He loves Himself, so likewise will He that we love Him: this is our principal operation, this is our last and final end, whereby we have forsaken the world, together with all whatsoever we have, ourselves, our bodies and our souls. For this it is we are enclosed in cloisters. For this it is we are clothed with this sackcloth, so to

[1] equivalents, i.e., those parts of the rule which apply to him.
[2] i.e., the writers of the theological compendia.

have this spirit and this love of God. This if we have not obtained unto this present, or at the least if we desire not to obtain it and do not enforce ourselves hereunto above all things else whatsoever, in vain it is that we have forsaken the world, in vain it is that we wear these contemptible habits, and in vain it is that we call ourselves Brother Minors. So that this is the chiefest science whereunto we all are bound and obliged, that is to say, to desire above all things to have the spirit of Our Lord and His holy operation." I omit many other excellent discourses which witness his singular zeal and his learning and which have wrought the conversion of many souls which now enjoy immortal glory in heaven, singing songs of thanks, giving praise to their Creator and Redeemer in the company of this blessed father.

*Of his voyage to Rome to the General Chapter
and what he did there*

THE TWENTIETH CHAPTER[1]

AFTER the death of Monsieur the Duke of Montpensier, the time drawing on that he, being now Provincial,[2] ought to be present at the General Chapter to consult with the rest of his brethren concerning the state of their religion and to give a particular account of the affairs of his province, he parted immediately after Easter from Paris to be at Rome before Whitsuntide. For the chapter was then to begin. And God by His special providence did so dispose that he was chosen General Definitor by the common consent of all the provincials met together.

The length of the way and the great heat of summer caused the King (that his journey might be more easy after he had stayed him) to prepare for him a galley to bring him from Marseilles to

---

[1] Chapters X to XIX, which lean heavily on Fr. Angel's sermons, have been omitted in this edition.
[2] For the second time. He was first elected from August 1602 till June 1604; his second term of office began 18 September 1607. The Duke of Montpensier died on the night of 28 February 1608; Fr. Angel was at his bedside.

Civita Vecchia, which was but one day's journey distant from Rome. They had the sea and wind against them all along their voyage and were shrewdly beaten with tempestuous weather, which ceased by means of his prayers, not without great wonderment and rejoicing of other passengers, who, being driven by the winds among the rocks, could expect nothing but a disastrous shipwreck. These incommodities of the sea made his companion fall into a fever when he was arrived at Civita Vecchia. Whereupon Father Angel was constrained to set him on horseback, going after him the rest of the way. This good religious man was much grieved at it, being ashamed to ride himself on horseback and his provincial afoot. He demanded pardon of him with all submission and Father Angel did seek to comfort him as much as he could, saying that God permitted this for a greater good and that He did draw sweetness out of bitterness as water out of the rock, that at their return they should have more leisure to repose themselves, that they should resign themselves to God's holy will; and with spiritual discourse he sweetened the rigour of the rest of the way, till they came to Rome. When he was come to Rome the first thing that he did after he had confessed and visited the holy places, was to humbly present himself to His Holiness, who seeing him prostrate on the ground to kiss his feet, he lifted him up and gave him his hand to kiss, showing extraordinary affection to him and rejoicing much to see him, which he witnessed by the effects. For whilst he sojourned at Rome, he sent him every day some confiture and such presents which might not be unfit for a poor Capuchin to receive, knowing well that his body, having been delicately bred and fed in his youth, needed some kind of restoratives after the travail of so long a journey. The good father received them with most humble thanks but he would never taste of them himself, but caused them to be given to the sick persons of their infirmary, as he was wont to do when he had received the like from his friends in France.

This General Chapter is an assembly of the provincials of the whole order, in what part of the world soever they are, with two guardians of every province, where there are such persons assembled that it may be truly said that this is the flower of religion, a mirror of virtues and an angelical army clothed in earthly bodies.

Here did Father Angel make known those graces which he had received from heaven and his burning zeal for the advancement of religion, and the excellence of his judgement in finding out means for that end, and his notable prudence in putting them into execution; which are the three pillars which uphold a regular building. Notwithstanding he ceased not sometimes to visit His Holiness, who gave him freely and with great contentment audience as often as he came. All Rome was filled with the sweet odours of his virtues; if he passed by the streets every man desired to see him, and his natural gravity, his comely tall stature and his port full of majesty appearing under the modesty of his poor habit, did show what he had been, without any intimation of those that knew him. If he entered into churches all admired his devotion. In the convent all the fathers desired one after another to have conference with him, to learn somewhat of him. The sick persons which lay upon their straw beds received great consolation by his visits. To be short, having no other time for himself but for to say Mass, he was fain to take the night time for the dispatch of his public business and other particular commissions which he had, yet was he as cheerful the next morning as if he had sweetly rested, and fell to the same task again.

His companion wondered at this, and taking brotherly liberty which he had given to him, admonished him and said that this great continual labour would overthrow his health, if he were not more provident in giving himself some rest. To whom he answered that God was too good as not to have care of His servants, and that it was for Him to dispose of them as it pleased Him, and for them to put in practice what belonged to them. And this was a thing very remarkable, that in the thick clouds of so much business he had always a smiling and serene countenance in token of his inward joy.

He was wont to say that God loved nothing which does not proceed from a joyful heart and contentment of affection, and all those that bear the Cross do not receive the fruits and benefits of it. "For," said he, "I find" (explicating the words of S. Paul: *God forbid that I should glory in anything than in the Cross of Christ*)

"I find herein," said he, "three sorts of persons, some that salute and adore the Cross, but do not bear it nor glory themselves in it; such are those which can well discourse of it and praise it much, but when occasion is presented they fly and abandon it. There are some others which bear it, but they glory not in it and these are they who suffer persecutions, tribulations or infirmities, because they can do no otherwise, herein like to Simon Cyreneus, which assisted Our Saviour in bearing his cross, but not of good will but by constraint.

"Thirdly there are others who do not only salute and bear the Cross but they glory therein, bearing willingly their necessities and afflictions, rejoicing in God's holy will and thank God who has vouchsafed to make them partakers of His chalice. The last of these three sorts do only gather the savorous fruits of the Cross and find glory in infirmity, life in death, sweetness in bitterness, joy in sorrow and an incomparable treasure in poverty. Whence it comes to pass many deceive themselves, thinking that perfection consists in enjoying their ease with gust and feeling, in visions, extasies and rapts, in great speculations of the understanding, in delightful sweetness of the affection. But alas, it consists in none of these. It is in imitating Our Saviour Jesus Christ upon the cross, where all the saints have searched Him and found Him, which is to travail for the love of God. This is the mark we ought to aim at, stirred up besides by the example of Jesus Christ, by that of our seraphical father S. Francis, which was a new-crucified man, and bearing these holy marks: *Ego enim stigmata Domini Jesu in corpore meo porto.*"

The chapter being finished, he being now to return to France, went to take his last farewell of His Holiness, who gave him audience with wonted and accustomed favour, and seeing by his humble thanks which he gave for his presents received that he was ready to depart, he renewed again the offer of his favours, which he refused with great humility as he had done formerly. After these refusals of honours he gave a great cross of gold with two chaplets of agates, one for his daughter Madame the Duchess and the other for Mademoiselle de Montpensier, her daughter and his grandchild, but this could not move his resolution, for he was not only

dead to all things of the world, but they were also dead in him, so that he had never accepted them if His Holiness and the Father General, who was present, had not absolutely commanded him to take them. Having taken them he prostrated himself and took His Holiness' blessing with all humility, who counselled him with fatherly charity to continue in his glorious designs, with promise to keep him in his remembrance and to witness his affection to him as occasion should be, either for his particular or the good of his religion in general.

His Holiness requested him often to go on horseback and not to expose his health to the extreme heat of the season and of the climate, to which he was not accustomed. Which he refused with great humility, being not willing to relieve anything of the austerity of his order. So being full of zeal, after he had taken his leave of the cardinals and some other eminent persons, he departed from Rome, the tenth of August 1608, leaving the whole city replenished with the odour of his exemplary devotion and admiration of his prudence.

Of his return from Rome and what happened to him
in the way

THE TWENTY-FIRST CHAPTER

MEN propose oftentimes and God does dispose; His sentences are hereby contrary to their determinations. The eyes of His providence see farther than the eyes of our affections. And because the present object, beguiling us often under the appearance of some good, does hinder us that we do not duly consider, nor understand the greater or lesser profit which will redound from the end; hence it comes to pass that God, seeing as well the success of our enterprises as the end which moves us, disposes often of our actions, contrary to our designs, when by His grace He imprints in us a desire to do nothing against His holy will and to rest ourselves wholly under His faithful conduct.

This blessed father, departing from Rome, had many good projects in his head which he could not finish, because God, seeing also that he had no other object but Himself, did dispose of all otherwise for His glory.

As he came down, the people in all places, being advertised that he was to pass by them, pressed much to see him, who after they had received the spiritual food of his exhortations, thought themselves happy if they could kiss his habit. So God would have his holiness of life testified by his actions to be known and to have some parcel of that honour which is now due to him and which he enjoys forever. You might have seen many principal men of the nobility to go forth to meet him, instantly[1] requesting him to take up his lodging with them. Which he did never accept, or very seldom, when he could retire himself to any convent. For although he were never so poorly treated, he took far more contentment to be there than he did where there was rich plenty of all things, having long since forsaken rich and plentiful means to embrace poverty with hearty and true affection. Religious men were as much cheered with his presence as secular; everyone was edified with the sight of him only, besides the fruit which they gathered by his discourse and conference.

As he came near to Turin he would not enter into the city, but said it was best to retire themselves to a convent of their order called Nostra Donna de la Campagna, distant about a league from the town, which he did the rather to avoid the occasion of visiting the Duke's Highness. For having banished all curiosity[2] from his affection, he declined as much as he could possibly the meeting of great persons. But he did attempt this in vain, for by what accident I know not, or whether by God's disposition for some good, he met the Duke's Highness in the way, who after he knew him, entertained him with all possible courtesy. He entertained about half an hour's discoursing with him about France, Rome, and some matters of state and religion. The good father excused himself as pressed and straitened by little time, whereupon His Highness told him that he would come to him the next morning, as he did, and passed the whole morning with him in the convent.

[1] insistently   [2] fastidiousness

This night the blessed father began to sicken and had a little fit of an ague, which broke his repose, yet thinking that it was a matter of nothing and it was only the weariness of his long journey, he ceased not the next morning after he had said Mass, to entertain His Highness again two or three hours, who offered him all courtesies that lay in his power and prayed him to be mindful of him in his holy sacrifices. Of whom, after he had taken his leave, he went on his way towards Rivoli, where there is a convent of Capuchins. Rivoli is a little town situated well for fertility, two leagues from Turin.[1] This good father, reposing there, purposed to have gone thence the next morning after Mass, which was the day of the marks[2] of S. Francis. But alas, he was defeated of his purpose, for as he was at the altar, he was taken with a great shaking and trembling of his ague, that he could hardly finish Mass. So that as soon as he had ended he was carried into his chamber and never went out of it till he had rendered his soul into the hands of Him that gave it him.

Of his death

THE TWENTY-SECOND CHAPTER

THE Duke's Highness had no sooner understood that his sickness had made this good father keep his bed but he sent presently[3] his best physicians and his apothecary to visit him and yield him all help and comfort they could, commanding them expressly to have a special care of him and to serve him with as much affection as they would serve himself. They signified so much to him and performed it in deed, sparing neither pain nor money, and employing their best endeavours to allay the heat of his fever, which was so violent that they could do him little or no good.

The blessed father, judging by the extremity of his disease that he could not continue long, and that he was come to the end of his pilgrimage, resigned himself into the hands of God. But as it is the

---

[1] Rivoli is about eight miles west of Turin.   [2] stigmata
[3] immediately

manner of the most perfect to mistrust their merits, esteeming themselves so much the greater sinners as they abound more in grace, he said that if it pleased God to have compassion on him he would yet live, having not done the penance which his sins required. Herein not unlike to S. Francis, who after many years of penance was always but upon his beginnings. And so, turning his thoughts to his end, he began with humble thanksgiving to God for the care He had of his soul, knowing that God's holy hand lays afflictions and diseases upon us according to our forces, wherewith He disposes to fortify and strengthen us. For when we consider dolours and afflictions in their own object with the eye only of nature, we have cause to be dejected with sadness. But since we are not only men but Christians also, we ought by the power of grace to consider them better, and piercing through the clouds of the accidents of this life behold clearly God's holy disposition, and lift up our spirits high, and so see the end which is designed to all, and comfort ourselves in the great profits and benefits which are to redound to us thereby. This meditation sank into the heart of this blessed Father, so that in the extremest pains of his disease he was as though he had been insensible.[1] "Blessed," said he, "are they who suffer anything for heaven; their dolours and griefs shall be recompensed with joy and gladness. The more we suffer, the more we satisfy for the pains due to our sins; this is the great mercy of God, which does punish our sins and crimes in this world. For so we depart out of it with expectation of more comfort." Afterwards he was visited by many that were well affected to his order, which, instead of giving him comfort, received it from him, in so much that they who entered to see him full of sorrow, departed from him with great contentment, wondering much of his great constancy. He made them understand how much it imports to live well if we will die well, and how hard it is to come to heaven, which is a place of so great purity. How likewise those abuse themselves who defer the amendment of their lives to their end, whereas it falls out that seldom he dies well who has lived ill. He did entertain them with these and the like discourses. All the religious of the convent one after another visited him, whom he instantly besought to assist

---

[1] i.e., as though he did not feel them.

him with their sacrifices and prayers, and to beg of God pardon for his sins, and especially that he might be helped by the Last Sacrament when they saw fit time, without waiting the extremity, wherein was danger of committing an irrecoverable fault.

His companion[1] was always with him and entertained him always in spiritual discourse. He prayed him to recite devoutly the prayers of the Roman ceremonial made to this particular end for the comfort and relief of sick persons. For among other prayers he made great account (as a good Christian ought) of those devotions which the Church does use and of the ceremonies of his order which have a particular virtue for those ends for which they were instituted.

He growing weaker daily by the violence of his disease, which grew upon him, he desired to fortify himself with the buckler of a true Catholic in this last action. Wherefore after he had confessed with his accustomed devotion, he prayed them that they would bring him the B. Sacrament, which he knew not only to be the strength of his soul and the food thereof, but also an appeasement of his bodily dolours. The reverend Father Provincial, yielding to his request, although he thought he was not in such extremity, brought it him after Matins, accompanied in procession with all the religious of the convent. O what elevation of his soul had he at the sight of his Saviour veiled under the Sacrament. His cheeks becoming vermilion red as the rose, and his tears trickling down his eyes, witnessed sufficiently what inward discourse he had with his Saviour, captivating all his faculties and powers to give Him thanks for so great a benefit. Before he received he would follow this last action of S. Francis, to die naked and deprived of all things, saving the love of God. Wherefore he besought Father Provincial that he might consign into his hands some small presents which His Holiness had sent to Madame his daughter. He put also those memorials which he had of the affairs of their General Chapter into the hands of his companion, assuring also the Father Provincial that if he did also commit to him the other presents that he should satisfy the intention of His Holiness, and as for himself, he desired nothing more than to deprive himself of the propriety of

---

[1] Probably Fr. Archangel Herbert of Pembroke.

the least things that could be imagined, to possess God more perfectly. Having often in his mouth the words of the Apostle: *Mihi
vivere Christus est et mori lucrum:Unto me to live is Christ and to die
is gain*. Moreover, he demanded leave of the Father Provincial to
renew his vows and to offer them afresh to God, the which he,
having once consecrated to God, never had any mind to change it,
although the violence of the people took him from his convent,
protesting now that it was against his will, and that whilst he was
out, he always longed after that which he did enjoy at this present.
He did all this with extraordinary devotion, and having pro-
nounced the words very distinctly, he made a brief exhortation but
very fervent to those that assisted him, and showed to them the
contentment which his solitude had caused to him. He commended
much the perfection and happy state of religion, saying that God
does draw His friends to it to feed them with the sweet milk of His
grace, not that they should live as they did before the life of plants,
for that is but earthly, nor the life of sensible creatures, for that is
but brutal, nor the life of men only, for that is but human, nor the
life of the angels, for that is but created, but to live the very life of
the Divinity, for He will make us live and enjoy His essence and
His essence is life and the spring of life: *With thee is the fountain of
life*, said David; so He will make them enter into the life which He
lives Himself with the Son and the Holy Ghost, in the company of
those among men and angels whom it has pleased Him to make
worthy of so great grace.

All his brethren standing about him as children about their
dying father, showing great signs of heaviness and astonished at his
fervour, seeming to hear the Holy Ghost speak through his mouth
and exhort them to their duty, in conclusion, he, with his eyes full
of tears and a spirit ravished with holy devotion, demanded
humbly pardon of all, both present and absent, which as soon as he
had done, he received the Holy Sacrament with so much devotion
that all the assistants felt their hearts touched with a sweet compunction and an ardent desire to make themselves worthy of so
blessed an end.

The next morning his companion, seeing him repose more than
ordinary in great quietness of body and spirit (as he thought) most

sweetly, and not knowing the reason of so sudden a change, thought that it was some beginning of an alteration whereupon his better health did depend. Wherefore he retired into a chamber hard by, and advertising the religious that they should not enter in to him, lest they should break his repose, which seemed to be better than he had all the time of his sickness, he was absent for the space of two or three hours, in which time he took a little rest upon a straw bed, having passed some nights before without once closing his eyes. While he took this little sleep or rather slumber, he seemed to be in a great churchyard, where a choir of angels made a most sweet harmony; he heard them with great attention, admiring at the beauty and behaviour of these heavenly spirits.

Afterward he seemed to come near a coffin all beset with flowers, whose odour was marvellous fragrant and sweet. Upon this he wakened suddenly, and fearing least the good father had yielded up his spirit (for in such cases dreams do much affright us), went to his chamber and opening softly the chamber door, he was presently spied by the sick person, who asked him from whence he came and how long he had been absent. "It is about two hours since," said he, "that I seeing you lie so quiet, I withdrew myself to take some rest." "I had thought," said the sick father, "that it had hardly been a quarter of an hour, for my soul was never in such a calm, being as it were rapt from me and full of such joy and contentment that I cannot express it, for it surpasses all kind of harmony and other contentment whereof the sense is capable." Then his companion, knowing that there was something super-natural in this action, told him what representation he had in his sleep and how that shortened his sleep, which the good father hearing said to him: "Speak nothing of it I pray you, but pray to God that His holy will be done." So did he fly ostentation and the more he weakened and abased his body in the outward man, the more strength and honour had he in the inward man.

This ravishing of spirit and extraordinary serenity of his counte-nance did increase more as he decayed in body and as death came on apace, which was a great proof to make us believe that he had already tasted some drop of that heavenly divine liquor wherewith the blessed souls are made drunk in Paradise. For this is the opinion of the best divines in mystical divinity, which is not contrary to faith or reason, that it is possible and also permitted to a good soul to have some feeling of the joys of heaven before death, so that it become capable thereof with a sincere will and due preparation. And why not? Since God, who is the object of our felicity in what state soever we be, in heaven clearly and in this life within the obscurity of faith, can, if it please Him, draw the curtain and represent Himself without cloud or obscurity, not to the eyes of our body, which are too terrestrial, but to those of the soul which are the same after death or during our life.

After this extasy he seemed to have a fresh constancy, as though he had not felt any evil at all, although the heat presently after retiring from him, he was deprived of the ordinary moving of his limbs. He earnestly requested that he might receive the Sacrament of Extreme Unction as the last buckler of defence against the assaults of Satan, which being more fierce at such times than at any other, make often those that are most strong to falter and faint. His desire was satisfied, and having received it with joined hands and his eyes lifted up to heaven and his heart to God, he spoke these words worthy to be graven upon the marble of eternity, or rather, in the hearts of devout souls, that they may make use of them in such conflicts: "God be blessed, I am now fortified on all sides and so well armed from top to toe that I do not fear my enemy."

The Duke's Highness being much afflicted for the sickness of this blessed father, besides the physician and apothecary, who were always with him, sent every day some of his gentlemen to visit him and assure him of his affection and to know in what state he was. Therefore he was accustomed to entertain them with spiritual discourse, giving them always some good rule how to live in God's grace amidst the great splendours of Court. His companion, seeing that one of these gentlemen would have driven him into a discourse touching nobility, and esteeming that the father drew on to his end, put him in mind of himself and said: *Ab hoc momento pendet eternitas: Of this moment depends eternity*, meaning the moment of death.

These words moved him so much that immediately, throwing himself down to the centre of nothingness, he esteemed himself one of the greatest sinners of the world, and upon this occasion he made an exhortation of the love of God, of the nature, quality and fruits of it, and of that which we are to render in exchange of His person, or in the person of our neighbour in whom His image is represented. And this he uttered with so much fervour, zeal and devotion and strength of lungs, as if he had preached in some pulpit in good state of health, and he witnessed to them that his heart put in practice more than his tongue did express, so that the physicians and other learned men who were present, hearing him cry so forcibly three times: "O love, O love, O love of God", his face being all on fire and his heart ravished on high, could not but exceedingly wonder at this, and said that this seemed to them rather to be the voice of an angel than of man.

Immediately after he called for the crucifix and, holding it devoutly in his hands, his spirit, which was not weakened, supplied to him matter of fervent and devout meditation of Christ's death and passion, till such time as, his forces wholly forsaking him, he contented himself to say "Jesus, Maria", with a wonderful tenderness of soul, and yet let not go his hold of the crucifix, but kept it in his hands.

Presently his tongue, which was the instrument of conversion of so many souls and the angel of consolation, benumbed in his palate, ceased to do its proper function half an hour before he departed. And then the sign of his eyes and hands were instruments of his heart, by which he witnessed to the priest that he understood and liked of those words which he spoke to him to assist him in so dangerous a passage, till such time as by a deep sigh coming from the depth of his heart, he yielded up his soul into the hands of his Redeemer and was received into the hands of angels.

This was the eight-and-twentieth day of September 1608, the six-and-fortieth year of his life and the two-and-twenty of his conversion among the Capuchins, that he rendered this his talent to God, who had given it him, and rendered it with hundredfold profit, which he had gotten by his travail. After his death his face changed not in colour, his eyes lifted up to heaven seemed to show some little smiling, his arms lay across upon his stomach. A man would not have thought that he had been dead, if his limbs being all cold had not lost all manner of heat and feeling. His companion, in whose arms he would die in witness of his affection, spoke to him as yet not having rendered his soul. The physician felt his pulse and put his hand on his mouth, thinking that his soul was not yet departed, when it was enjoying the recompense of his merits. In fine, his soul went from him so sweetly that it gave no sign of departure by any contraction of the body (as is ordinary), but only that it lived before and now had no life.

The Duke's Highness having heard the tidings of his death, being much grieved for the loss of so worthy a personage, purposed to go and see him and honour his funeral with his presence. But his physician diverted him, because he had seen some spots upon the body of this good father, which he thought might be tokens of the purples,[1] and so His Highness might incur some danger thereby. Whereupon he gave charge to his physician to see him embalmed and to put him into a coffin of lead and cover it with a cloth of black velvet, desiring that he might be so buried, as he was in the chapel of that convent.

Of the transporting of his body to Paris

THE THREE-AND-TWENTIETH CHAPTER

WHILST the body of this blessed father did repose at Rivoli, the heavy news of his death was brought to his daughter Madame the Duchess, who was much afflicted with the tidings of it. Her love, answerable to his fatherly love, would not permit her to leave his body so far from her, and therefore took order that it should be transported to Paris. She sent for this purpose the Governor of Dombes in Savoy to request the Duke's Highness, both in her uncle's name the Cardinal Joyeuse as also in her own, that he would not refuse his consent to the removing of her father's body. His Highness accorded to it, yet very sorry he was that Piedmont should be deprived of that rich treasure, having already found and

[1] the plague

known the profit of it by many effects, whose soul was powerful to assist the necessities of those who had recourse to him for his intercession to God. He was taken thence with many tears and great sorrow. The Duke's Highness had three sons: Monsieur the Prince Major, Monseigneur the Cardinal and Monsieur the Prince Thomas, who assisted there with all their train, and bearing great torches of white wax in their hands, accompanied the body on foot two miles from Rivoli, doing him this honour due to his piety, at the remove of his body, which they could not do before at his death, nor at his burial.

There were four religious of his order who were always about his coffin and followed it (as they had commandment to do) even to Paris. Through the villages as they passed, the curates with the people came out to meet the corpse in procession. The towns where there were many ecclesiastical persons assembled, did the like in general processions, and did think it a favour from heaven that this precious jewel passed by them, hoping to obtain thereby the influence of some particular grace by his means.

When he came to Lyons the principal persons of the city came to receive him, and all the clergy and religious went out with a great number of torches and lights to conduct him to the convent of the Capuchins, who were attended with such multitudes of people that they could hardly pass.

Madame the Duchess of Mercoeur earnestly entreated Madame the Duchess of Guise that she would let her have for a present the heart of her father, to be kept as a precious relique in the convent of the religious women of S. Clare, called otherwise Daughters of the Passion; which is one of the most goodly monasteries of this order, and a witness of the great piety of this princess which caused it to be built in the suburbs of S. Honoré, right against the monastery of the Capuchins, to the erecting whereof this good father had contributed all he could by his good advice and employment, and had preached there the first day when the first twelve were closed up,[1] at which time Monseigneur the Cardinal of Gondi performed the rest of the office.

There was some difficulty made in yielding to this demand, for

[1] 9 August 1606

as much as the heart having been put and closed within the body covered with lime and some sweet herbs, when His Highness caused it to be embalmed, it was thought that besides the natural course of all the parts of the body, there had been some corruption caused and hastened by those things applied. Notwithstanding these reasons, his body was opened again at Lyons in the presence of the Governor of Dombes, of Monsieur President and some others, and his heart was taken forth, fresh and blood ruddy as at the hour of death, not without great astonishment of those that saw it. The same day the Office was said for him (as it was in all other places where his body stayed) and the press of people was so great and the clamours and cries so loud, both of people without and within the church, that a father of the order being to make the funeral oration, was constrained to begin with these words: "Silence, people, silence".

After the Office they departed and went on their way towards Paris, whereof the inhabitants of Nevers being advertised and seeing so precious a jewel at their gate, went out to meet him in great troops with an incredible reverence and devotion. They did him the same honour as he had at Lyons, and the next day the Bishop with all solemn ceremony conducted him after to the bark, not without the great shouts of many and tears of others: in the like manner he was received in all places. The eleventh of June his body came to Paris and was received with that respectful devotion as may be well admired but not expressed. The Capuchins went forth to meet his body a league out of the town, accompanied with a great press of people. All the household servants of Madame the Duchess his daughter went forth also, two and two on horseback in mourning weeds. The Capuchins came after in the same order, every one carrying a light of white wax in his hand, singing the Office and suffrage for the dead according to their ordinary manner of plain song. After followed the body carried between two mules, covered with a grey cloth, as the bier also was, with a white cross of cloth (for so it was ordered by Monseigneur the Cardinal of Joyeuse according to the direction herein from His Holiness). And there followed a great company of knights of the two orders of the King. Among others Monsieur the Duke of

Espernon, his brother-in-law, Monsieur le Grand, the Master of Horse, Monsieur de Roquelaure, and many others in whose face men might have read the sorrow of their hearts, not for the loss only of so worthy a kinsman but such a spiritual father, who during his life taught them the way to heaven by his holy exhortations, and encouraged them to surmount all difficulties with manly courage, whatsoever they were, by his extraordinary manner of virtuous life. It was thought that there was above a hundred thousand persons within the street or in windows or coaches, who were the beholders of the reception of his body. And besides these great multitudes at Paris there were fourteen parishes which accompanied him from the country round about, and the devotion of many was so great towards him that they could not be kept from cutting some little pieces of the cloth which covered the bier, taking all the flowers wherewith it was set, to keep them as relics.

The Capuchins watched all the night about the body and the next day had a solemn service whereat Madame of Guise, his daughter, was present, who by her constancy made known a virtue surpassing nature. All the principal seigneurs were also present. After the service he was buried before the high altar of the Capuchins, where they have permitted, contrary to the custom of their order, that this inscription should be graved upon a marble stone.

Hoc tumulo sunt ossa Reverendi Patris Angelis de Joyeuse olim Ducis, Paris, ac Mariscallis Franciae, & in Provincia Occitania proregis; qui in ipso aetatis flore, ut totum se Christo addiceret, tot honores, & opes abiecit, & ordinem Capucinorum ingressus in eo reliquum vitae transegit, singulari pietatis, & humilitatis exemplo, in quo tandem obiit, cum pro secunda vice esset Provincialis Provinciae Franciae, & Definitor Capituli Generalis, anno Christi 1608. 4. Calend octobris.

Henrica Henrici Montispenserii Ducis vidua Patri charissimo maerens posuit.

"In this tomb are the bones of the Reverend Father Angel of Joyeuse, heretofore Duke, Peer and Marshal of France, and Lieutenant of Languedoc, who in the very flower of his age, that he might give himself wholly to God, despised so many honours and riches, and entering into the Order of Capuchins, spent there the rest of his life in it with singular example of piety and humility; wherein he died at length when he was the second time Provincial of the Province of France, and Definitor of the General Chapter, in the year of Our Lord 1608, on the fourth of the Calends of October.

"Henrietta, the widow of Henry, Duke of Montpensier, caused this to be done in mourning for her most dear father."

THE MIRACULOUS LIFE, CONVERSION
AND CONVERSATION
OF THE REVEREND FATHER BENET OF CANFIELD,

an Englishman and preacher of the Order of Capuchins.

Of his country, birth and education

THE FIRST CHAPTER [1]

THERE are not more virtuous effects than those of God's providence, which are powerful to rouse up a soul and to draw it from
the vanities of the world to the search of the Sovereign Good, but
they are so full of excellence and obscurity, either in their cause or
their essence or in their end, that we must have our understanding
wholly perverted or else ingenuously confess that they are beyond
the bounds and limits of our reason and knowledge to comprise[2]
them. There is no man ignorant that they are, for we feel them and
taste the fruits daily. But to judge of the worth and value of them
or to know what particular motive induces God to bring them to
light, this is a matter that the angels themselves do not know.

The reverend Father Benet of Canfield, whose life, conversion
and conversation has not only been miraculous but a continual
miracle, will serve for an evident proof of this truth. For he which
had sucked heresy with his mother's milk and in his birth was
seized with death, grew to be nourished and fed with the sweet
liquor of grace within this seraphical order, the most hard and
austere of all others, to subdue the passions of the flesh, wherein he
lived many years. In his death he was made partaker of a true and
happy life. He which from his cradle was tainted with the impuri-
ties of Puritans and took contentment therein, was cleansed from
his filth and brought into the bosom of the pure and true Church

---

[1] A translation of a Latin hymn to Fr. Benet of some two hundred lines,
composed by Agatha Wiseman, O.S.B., and received by Brousse after her death
in 1613, has been omitted.
[2] comprehend

of God, the Catholic, Apostolic, Roman Church. And his soul shining with an extraordinary purity by an extraordinary measure of God's graces and benedictions, vowed an irreconcilable enmity, both in tongue and heart against such impurity, after he had discovered the odiousness of it. He who in his former thoughts and designs aimed at nothing but at the glory and greatness of the world and had no feeling or care of heavenly things, suddenly was so changed that he despised all the pomps and vanities of the world and fixed all his thoughts upon the bettering of his soul and aspiring to heavenly things. He persevered in these holy desires and never grew faint or weary in his affection. He only changed the object, and like repentant Mary Magdalen gave all that unto God which he before had prodigally employed upon the world.

This was God's providence which wrought this extraordinary change, which in the beginning cannot but produce astonishment and likewise humility and astonishment in the ignorance of the time.

He was an Englishman by nation and I may say by predestination and benediction, whence those that are drenched and buried in error may see that God does never refuse sufficiency of grace to draw them forth, seeing that even in this realm (heretofore a dear child of the Church and afterward separated by God's secret judgement) there are those whom God does extraordinarily call unto Him by special grace. For although the exercise of Catholic religion be forbidden and suppressed, yet are there many fervent and zealous souls which will not (though it be with peril of their lives) do anything which is contrary to God's and the Church's commandments. Therefore, as the story of Job notes very particularly to his great commendation, that he was of the land of Hus, where the people were malicious and great sinners; so he, born and bred in heresy, which is so much the more venomous and dangerous because it is masked with the name of a pure religion, merits the more honour and praise in that he was an Englishman, in that he did overcome the corruption of nature and nurture and afterward attained to such heroical virtues, preferring banishment, poverty and austerity of life for the love of Christ, before his dearest country, his plentiful means and delights wherein he had been bred and pampered.

He was born at Canfield in Essex, of a good family and parentage, his first name was William Fitch, by which he was called till he became Capuchin. From his infancy he was of so sweet and lovely a disposition that he drew all men's affections to him that knew him. His parents loved him more dearly than they did the rest of their children and cherished him more tenderly, not knowing to what end God had destinated their natural favours. He was the second brother of three of them. The eldest who was heir of the revenues and lands according to the laws of the country, was called Thomas, the third was Francis, who having little left him by his parents, married a rich widow, by whom he advanced his means and fortune and afterward for testimony of his gentry and recompense of his public service was made a knight.[1] These two brethren, though brought up in good letters, were no way comparable to Father Benet, who beyond his natural inclination, wherein he did exceed, did show by effect that he was carried to his studies with an extraordinary desire. He spent in his tender age whole nights at his book and did not willingly converse with any but those of whom he might learn somewhat. He took no pleasure in any recreations that drew him from his studies, insomuch that when his brethren and some other gentlemen, who were brought up together under the same master, would take him to go a-hunting (in which sport he more delighted than in any other) he would either refuse to go with them or if he went, he always took some book in his pocket, which he opened and read as often as the least occasion was offered to him, taking more contentment in reading some passage or sentence in such a book as he carried with him, than in that delightful sport. Many such things did he in his tender age and in the darkness of error and heresy. What would he have done if he had been a Catholic and had had the light of true faith?

When he was grown to better age and was capable of greater knowledge, he gave himself to higher studies, which occasioned his parents to send him to the Inns of the Court,[2] there to study the common law. This good father advanced himself so much herein

[1] Thomas (1559-88), m Agnes, da. of John Wiseman of Great Canfield and had six children. Sir Francis (1563-1608), m Margaret, heiress of Edmund Tirrell of Beeches, widow of John Daniel Esq.
[2] He studied at the Middle Temple from circa 1578/9 till 1586.

in a short time, that those who were not witnesses of it, could not believe it. But when it pleased God of His infinite mercy, to show him the beams of His truth through the clouds and fogs of heresy, wherewith his soul was infected, they did so lighten his soul, that in one moment he was wholly changed into another man, for whereas before he was fervent in his study of the law, he became slack and cold, and whereas before he was pleasant and a lover of company, he became melancholic and a friend of solitariness and much retired. Yea now he began to enter into mature consultation with himself, being driven into many perplexed thoughts. For on the one side, the belief and religion which he had learnt from his infancy, held him as it were fettered and manacled, besides that, it was the common religion of his country and of the greatest part of his kindred and friends. On the other side, he conceived great scruple and matter of doubt concerning the truth and verity thereof, so that he knew not what resolution to make. But God made His divine inspiration to consider the glorious crowns which are reserved in heaven for the recompense of good works and the eternal torments which are prepared in hell for the souls of sinners, which of all good inspirations is the best and the most forcible.

He continued some few days in this state, feeling the spiritual combats in his soul, which God did more and more augment. The cause whereof he could not comprehend till his miraculous conversion was effected, which it has pleased God that he has left written with his own hand to serve for a motive to others that stray out of the right way and to give occasion to Catholics to admire the effects of God's providence, to humble themselves and to give unto God immortal thanks for those graces which He has so freely and graciously given to His creatures. It has been already printed by someone[1] (who desirous to conserve the memory of this blessed man, has prevented[2] me) but because the rest of his life and actions which are of very great importance to serve for a notable example unto others, was not adjoined to it, I have thought it fit to put all together in one story, that so it might be more perfect and more available to the edification of others and thus the story does begin.

[1] It was first published by M. de Nantilly in the sixth French edition of the *Reigle de Perfection*, Paris, 1614.
[2] forestalled

★

His exclamation upon the state of this present life

THE SECOND CHAPTER

ALTHOUGH the disorder of my life past, compared with the strict life of ancient Christians, or examined by the judgement of those of our time, may seem evil, wicked and monstrous, yet it was so shadowed and covered with the iniquity of the time, abounding with vicious and lewd libertines, that it could hardly be discerned and condemned for such. For even as black being near to white does more plainly appear, so when it is mixed and confounded with black it can hardly be distinguished. The same may I say truly of my life, the darkness whereof compared with the candour of the life of old Christians, or the purity of those that are good in this age, would presently be discovered. Yet having led my life in the black darkness of this present age, it seemed not so foul as indeed it is. For since the lamentable change of the Catholic faith into heresy, since the overthrow and contempt of the universal apostolic Roman faith in our realm, the consciences of men have been so stretched and enlarged, the rein of concupiscence has been so slackened, that all honesty, virtue and good life has been forsaken and abandoned, and on the contrary side vice and iniquity has wholly swayed and overruled the same. I would to God my words were not true, but experience does manifestly show what I say to be but truth.

For first of all, how are men's consciences stretched in trafficking one with another? How little or no fidelity is there now in mutual promises? What cunning dealing and cozenage is there practised everywhere? What small hold is there of men's words and credit? Need we not now more bonds and writings to borrow but twenty angels,[1] than was needful in time past to buy so much land forever? No man trusts his neighbour, neither would I counsel him to trust him. As for sacred oaths, which ought to be inviolable, alas men make merchandise of them and sell them for money. And for concupiscence, who sees not that it is withheld by no bridle, men

---

[1] About £10 (pre-devaluation).

following their liberty and pleasures like brute beasts? But for this I had rather pass it over lightly, than to prove it by many particular examples. And why should it be bridled or kept in, if (without giving any consent unto it) it be judged a mortal sin, as Master Charke[1] and other ministers his companions do teach? And that all we do, are mortal sins, as Protestants hold?

Moreover, if any man give alms or do perform any other good work, he shall not be reputed a friend of Protestants, but be esteemed (as they ordinarily term it) a merit-monger and one that seeks to save himself by his merits. As for hospitality and relief of the poor it is almost quite neglected, especially among their churchmen, who either maintain their wives or concubines upon the goods of the Church. And as for fasting and prayer, which Our Saviour has so often recommended to us by words and works, they are so little esteemed that he which fasts upon the eve commanded by the Holy Church, is called a Papist and long prayer is styled a monkish act. And finally, to use the help of the sacraments against sin is reputed enmity against the State. But to confess, to reconcile others or to be reconciled, yea but to carry about him holy things, as *Agnus Dei*, medals, a crucifix or grains that are blessed, or but to be in company with a priest, this is no less than a crime of treason to his prince and country. But he that will take a more clear view, how vice and iniquity are exalted, let him but observe how sin now reigns in all states and sorts of life and he shall find that all manner of grievous sins are committed as freely and loosely as if they were not such. So do they (confirming the words of Holy Scripture) *drink sin as water*, which is one of the great sins of the world; and of the six things hated of God, the one is, to have our feet light and swift to run to evil.

And to examine further some other points, what little honour is that given to God's majesty, whose name is so blasphemed in swearing and forswearing in all discourses, that he is scarce esteemed a gentleman or a man of courage, which has not learnt to interlace his words with many oaths and blasphemies. Their Sundays and feasts, how are they neglected when on these days, there

---

[1] William Charke, puritan minister, preacher to Lincoln's Inn, 1581-93. He wrote against Bl. Edmund Campion and disputed with him in the Tower (*DNB*).

are more idle persons walking up and down the streets, and in Saint Paul's Church (which is made a walking and talking place) than there is on others.[1] Nay, even Sunday is a day designed for bear-baiting, and even the hour of their service is allotted to it, and indeed the time is as well spent at the one, as at the other. I need not speak of profanation of feasts, which the Puritans will not approve at all. For rancour and malice, do they not reign universally through the whole realm? As for defamations, detraction and rash judgements, men make no account or reckoning of them, what divisions and debates are there in every parish. And for the most part the minister is a principal man in maintaining them. If we speak of covetousness, is not he to be judged a thief, which desires the goods, lands, and possessions of his neighbour, I mean in the presence of God? and who be there among them, who lie not still in ambush, and secretly suborn spies, to inform them how they may take any least advantage how to seize upon other men's goods?

I will omit to speak of justice, which is corrupted among the principal justices, and it is not long since they accused one another in their highest court of justice. This is but too evident, when we see daily so many just persons, priests and other Catholics, unjustly imprisoned, their goods spoiled, and in the end themselves cruelly put to death, and all under the cloak of justice.

I will not discover more detestable sins in the greatest persons, who will not abide that they be touched. But all the other former sins and many other, are so common in all forces, as if they thought there were no God at all, or if there be, they seem to be of those of whom the Prophet speaks, *Our Lord will not see it, neither will the God of Jacob behold it.* Neither is it to be wondered, that they keep God's commandments no better, since they are not incited and moved by their ministers to keep them, but they boldly preach, and teach by their lives, and by their doctrine, that they cannot be kept. Our Saviour says, *My commandments are not heavy,* and they say they are most heavy, yea impossible. Our Saviour says, *My yoke is sweet, and My burden light,* and they teach that it is sharp,

---

[1] The use of the precincts of St. Paul's as a market place, and the generally unspiritual atmosphere in and around it, was a common topic for the satirists of the period, and, it must be admitted in all fairness, of pre-Reformation times as well.

yea unsupportable. Our Saviour says, *If thou wilt enter into eternal life, keep the commandments.* And they teach that we must enter into it by only faith; is it not like that such a life proceeds from such doctrine? For what wonder is it, if such fruit grow from such seed? Heresy and schism bring forth no better. Heresy and bad life do go together. Therefore Saint Ignatius[1] says *Fly the breath of iniquity, fly the devilish doctrine of heretics out of whose mouth proceeds an infection which poisons the whole world. Heresy is without God. Heresy is an invention of the devil.* What faithful English heart is there which does not weigh the complaint of Saint Basil in his time, saying: *Good doctrine is subverted, those who ought to feed the flock of Christ with the truth are forced to be silent, the mouths of good teachers are closed up and blaspheming tongues do riot, holy places are profaned, the better and wiser sort of people come not to the churches where doctrine acceptable to God and good people is taught, but they are forced to live in deserts, lifting up their hands to God with sighs and groans and many salt tears.* This is the state of our poor country since Catholic religion has been overthrown. There has been as it were the general deluge of vice and iniquity and the very outward face of all virtue and honesty has been thus disfigured. Whereupon it came to pass that my enormous manner of life appeared not so foul in this miserable country as when it was in another Egypt, the darkness whereof were so gross and so palpable that it might in a manner be cut with a knife.

What he was and what he was become, how he does detest his life past and embrace a new life

THE THIRD CHAPTER

JUSTLY may it be said with Saint Policarp: *O God, unto what time hast Thou reserved us! Alas what time is this, what people and what manners do we now behold! Faith is exiled, the Church despised, virtue is trodden under foot and vice is exalted! Alas say I, sin, heresy and*

[1] St. Ignatius, Bp. of Antioch.

schism do now reign. This is the time wherein I was born, brought up and nurtured among these people and infected with their manners. This was Thy ordinance O God, so it pleased Thy divine majesty and providence, that I should be born in these unhappy times and participate of their miseries by following them. Thy ways and judgements, O Lord, are inscrutable, Thy wisdom is infinite and Thy mercies without number. O depth of the riches, of the wisdom and knowledge of God, how unsearchable are His judgements and His ways incomprehensible! There is no number of His wisdom and His mercy is above all His works. To Thee will I always sing a canticle of praise and offer to Thee thanksgiving. For notwithstanding all these dangers, Thy bounty has not forsaken me, but cast me into another mould, and changed my sin to my benefit. I cannot but consider my headlong course and desperate life which I led wandering from Thee. As a lost sheep I strayed, when Thou ceased not to look after Thy servant. For how barbarous and brutish was my life which I passed over out of Thy Holy Church and without the help of her divine sacraments? Can he be styled a Christian which never received the Sacrament of Penance nor of the Altar? Never heard Mass, never assisted at Matins or Evensong, nor ever saw priest in all his life? Such a one was I, wretched and miserable man and unworthy the name of a Christian. O Lord remember not the offences of my youth, nor my ignorance. There was nothing else to be seen in me but a superficial show and outward appearance of a careless Christian. For if I were not then a branch of the true vine, how could I bring forth good fruit? If I were not a member of the body, what service could I do to the head? But such I was not then, for he (as a venerable author well observes) is not worthy to have God for his Father, who has not the Church for his mother. So then I lived in body, but was dead in soul. I daily broke Thy holy commandments, I daily committed mortal sin. All my life past was nothing but a heaping up of sin and horrible offences. I provoked daily Thy wrath and indignation against me. My conscience did torture me and the inward and secret parts of my heart did reprove and fret me. Avarice and covetousness did wring me, pride did overwhelm me, envy did consume me, concupiscence did inflame me, luxury did imprison me, gluttony did transport me, drunkenness did confound me, detraction did rend me, ambition did supplant me, discord did trouble me, anger did vex me, lightness did carry me away, negligence did oppress me, hypocrisy did deceive me, flattery did abuse me, favour did puff me up, and calumny did prick me. But Thou, O Lord, art He which wilt deliver me from all these perverse nations. These are they with whom I have haunted, whom I have trusted as my friends, obeyed as my masters, served as my lords, believed as my counsellors, conversed withal as my citizens, and dwelt friendly withal as my domestical companions. And yet, O Lord, Thou tookest not away Thy grace wholly from me, neither didst wholly abandon me, not then when for the space of seven years I lived so perilously, in a place so full of dangerous snares, which time I spent in feeding my fancy with the vanities of this place and took my delight in the ordinary pastimes of that place. Alas, how often have I beaten the streets in idle walking? How often have I run to plays and comedies? How many an idle turn have I made in Saint Paul's Church, now so profaned. How often have I run to dancing and fencing schools? If I spent any time better than other, it was when in the Inn of the Middle Temple I read for fashion's sake some book of the common law. In this extremity of danger did others despair of me? No surely, for such was alas the blindness of men that I was esteemed forsooth a young man of great good hope, when it did not appear whether I lived like a Christian or no. For can I hold this a Christian life, or think that my sins were but small? No surely, but rather with the prodigal child am bound to say: Father, I have sinned against heaven and before Thee, I am not worthy to be called Thy son. Alas, I took the broad way which led to hell and destruction and no man reproved me, no man forbade me, no man admonished me. Thou only, O Lord, hast cried to me aloud that I should leave this monstrous and dreadful life, but I, alas, was so asleep that I heard not Thy voice. There was such a thick cloud of vanity before my eyes, that it was almost impossible to see the true Sun of Justice and Light of all Truth. I was so wrapt in darkness (being the son of darkness) that I loved nothing else but it, because I knew not the light. I was blind and contented myself in that state and went on through darkness to the profound and obscure pit of darkness, till such time as it pleased Thee to pour into the inward ear of my heart and instil Thy most holy and soul-saving commandments, saying, *Fiat lux*, let light be made, and presently there was light, and so the thick and foggy clouds which veiled my eyes vanished away. I saw Thy light, I acknowledged Thy voice and said: O Lord, Thou art my God which hath drawn me out of darkness and the shadow of death, called me to the knowledge of Thy certain and clear light and caused me to discern it. For this I render Thee immortal thanks, that it pleased Thee so to illuminate and convert me. I have now a horror of the darkness wherein I was and more of the dark abyss, whither I was going. I have said in my heart, woe be to that darkness which took hold of me so long a time, and cursed me that blindness which would have hindered me from seeing the glorious light of heaven, and unfortunate and disastrous be that ignorance which impeached[1] me from the knowledge of Thee, which art my only God and Lord, light and joy, the hope of my soul, which hast at length so mercifully converted me and turned my heart from the vanities of this world, that shortly after I made three vows, of obedience, poverty and chastity, which I purposed to keep in the religion of Thy faithful servant holy Saint Francis. But by what means has this been done, O my Lord; from how many dangers hast Thou preserved me and succoured me in all my necessities? How many great temptations have I found in this affair, and how powerfully have I been delivered? How often have I delighted in vain and frivolous things? How great have Thy mercies been in this my sudden change? When I wandered Thou didst bring me back, when I was ignorant Thou didst instruct me, when I was heavy Thou didst comfort me, when I did despair Thou didst strengthen me, when I did fall Thou didst lift me up, when I was up Thou didst hold me, when I did walk Thou didst conduct me, when I did come unto Thee Thou didst receive me, when I did sleep Thou didst watch over me, when I did cry unto Thee, Thou didst hear me. These and many other infinite benefits Thou didst confer unto me in my conversion. Thou which art the God of my soul, make me (O Lord) to know and acknowledge

---

[1] prevented, hindered

Thee and that I meditate day and night on Thee so that no time pass from me wherein I may not continually give Thee thanks for such inestimable benefits received from Thee. For what should be more pleasing to me and more sweet than to speak and think always of Thee and so to render thanks unto Thee, to the end that for them I may always love and praise Thee with all my heart, with all my soul, with all my understanding, and with all my force, and with the inward marrows of my spirit and of all my faculties and powers, and resign myself wholly to Thee (my Lord, my God) which art the bliss and contentment of all those which trust in Thee?

*By what means he was called from his worldly
and heretical temptations*

THE FOURTH CHAPTER

AFTER I had long lived in this licentious manner like a libertine and that it pleased God of His infinite mercy to recall me, in the summer time, according to my wonted[1] manner I purposed to go into the country to my friends to recreate and delight myself with those sports wherein youth delights, and being come to the house of a friend of mine, my mind was wholly changed and alienated from any sports at all. For three or four days after I came thither, it happened that I lighted on a little book which I was curious to look upon, and finding that it was a book that I had heard much commended, treating of a resolution to live well,[2] I was presently moved to read some few passages in the same, yet without any purpose to read exactly all whatsoever might be contained in it. And after I had read some little thereof I began to see the end

---

[1] accustomed
[2] i.e., *A Book of Christian Exercise appertaining to Resolution*, by R.P. Perused and accompanied now with a Treatise tending to Pacification by E. Bunny, London, 1584. This was a Protestant version of *The First Book of Christian Exercise, appertayning to Resolution* (Rouen, 1582) by Father Robert Parsons, S.J. Parsons altered the title of subsequent editions to *A Christian Directory, Guiding Men to their Salvation.* Both in the Catholic and the Protestant form this work passed through numerous editions.

whereat he aimed which was a present and speedy reformation of the life of the reader. Whereupon I was desirous to see what arguments he used to persuade thereto and if peradventure I liked them well I would put them in practice. But in reading I began to have a remorse of conscience and therefore I left the book for the present with a purpose to read more thereof the next day, the which was Sunday. But when Sunday was come I spent it in going to the prayers of heretics and partly in some recreations and the day after I read very little or nothing at all. But on Tuesday I took the book again into my hands and I read therein many pages, during which time I laboured to favour myself as though those torments which were threatened to sinners were not touching me, although my conscience reproved me therein. But the more I read, the more my conscience accused me, so that I began to assign and limit a time wherein I would amend my life.

But what shall I say O Lord, whilst I did not answer sufficiently to Thy holy inspirations, Thou didst not cease to knock harder at the gate of my heart, so that I began to find my conscience extremely oppressed and by that means I became sad and melancholic. Then did I feel my heart pierced with grief and anguish, knowing that with these pleasures on the one side I lived ill, on the other side I would not forsake them; and reading on still I found evasions to pass them over the more slightly. At the length, having read the chapter which treated of the account which we must make to God, I was forced in spite of my teeth to apply this to myself; this touched me so near, and so shook my conscience, that I being not able to dissemble or colour the matter any longer was driven to confess that I was the sinner against whom these horrible pains and torments of hell were denounced. And from that time I saw the miserable state wherein I was, and so sought to amend my life past. But alas how many blocks lay in my way? How subtly did the old serpent show himself? Hereupon what inventions and stratagems did he not use to hinder me? He began thus with me: "Hereafter you shall have better opportunity and shall do it more easily; you are yet in the flower of your age, and what a folly is it to deprive yourself wholly of your pleasures and comforts? And what will your friends say to this, when they shall see you grow so sober and sad? You will lose your credit among those who esteem you and among the wise you will be reputed for a fool. Again, when you shall have tried you will find it impossible to abstain from your accustomed sins. A good life is extreme hard and unsupportable. Look about you, and see if there be any that live in that manner that you determined to do. How can you live without great or small sins, since all ministers say: All sins are mortal? Away with these peevish thoughts; by only faith thou mayest be saved. What need is there of so many things?" In this manner my enemy assailed me and I believed a long time that those were great arguments of right reason, rather than suggestions of the devil.

I was vehemently tempted by transitory pleasures and the vanities of the world held me in thraldom. So that this my new desire was not yet strong enough to overcome the contrary, which was rooted in me by long custom. Delights of the world did allure me and the torments of hell did affright me. God's inspirations did call me, but the flesh, the world and the devil stayed me. So that my two wills, one new, the other old, the one spiritual, the other carnal, divided my soul. Finding by experience in myself how the flesh coveted against the spirit and the spirit against the flesh, I continued three or four days in this perplexed agony, but I would not in this conflict avoid the occasions. I lamented and bewailed with tears this my unhappy state, yet my soul refused to be resigned wholly into Thy hands. It feared like death a perfect renunciation of the world and while this combat endured, I thought I could not subsist without my wonted pleasures.

Thus the tempter, being very strong and well-armed, invaded me. But Thy goodness, O Lord, bridled his fury and strengthened me, that he did not wholly overcome me. This devil, I say, appeared unto me, transformed into an angel of light, but Thou didst enlighten me to know him well and in the end among these dolours and oppressions Thy goodness gave me this inspiration, that although a virtuous life were very hard and sharp, yet living well I should have some good hope to enjoy heaven, whereas living in that state I had no hope at all; this little sparkle of hope in these difficulties was like a little beam of light coming from the stars, which shine afar off and did appear to me in this misty and thick

fog of darkness. By reason whereof I took heart and broke with violence all those chains and cords which held me so fast tied to the
world. Which mine enemy seeing, began to lay a new battery
against me, which was to set before me his dangerous doctrine of
predestination, telling me flatly that I was predestined to be
damned and all that I could do but vain, and saying to me that
although I were forward in well-doing and continued some years
therein, yet if I were not predestined to be saved I should be
damned in the end. O how this troubled me; I was very near to
have been swallowed up in this dangerous abyss. But Thy hand,
O Lord, delivered me by this inspiration, that on my part I ought
to do my duty and so I should try whether I should be saved or
damned, which whosoever does he cannot perish. After all this he
laid another trap for me, labouring to make me believe that all my
good purposes even to this time would come to nothing and that it
was but a brain-sickness, stirred by the reading of this book and
the like had happened to others and passed like a dream. "For,"
said he, "are there not many others that have read the same as well
as you and have they not had vehement persuasions? But who I
pray is become the better for the reading? Do not they live as they
did before?" And I was driven to confess this, having known
many that had highly commended it and yet profited nothing by it.
"Presumest thou," said the enemy, "that thou hast more force than
they?" While I was thus troubled, I retired myself as I was
accustomed into a solitary place to the end I might have better
commodity[1] to bewail my miserable condition. Thou, O Lord,
knowest with how many tears, sobs and groans I poured forth my
soul unto Thee. At length, lying down under a tree near unto a
hedge, where I purposed to continue my tears and lamentings till
I received some experimental grace, as indeed I found, Thou
heardest my prayers. In this course of temptations I cannot but
remember how every morning as soon as I awaked, this onset was
given me afresh and then I felt myself very melancholic and almost
unfit for so good an enterprise, yet on the one side the unsupportable torments of hell were so fearfully represented unto me and so
rigorously threatened against me. And on the other side the

---

[1] opportunity

inexplicable joys of heaven were so plentifully offered unto me and Thy grace did so powerfully assist me, that all these hindrances had no power to stay me or divert me from promising frankly and freely to undertake this happy course which I have begun by Thy holy inspiration. After this time I had so abandoned the world and worldly affairs that when I heard any speech of them, I thought they were like speeches of mad people or at the least like the talk of young children, who talk ordinarily of vain and ridiculous things and always impertinent.[1] Yea, those that had such communications seemed to me to be as far from me as though they came out of another world, or out of a region far distant. So far had God's grace now prevailed with me to draw me from the world.

How he was doubtful in faith and how he purposed to study.
What a vision he had while he was abroad in the fields

THE FIFTH CHAPTER

HAVING abandoned all lets and hindrances caused by the vanities of the world, I resolved now to put in practice how I could serve God, but presently another temptation took hold of me which afflicted me worse than all the rest, to wit, what religion I should embrace. But Thy mercies, O Lord, which aided me before, showed themselves more clearly herein. For when I had considered how the Christian world was lately divided into divers forms of religion, and seeing how our country of England did hold a kind of religion differing from the rest, and reflecting how I had been always bred and brought up according to that religion, without ever knowing any other, these things, being debated and discussed in my understanding, occasioned in me much doubt, which of these I should embrace. As I thought I saw wise and learned men on both sides, which made me doubt so much the more what I should do. And this made me so much the more anxious, because I feared that I could not attain to the perfect knowledge of this matter. "O," said

---

[1] to no purpose

I, "what an infinite labour is this? Into what an intricate labyrinth am I fallen?" But Thy holy inspirations, O Lord, always assisted me, which willed me not to despair, but rather to assure myself that in using good means I should obtain my desire. Whereupon I returned to London the Monday following to get some book which handled the controversies of religion, that being at my lodging I might examine them better, and also more conveniently pray, fast, watch, lie hard and do such things as I thought good to join with my studies. And although I knew that in the opinion of Protestants (to which I myself was then also inclined) such exterior acts would little avail me, yet I would needs see what fruit might follow hereby, descanting in this manner with myself: "If they do not profit me, yet at least they cannot hinder or hurt me." Being thus resolved to study and to bend all my wits to the search of these difficulties, I felt my heart much eased. Notwithstanding, I doubted what the end would be. But calling to mind those words of consolation: *Seek and ye shall find, knock and it shall be opened unto you, come unto me all ye that are heavy laden and I will refresh you,* and likewise the example of Cornelius the Centurion who before he believed was out of the right way, yet by reason of his good life and good intention he obtained to be instructed in virtue, by these words and this example, I say, I was much raised up and comforted. Furthermore, because I feared lest the circumstances of my sinful life might bar me from obtaining this grace, I examined myself often by the rule of the Twelve Fruits of the Holy Ghost, which were written in this book, and when I found myself defectuous I strived to amendment.

The Friday after dinner I ended the reading of this book of resolution and the same evening I went into the fields to walk and meditate of this matter which occupied my head. Where having stayed a while I returned homewards and as I came near thereto, by accident I looked on one side of me and seemed to see in the same field a company of horses going all together in a fair green alley. At the first view I thought in truth that this was that appeared unto me, and thereupon I went forward, and having gone but two or three yards farther I saw them behind me, and viewing them again they seemed not to be horses but spirits, and then I made

haste to them, and after I had gone some few paces I judged them
again horses and suddenly stayed upon it and, reproving myself, I
spoke inwardly to myself, "What is it I may think of this? Are not
these horses some spirits?" Having gone some dozen paces and
looking behind me I saw nothing of that which I formerly saw, but
there succeeded in the same place a great company of poor people,
ill-clad in brown colour, of whom some carried white wallets on
their shoulder, some other great leather bottles in their hand. I was
more troubled at this sudden change than I was beforehand; therefore, turning myself towards them, I set myself to behold them
wistly,[1] and having taken a good view of them for a good space as I
went on, I thought that they might be haymakers, for that it was
the season wherein such did travail. And so I persuaded myself in
very deed. In this persuasion I held on my way and could not but
wonder what that might be that seemed to me a multitude of
horses and what was become of them. Which although I had discussed with myself a long time I could receive no satisfaction.
Immediately I turned again and looked back towards the same
place and all was vanished and in their place I saw a well-ordered
company of men and children all clad in a whitish colour. Upon the
sight of them I made as much speed as I could to go unto them, but
I could not approach them for they went as fast from me as I came
towards them and seemed to keep the same pace in retiring from
me as I did in advancing. At length I saw them clearly and beheld
them perfectly. They were all clad alike with a kind of vestment
like to long gowns with wide sleeves. The colour of their garments
was a white grey. Their robe had upon it from the neck to the
girdle a thing which I might liken to a Spanish cloak. They had
their robes girt to them and some of them under their garments
wore as it were a white robe like to a surplice, with great and wide
sleeves made of linen and upon their head they wore great hats all
of the same fashion and of the same colour as were their robes. The
men were in the midst and the children on both sides. So went they
in order all along the breadth of this alley. They seemed to me to
go very cheerfully and graciously as it were dancing and rejoicing;
they shook their sleeves in token of joy. I would gladly have

[1] attentively

accosted them, but they made from me, if I moved never so little and when I stayed they stayed also, imitating herein the former visions, by all which signs I conjectured that they would draw me after them, that I might follow them. After a good space of time I stayed myself and closed my eyes to the end that I might behold them better and more clearly. Then opening my eyes I beheld them as before and then I mended my pace towards them, thinking that if they went on, they would stay at a hedge which was now very near to them and then I should understand what all this meant. But being come thither, I saw nothing at all but in another close[1] before me I saw one of the greatest of this company all alone and presently he vanished and I returned home. In going homeward I was musing with myself and earnestly laboured to search the meaning of this and framed divers conceptions. But O good God, Thou wouldst not that I should know the exposition of it, Thou knewest that it was much better for me that the knowledge of it should be suspended. And therefore all the declarations that I or others could make were little to the purpose, till such time as it was manifested to me in fit time and place, according to Thy holy preordination.

*Of his conference with the Catholic and of
his dangers escaped*

THE SIXTH CHAPTER

BEING come home, although I would willingly have fasted, yet I sat down to supper in company and because I did eat very little, as I had likewise done some days before, the company asked me if I were sick, as indeed I was, but they knew not of what disease, neither could they guess. After supper I went to bed and after I had maturely considered this matter I imparted it wholly to a Catholic which lodged with me, to whom, although he were my

---

[1] enclosure, open space

familiar and inward friend, I had communicated nothing as yet. When I had told him briefly what I had done all the week past and what temptation I had had, how I was affected and how I purposed to employ my time for the searching out of the true faith, how to that end I thought to go to London on Monday, how I had disposed of all my business and lastly that which I thought not to have done, I revealed my vision also to him.

He rejoicing to hear this, entered into conference with me, saying: "As for religion, I think there will be but small doubt of it, the truth itself is so evident and apparent, and for you to bolt[1] it out by study, being of so small learning and judgement for this purpose, I hold it no ways expedient, for it will be long ere you will by this means take a firm and good resolution." To whom I answered: "Do not dissuade me from this search of the truth by mine own study, for the matter is of too great importance and too doubtful for me to give credit to one side or the other."

Upon this we resolved the next morning to go towards London where by his means I might confer with some Catholic priests, but he told me: "There may be some difficulty in bringing a priest to confer with you, because he may mistrust you; if you become not a Catholic, you may occasion his taking. For although priests do not fear the affliction which may befall them for so good a cause, yet for the security of them with whom they converse, they are and ought to be circumspect to whom they discover[2] themselves." To whom I made answer: "In truth I do believe that, when I shall be fully resolved in one religion I shall not forbear to hate and persecute the contrary." The next morning early we went together towards London and on the way he took occasion often in discourse to persuade me to his religion. Among other matters of discourse he spoke of a book which the Protestants feigned to have been found in the corner of a wall which was of an old date and as they say proved evidently their doctrine. He said that this book was alleged often in pulpits as a book of great authority and of no small moment to maintain their gospel and yet the same book a little after was recalled by themselves to their shame and confusion. Afterwards I understood that this was a true history.

[1] sift   [2] reveal

He spoke also of a certain exorcism done by a Catholic priest[1] and related many other strange and marvellous things done in it and how finally the devil was cast out of the possessed person and restored to former health. But of this I doubted much. O Lord, I confess to Thee my infidelity in not believing the power and authority which Thou gavest to Thy disciples saying, *Have ye power over the unclean spirits*, but by the multitude of Thy mercies I saw afterward so many examples, that there was no cause to call this in doubt, for which Thy holy name be ever praised. He had this speech with me and much other to draw me from the new religion, although I yet held my firm purpose to follow the course of my study as the principal foundation upon which I would build my knowledge.

All this time that we were together, I did call to mind my life past and in the end breaking out of a depth of my inward thoughts I suddenly cried out and said: "O if I had died heretofore, what had become of me for all eternity! Alas, how many dangers have I escaped! O Lord, I beseech Thee, give me grace that I may never cease to thank Thee for so great and marvellous deliverances from such extreme and desperate dangers." Then I began to recite to my companion, how when I was very little, I broke by chance my backbone and yet by the goodness of God I recovered my health. Another time how falling into a dangerous malady and almost despairing of recovering myself, by reason of four or five incisions which were also to be reiterated insomuch that my bowels were seen and therefore the physician said that he had little hope of life, notwithstanding by God's great goodness I was healed and escaped this danger. I likewise recounted to him how at another time, I, being very tender and young, fell into a vat of boiling beer where I had been suffocated, had it not been that by God's providence one was there at that time which took me out instantly. Another danger greater than the former I escaped when being come to the blossoming of youth, stirred and moved by proud folly, I adventured myself into a desperate combat, that I could

---

[1] Presumably this refers to the exorcisms of Fr. William Weston, S.J., who had landed on the Norfolk coast in 1584. An account of these is given in Samuel Harsnett's *Declaration of Egregious Popish Impostures* (London, 1603), the well-known source for Shakespeare's references to devils in *King Lear*.

hardly pass out of it with my life; seeing my companion so wounded that he lay for dead and myself also laid on the ground.

These dangers I could not call to mind without great fear and trembling, saying: "In what case[1] had I been if I had died then? I confess, O Lord, that Thou hast delivered me from all these, and therefore I render Thee all humble thanks and not only for these, but for no less deliverances since that time by sea and land and especially in a great sickness where I lay speechless. Thou hast shown thy fatherly care over me, when I, a wretched and unhappy creature, had no fear of Thee. Thou hast used great means to make me know the fearful state wherein I was. But alas I, being blind and obstinate, neglected them." I fell into so deep meditation of these things and of my life past, that I did not suffer my spirit to occupy itself in any other thing. And if by chance I looked upon the fields to take a little recreation, I did presently reprove myself sharply for it, fearing to offend Thee, O my Lord. And in considering these things I could hardly forbear weeping and chiefly when I came to the city of London, where those places were represented to me, wherein I had vainly delighted myself; and at length, restraining tears as long as I could, I shed them in great abundance, so that meeting some of my old companions I plucked down my hat and held down my head through shame and confusion in myself. From that time, O Lord, Thou didst humble the pride of my lofty heart and madest me see the lamentable state wherein I was, so that of an unbridled wild colt and a furious bull, Thou madest me a poor and contemptible ass, willing to bear burdens, and a sheep disposed to hear and follow Thee.

Of the manner which he purposed to himself for his studies and how he wished and sought conference with a Puritan

THE SEVENTH CHAPTER

WHEN we were come to London we would not go together, but we concluded he should go on one side and I on the other, to the end

---

[1] condition

that according to our design he might confer with Catholics and I with Protestants so that we might cull out the reasons and arguments of both sides and so the next morning we might compare them together. And in the mean while I went to my lodging where instantly I knelt down to pray, giving now full vent to my tears which I had restrained before. In my prayers I prayed that God would give me light and favour to be able to find the truth and sincerity of true religion, which afterwards was mercifully granted to me. Afterward I lifted up myself and took my pen in my hand to write down the points of controversy which I did purpose to study and in the end I resolved to meddle but with some of the principal points, as for example that of the real presence of Jesus Christ in the Sacrament. The reason which moved me so to do was this, that if I did find that Jesus Christ were not really there, then certainly that could not be a true religion, neither could that Church be holy which had so great an error to believe that He was where He was not and which does honour a creature with that adoration which is due to the Creator. On the contrary side, if Jesus Christ be truly present in the Sacrament, I thought it impossible that that could be His spouse and the Holy Church which says that He is not where in truth He is, and so refuses a benefit so great and so unestimable. I resolved therefore to give no credit to that Church which I found failing in this high point, and besides I knew that he (as Saint Augustine says) which errs in one point of faith cannot be saved. Hereupon I wrote down this point of the Holy Sacrament and some others. Afterward I sought what I could say against the Catholic opinion.

Having my head fraught with these matters I went to a Puritan of my acquaintance, with whom after I had discoursed a while, he asked me if I would receive the Lord's Supper with him the day following. I was glad to hear speak of this to the end that I might have occasion to debate this question, which I purposed to propose unto him. I answered him, "If we go to any sacrament we first ought to be well prepared." But now the time was very short. Notwithstanding (he said) that that was sufficient time, to wit, to eat His bread and drink His wine; then, thinking with myself of the danger of the time and the quality of the man with whom I spoke,

I saw it perilous to meddle, but considering that such peril could not be avoided, to wit that either I must use such conference or hazard my soul in living in ignorance, I concluded[1] to enter with him into the question of religion and principally touching the Sacrament, he having given me occasion of treating thereof.

But Thou, O God, which directest all the ways of those which seek Thee in simplicity of heart, wouldst not permit that I should have conference with this heretic, who was disposed, if not to kill the body, yet at least to kill the soul. For even as I thought to enter in this conference there came in a third person which broke off my discourse and frustrated me of my intention, though I waited a while the departure of this party. But while I thus attended, other friends of this Puritan came in also, who took him away into their company, and yet I followed him to the place where he went, hoping that he would quit his company that so I might have opportunity to speak with him, but I lost my labour and my pain. O good Lord how merciful wast Thou herein unto me, for Thou preservedst me from a great evil, foreseeing how I might have been troubled with his false objections and so haply more inveigled in his heretical opinions.

Of his spiritual temptations

THE EIGHTH CHAPTER

SEEING that I could not be partaker of my desire in having conference with this Puritan, I was disquieted in my spirit and hoping that the next morning I might have better opportunity of conferring with him, I went to a friend which was well affectioned to the Catholic religion, to arm myself the better to dispute with the Puritan, that having conferred their opinions together I might better discern the truth. So I went to his lodging, but I found him not there. Therefore to advertise him that I had been there, I put a little piece of paper in the keyhole of his door in which I re-

[1] resolved

quested him that as soon as he returned, he would come to me to my lodging. So I went home and sat me down and began to think seriously of this business. As soon as it was evening I retired myself into my study, where on my knees I prayed to God. Then had I a sharper conflict than ever before, then did my enemies seek to entrap me with new intentions, then did they give a hot and fresh assault to divert me from my good purpose and to hold me captive in their possession.

O good God, how little force have we when Thou dost never so little withdraw Thy hand from us! Thy grace so fortified me a little before that I thought there was nothing able for to shake me. Now Thou hast turned Thy face from me and I was presently[1] troubled. I persuaded myself that I was somewhat, although I was even less than nothing. I said, "I will become wise," and straightway I became a very fool. I do now know that without the aid of Thy holy grace we can do nothing. It is certain that unless Thou keep the city, in vain does he travail which thinks to keep it. The grace which Thy goodness does communicate to us is measured by Thy wisdom, which will not permit that we be always assisted alike in our prayers. So that now putting myself on my knees to pray, I had not the feeling of my wonted fervour, but contrariwise I found myself very unapt and loathed more and more to persevere in it. Besides, I felt a discontentment and anxiety of spirit which did much trouble me.

Now my enemy began to play his parts, for he seeing that nothing held me but ignorance of the true religion, he took occasion to vex me, that so he might more easily overwhelm me. Therefore he objected to me that I undertook too hard a matter, saying that the resolution of it is too high a matter and far exceeding my capacity, "for if learned and judicious men do not attain to it, what hope canst thou have? Well may you have some conjecture, but never such knowledge as to assure your salvation thereon."

In the end I rose and took the foresaid book of resolution again into my hands and read somewhat of the pains of hell, thinking by this means to kindle my devotion in prayer, but it profited nothing. Afterward I felt more devotion, but I found my spirit more vexed

---

[1] immediately

and afflicted than before. For then were suggested to me by the enemy so many sorts of temptations, so many new sleights and inventions and with so wonderful a liveliness, that I poor wretch all astonished, was miserably overcharged with fear. And while I was in this state he did not cease to object strangely to me, that not only I should never attain to know the truth by my study, but that my spirit should be so turmoiled that I should be in danger to lose my wit, and that my brain was already somewhat cracked, and that I should never be so well settled in my wits as I was before. O good God, how wily is the enemy of mankind? These things were objected unto me with such unknown subtility that I was not able to reject them, yea the more I laboured to put them from me, the more did they assail and afflict me and they were the more violent against me, because I was alone and unexperienced in spiritual combats.

After I had been sorely beaten by this fierce battle, at length I lifted up myself, thinking because I had rested little or nothing the nights past, that the heaviness of sleep would drive all these turmoils out of my head. But after I had stripped myself and laid myself down, not upon my accustomed bed but upon the ground with a single coverlet, all these molesting thoughts represented themselves with such eagerness that my soul was wonderfully weakened and oppressed, insomuch that I was hardly able to subsist any longer.

This was the sorest conflict that ever I had, so that I became as a man deprived of his senses; yea, the force of these temptations was such that it brought me even to the next door of despair. And the fear which I had to fall into it wonderfully disquieted my soul. Tormented in this manner, I could find no ease from these terrible dolours; my body, also subject to it, could have no manner of repose, but tossed and turned itself on this side and that.

This manner of lying was so unpleasing to my enemy (as I afterward knew) that he ceased not to suggest unto me that if I went unto my bed I should find more repose. And Thou, O Lord, sawest mine affliction and permittedst it. Thou hast tried my heart and visited it by night and hast examined me by fire, for as much as Thou didst forsake me to prove me, but it pleased Thee that I should know myself, nor for the love of Thee, but for myself, for mine own great good and profit. For I presumed before of mine own person and I thought myself of myself able and sufficient enough, and, silly wretched fool that I was, I did not perceive that I was governed by Thee. And herein I abused myself till I saw that Thou wast gone a while from me, then I saw that my error and failing proceeded from myself, and my rising out of this misery wherein I was plunged came from Thee. O glorious Clearness, Thou hast opened mine eyes and illuminated them. I have seen and known that the life of man upon earth is nothing but a temptation and that no flesh can glory before Thee, much less to justify itself, for as much as if there be any good in it, great or small, it comes from Thy bounty and if there be any evil it comes from ourselves.

The temptation being overcome, the consolation follows; the truth was revealed to him. And how he with another by his means being converted, were reconciled to the Church

THE NINTH CHAPTER

BLESSED be Our Lord which delivered me, not into bondage, nor into their teeth. Our soul as a sparrow was delivered from the snares of the hunters, the nets are broken and we were delivered. Blessed be Thy holy name, which art near unto the afflicted and dost not permit that they should be tempted above their force. In the midst of this so great desolation, and danger, in the midst of so great obscurity, Thou causedst a beam of Thy goodness to shine upon me, by the light whereof I discovered this heap of fraud and of illusion and loosed the knot of all the subtilties of my enemy, seeing clearly that this vexation was nothing but the temptation of the evil spirit; and blessed be Thy holy name for it.

After these tribulations ceased I rested in great tranquillity and quietness of spirit, yea, I became more constant and resolute. And it pleased Thee so to recompense these tribulations and afflictions by abundance of joys and consolations, for the consolations of the Holy Spirit prevented[1] me in such manner, that I felt such plenty of joy and peace poured into my heart, that being replenished with it I had forgot all the world and so I knew no more that which I was. So was that saying of the Holy Prophet fulfilled: According to the multitude of my dolours in my heart, Thy comforts have rejoiced my soul.

Moreover, as if this had not been sufficient, Thou didst reward me with another rich benefit, which was, Thou didst reveal by an inexplicable manner the clear and perfect sight and assured knowledge of Thy only most pure and holy religion, and that with so great certainty that I was not only confirmed therein, but I thought that all to whom I did speak thereof could not any way doubt of it, which when I, poor worm, did manifestly see not without great admiration and astonishment, I cast forth these words: "O Lord, I now know that Thou dost never forsake him which calleth upon Thee in truth"; for the multitude of so great benefits I confess it was impossible that I could be sufficiently thankful, yet burning with the ardour of charity which Thou didst impress in my heart, I used these words: "Goods, lands, life, and all other things are nothing", all which I was no less willing to leave for Thy love than the cruel and barbarous time was disposed to take them from me, as they did from other Catholics.

But O Lord, what is become now of my study to which I was before so bent? What am I to do for those conferences which I purposed? Where are the propositions and questions which I had written down to use for arguments? Likewise where are my fastings, prayings, lying upon the hard ground, which I used as means to come to the knowledge of the truth? O my God, Thou hast prevented all these before I began them, so gracious art Thou to those that seek Thee faithfully. The prophet says: *Reveal thy way to Our Lord and hope in Him and He will do it*. And in another place he says: *He will not permit that the just be continually tormented*. Thy mercy also showed itself more in this effect, for in the time of this gracious visitation, being well confirmed in the truth of true religion, I heard one knock at my chamber door and seeing that it

[1] anticipated

was late and my manner of lying undecent,[1] I durst not open the
door, yet hoping in this time that all would succeed well with me,
when I understood who it was I did almost foresee a good end and
issue of his coming, so I let him in and received him joyfully, for
this was he whom I had searched after to collect some arguments
for the search of the truth, who came not to me without God's
especial providence, so that as soon as he was entered I commended highly and exalted the Catholic religion and I spoke to
him with extraordinary fervour, saying: "Assure yourself that there
is no other truth but this," and he, wondering to hear this of me,
at length was won by me to confess the truth. Then did I ask him
if he were reconciled to the Church. He, much wondering at this
question, said, "No, but God willing I will be," whereupon we
resolved to go both together and reconcile ourselves unto the
Church, and so conferring together all that night we passed it in
discourse upon this matter, without once stripping ourselves out of
our clothes.

The next morning, which was Sunday morning, at the break of
day we prosecuted our design of reconciliation and went to an old
and infamous prison called Newgate, which was commonly filled
with priests. Among whom we found a priest which had been of
my friend's acquaintance, who after his banishment out of England became a Charter monk at Antwerp;[2] and this good priest put
us both into the haven of our souls' health, reconciling us to the
Holy Church. Who is able, O Lord, to comprehend the greatness
of Thy mercy which was shown to us both, in making me (being
without knowledge of religion and one who lived according to the
wickedness of the time) in the space of a week a true Catholic, in
so much that I did abhor the course of my life past and despised
all the pleasures of the world and feared no dangers of the time,
and that he also should be persuaded with so few words, who had
not hearkened before to any persuasions.

This happened on the day of Saint Peter ad Vincula,[3] which

---

[1] unsuitable
[2] Presumably Fr. Robert Darbyshire (or Darbysher), who became a Carthusian at Sheen Anglorum in 1592 and was elected Prior in 1596. He died in
1611. (L. Hendriks, *The London Charterhouse* . . . London, 1889, pp. 313-14).
[3] 1 August 1585

saint I do believe did much assist me herein, because I entered into the Church whereof he was the chief when he lived, and the chains and bands of my sins were loosed by confession on the same day that the Church does celebrate the memory of his chains, broken miraculously by the angel, so that I might say with the Church in great exultation of heart: *This is the day which Our Lord hath made, let us rejoice in it. For Thou hast broken my bands, I will sacrifice to Thee a sacrifice of praise, for now I am Thy servant, O Lord, I am Thy servant and the son of Thy handmaid the Holy Church.*

How he studied controversies and, having assigned a great part of his means to his kinsmen, he passed beyond the sea; and of the motives which induced him to enter into religion.

The Tenth Chapter

When in this manner Thy mercy, O Lord, had delivered me from heresy and schism, revoked me from my life past and established me in Thy holy Church, and when I saw that I could not for all this avoid the dangers and poisonous speeches of heretics, I began in good earnest to give myself to the reading of the Holy Scriptures, that by this means I might confute their fond objections. Wherein having spent some time, I found manifestly how weak their arguments were, so that I did not wonder if according to the saying of Saint Paul: *A heretic is condemned by his own proper judgement in oppugning wilfully the truth.* But because I feared lest conversing with them, I might have that verified in me: *With the wicked thou wilt become wicked*, I did design nothing more in my soul, than to find some other of better life, to the end by the assistance also of Thy grace that might be said of me: *With the elect thou shalt be elect.* Wherefore after I had consulted a while I determined speedily, that abandoning honours, kindred, friends, goods and country, yea hazarding my life, I would go into some other country where God's servants do honour Him publicly.

After I had waited for means to accomplish my desire, a commodity[1] was offered me, not thinking of it, of which I was exceeding glad; and so assigning about the half part of my means for the comfort of poor Catholics and disposing of my affairs, I took leave of my friends, who permitted me to go, though it was not without much sorrow and mourning after me. And not only my friends, but one which had been as an enemy to me, a counsellor-at-law, who, understanding my drift and that I had forsaken my friends, my means and my country for God's sake, took my departure no less heavily than my best friends, and said that he was very sorry that he had conceived any such opinion or suspicion formerly of me, and declared my innocence with a protestation that he had rather have lost his advancement, which he did hope for by his practice in the law, than my company.

Then I embarked myself to go into France, but by reason of contrary winds we rode to and fro upon the sea a long time and were often in very great danger of being cast away. But O Lord, Thou, which art the defence of them which trust in Thee, didst deliver and bring us to the desired port in a Catholic country, where I first saw that which I had never seen, to wit, the majesty, beauty and magnificence of Thy Church. And with great contentment, I did first consider the comely order which is in this militant Church and heavenly hierarchy, from the highest degree of the Chief Pastor, even to those that are but newly entered into orders, having as yet but simple tonsure, and even to the secular persons, whence every inferior degree is subordinate to minister to that which is above it, in imitation of the heavenly hierarchy; though not like in all things, for even as the heavenly hierarchy is divided into three hierarchies and every one of them into three orders, so is the earthly. As the first consists of seraphims, cherubims and thrones, which do illuminate the second hierarchy, every one according to his order and degree, so the first earthly has three orders, to wit, the supreme bishops, the archbishops and bishops, whose office it is to illuminate and authorize others which are under them. The second heavenly hierarchy consists in three orders, dominations, powers and principalities, and these are

[1] opportunity

illuminated not immediately from God but from the superior angels, and they illuminate those that are under them. The second hierarchy of the militant Church is also of three degrees, of abbots, friars and curates which receive their authority, direction and light from those of the first, as from their superiors and do govern, teach and illuminate those which are subject to them. The third heavenly hierarchy consists of virtues, archangels and angels, which are only illuminated and do not illuminate others, so has the third earthly three orders of virgins, continent persons and married, who do receive the word of God, the sacraments and light without administering them to others. These things I did not altogether so exactly consider then, but according to the little light I had.

Secondly when I saw the goodly and magnificent buildings of Thy temples, the beautiful monasteries, the exquisite painted and graven images, which adorned and enriched the churches, both within and without, I could not but behold the glory and gravity of Thy Holy Church. And although Thou dost not dwell in temples made with hands, as within a place which does contain Thee, yet, O Lord, I say with the holy psalmist: *I have loved the beauty of Thy house*, and that it is pleasing to Thee and that Thou dost dwell there with Thy Son Incarnate Jesus Christ, and the Holy Ghost. And therefore we may sing with the prophet: *Holiness becometh Thy house for ever;* that is, to the end of the world. And by these great and glorious structures of monasteries richly rented and endowed, I could not but behold the great piety and devotion which the Catholic Church showed, as by the ruins of them in our country I saw and bewailed the unhappy calamity of heresy.

Thirdly, the beautiful and majestative services of Thy Church seem to me to give much splendour to it. For when I saw the solemnity of the Mass celebrated with priests, deacons, sub-deacons and acolytes, every one in their ornaments according to their degree and everyone administering according to his office; when I saw the altar richly dressed and adorned, the multitude of lights upon the altar and round about the choir, with what devotion the altar was incensed, the solemn procession so well ranked and so many devout people following with torches and lights, the choir so well furnished with priests, clerks and chanters, everyone in his place and clad in white, preparing to celebrate the Divine Office; when, I say, I saw all these things, I could not but behold them with great devotion as if I had seen in a lively glass the magnificence and majesty of Thy Holy Church.

Fourthly, good Lord, so great was my inward melting sweetness when I heard the harmonious music of voices and organs, which with hymns and canticles were offered to Thy divine majesty, that my heart could not but leap with joy and was violently drawn from all worldly thoughts and could not contain the joy, but often melted into abundance of tears, so that my eyes seemed to be two channels running from a plentiful fountain and that I might truly say with Thy servant Saint Augustine: *How often have I wept, feeling myself lively touched with those sweet canticles and hymns which are sung in Thy church, with so sweet and well beseeming harmony.* Thou seest, O God, how my heart trembleth, when I call to mind these so great benefits; pardon therefore my ingratitude.

All these former things seem to me to be full of gravity, beauty and magnificence in Thy Church, and the rather being now delivered from those infernal blasphemies, which are belched out of the mouths of many heretical ministers, and now living in a Catholic country with great tranquillity and repose of spirit, I heard also, O Lord, Thy sweet voice, which did invite me more clearly to the embracing of the religious, solitary and private life, by quite abandoning all worldly affairs. Yet doubting of a matter of so great importance, for as much as I had heard it said that it was not lawful to believe every spirit, I communicated it to some of my best friends, asking their advice and judgement herein, who being many, differed in their opinions. Some persuaded me to one thing and some to another and all of them were little or nothing inclined to this kind of life, which I was desirous to embrace. For they persuaded me rather that I should continue in the world, whereas I was minded to forsake it.

But, O Lord, Thou gavest me so many considerations and emotions to follow Thy holy inspiration, that in the end, after I had borne much affliction by contrary persuasions, I resolved to put it in execution. My first consideration was founded upon the words of the Gospel, which sayeth: *The way is strait and narrow which leadeth to life and there are few which walk in it.* And I set before my eyes the great debauchments and disorders of most men's lives in this time. I afterward considered the extreme danger that is in the world, where there are occasions of falling and plunging into sin, and how for this cause the Christians of the primitive Church (which in respect of these of our times were saints), how, I say, they sequestered themselves from the world, and how some striving to be more perfect fled into deserts and wildernesses, fearing lest among men they might defile their souls with some foul stain of sin. How much more ought I, poor and frail creature, retire myself to some monastery to separate myself from Christians who lived so licentiously.

Besides, I called to mind the great multitude of souls which I had left in England, my familiar friends with whom I had lived and many millions of others, seeing them all to pass this pilgrimage in miserable blindness, going like straying sheep through the thick darkness of heresy and schism and myself worse than others, to be delivered from such captivity. When I considered this I felt such a fire of charity kindled within me, that immediately I was forcibly moved to retire myself from the world. Moreover, although I was called to Thy holy service, yet I was not unmindful of those words which say: *Many are called but few are chosen.* This served for a spur and goad to drive me to a more assured and perfect life than that which I did lead. To these considerations I added that it was no small thing to expect eternal glory, to come to which, we must pass through water and fire.

And lastly to answer well to my extraordinary calling, I thought I must embrace and undertake more than an ordinary life, and my life past licentiously spent ought to be recompensed proportionably by penance in this life or the next. For this is agreeable to that which is written in Holy Scripture: *As much as she hath glorified herself and hath been in delicacy so much give her torment and mourning.* And an ancient doctor says that *a deep wound requires a deep rent.* These things, I say, stirred me up to do penance and to follow the counsel which Our Saviour giveth in the Gospel: *If thou wilt be perfect, go and sell all that thou hast and give them to the poor and thou shalt have a treasure in heaven.* These and such things, O Lord, came not from me but proceeded from Thy pure and free liberality, to strengthen me in the course of my begun life and to confirm in me that which Thou by Thy goodness had begun in me. For which all praise, glory, and honour, be rendered to Thy holy name.

Of a certain spiritual ravishment, wherein it was revealed to him what he should do. And of the total obligation of all these things

THE ELEVENTH CHAPTER

ALTHOUGH these precedent considerations moved me greatly to forsake the world, yet was I tossed oftentimes with contrarities, before I could attain the end of a small resolution. But Thou, O Lord, art near to those which have a troubled heart, for Thou hast not despised a contrite and humbled heart. So that after I had been occupied in the consideration of my life to come, and not without great anxiety and perplexity of spirit, after I had my recourse to Thy goodness by continual prayers, and, finally, after I had resolved to cause three Masses to be said in honour of the Most Holy Trinity, with intention to pray Thee to give me Thy grace to abandon the world, Thou didst then call me with so clear, manifest, and loud voice, that I could not resist so powerful and effectual will and calling. For about midnight, being all alone in my chamber and lifting up my spirit towards Thee in this affair, I felt myself drawn by Thee and my spirit so filled with a sudden supernatural light, and was so surprised with so great a fire of charity, that being out of myself and transported into Thee, I rested like one that had lost all feeling of myself and the world; in which ravishment and alienation of sense I knew after an unspeakable manner Thy holy will touching my vocation, so that if an angel had appeared visibly to me to have declared it, I could not have better known it, nor more certainly believed it. So that with great astonishment I could not contain myself but cried out saying: "O Lord who is like unto Thee, who is like unto Thee". O Lord, Thou didst so abundantly distil the dew from heaven even into the bottom of my soul, that by the means of it, spending all the night in thinking of it, I passed the night in great sweetness, and spiritual delight. And so being overcome by the excess of Thy goodness, I protested before Thee and all the heavenly Court to abandon the world wholly and to distribute all that I had to the poor, which are Thy members; of which promise I never after repented me, but, which is more supported and favoured by Thy special grace, without any contrary temptation, the time being prolonged, I desired nothing more than to have opportunity to effectuate it perfectly, which happening afterward at the feast of the Blessed Trinity, I believed piously Thou didst vouchsafe me this grace by reason of my devotion in honour and praise of It; to wit, because in the day of my reconciliation it was enjoined me for penance that I should fast three days and that I should give three alms to three poor persons. And likewise, the day before, I determined to have three Masses celebrated, offering all to the honour of that Most Holy Trinity.

How he entered into religion, with an exposition of the foresaid vision

THE TWELFTH CHAPTER

ALTHOUGH I had made before with myself a firm resolution to become a religious man of the Order of St. Francis, yet I was in great doubt whether I should take the habit of the Cordeliers[1] or of the Capuchins, not knowing well which of these two did most follow St. Francis. I saw well the life of the Capuchins to be more austere and strict, yet I knew not whether they did more perfectly observe the rule of St. Francis and whether they did wear his true habit or no, and inclined rather to think that they did not. So I thought to enter into the religion of the Cordeliers, and yet observing that they lived not so austerely as the Capuchins, I was

---

[1] The Conventual Franciscans.

troubled and thought I should hardly satisfy myself in following St. Francis so perfectly as I desired. After I had a long time made a diligent and exact inquisition hereof, I found myself notwithstanding very doubtful, so that I once purposed to have gone to Rome to understand it more clearly, even from His Holiness'[1] own mouth. But I thought it best at length to go first to Paris and there to confer with men of the one and of the other religion, where I took resolution to take the habit of a Capuchin, following the advice and counsel of a Capuchin which before had been a Cordelier and came out of that order to live more austerely.[2]

But I did not so wholly rely on him, but that I used all other good means to be well informed of the truth and by those whom I knew to be very learned and pious, who although they assured me that the Capuchins lived according to the rule of St. Francis, yet they did dissuade me to enter into this religion, by reason of their great austerity, saying to me that it was exceeding hard to pass from one extreme unto another, and besides that I should make a conscience in embracing such a life where there was little likelihood that I could continue. Which they said because they saw I was but of a weak constitution of body. So that one day parting from Paris to go to Meudon, to a convent of Capuchins, in some anguish of spirit, to speak with the foresaid religious man which had been a Cordelier, I ceased not to pray fervently, till such time as coming near the convent I felt myself much eased, and such a vigour and force of spirit was given unto me that I resolved immediately to become a Capuchin and instantly I had an inspiration which said to me: "*Lo, now all the vision is accomplished*", as it may be seen by that which follows.

Hereupon I felt myself rid of all afflictions and whereas I came from Paris to have some assurance by way of his advice, I entered into the convent of the Capuchins, now fully resolved; so that instead of consulting with him, at the first word I asked of him when I might take the habit. Then was, O Lord, all that fulfilled which Thou hadst foretold me by the foresaid vision, when by the

---

[1] The then Pope, Sixtus V, was a Conventual Franciscan.
[2] Fr. Optatus (p. 78) suggests that this was Fr. Pierre Besson de Dreux, then at Paris. He was assassinated on 26 June 1589 by a lifeguard of Henri of Navarre, in mistake for Pierre Deschamps.

horses which I had formerly seen was represented to me all mundane vanity past, in which I was long delighted. By the men so poorly clothed was represented to me the contempt of the world and the poverty in which I should take contentment. By the colour and fashion of their attire, with their bags and bottles, was signified to me my vocation, which should be the life of the Capuchins. By the men and children clothed in grey and some wearing white surplices, were signified to me the Cordeliers, and that so perfectly that when I saw them sing together at the desk,[1] methought I saw the very figures of my vision. And that I followed them, this is also effected in that the Cordeliers have much invited me to follow them. And I having a long time rested myself upon their persuasions and because they stayed for me when I made any stay, this signified that when I was in doubt concerning the observance of the rule, they laboured to resolve me, saying that with them I should observe well the rule of St. Francis and that they would answer for me at the Day of Judgement for this point.

Concerning him which left his company and, getting before them, went straight before them in another close where he appeared to me, that which happened after did seem to me to point it out directly when a Cordelier having left his fellows did exceed them in austerity of life and went into another close, that is into another congregation, to wit the Capuchins, right before us, which is towards perfection. Lastly he appeared to me as drawing me after him and inviting me to pass over this company, to wit the order of the Cordeliers, and to follow him to the Capuchins, as I did afterward according to his advice. When at Paris a little after on the 23rd of the following March, 1587,[2] I took the habit where two others of the same country and born of noble families, which were come into France for the same end, followed me and by my example and my counsel received also the same habit.[3]

[1] in choir   [2] The text reads "1586".   [3] See above, p. xxiii, n 3.

*A brief repetition of the foresaid principal points
by way of thanksgiving*

The Thirteenth Chapter

Now, O my God and Saviour, when I call to mind all these marvellous works and Thy exceeding benefits bestowed upon me, poor worm and ungrateful, unprofitable and negligent servant, when I remember them to imprint them the rather by this means into my heart and to engrave them in the bottom of my soul, I am forced to confess that I find nothing more sweet and savorous to my soul, nor know nothing that is more pleasing to Thee than to praise and laud Thy holy name for them.

For Thou hast compassed me about, Thou hast taught me and kept me as the apple of Thine eye. Thou which art the Way hast led me into the way of Thy holy truth, so that I strayed not. Thou that art the Truth hast taught me, so that I erred not in things that were hard and profound. Thou that art the Life, hast preserved me so that a multitude of mortal darts of the world, the flesh and the devil have not wounded me to death. *O my Light, Thou hast found me out in a desert land,* that is, in England which is unpeopled of Catholics, *in a place of horror,* that is in horrible sins, *a land of great desolation* where is there scarce seen any trace or footstep of Catholic religion.

O my Love, Thou hast spread the wings of Thy mercy and hast taken me into Thy favour and service, and *hast carried me upon Thy shoulders, for I am a most vile sinner, I have built upon Thy back.* O my Sweetness, *Thou hast taught me to draw honey out of the rock of penance and oil out of a most hard flint stone,* to wit out of a most strait rule, and in all this, O Lord, *Thou hast been my only Guide,* so that I may justly say: *He hath not done in like manner to any other nation.* Give me grace therefore, O Lord, to think of them often and to express them so that I, being ungrateful as I am, yet others may praise Thee for them. How great a benefit was this to convert me at that time and place in which I determined to take my recreation, seeing for that end I walked forth into the fields?

The multitude of my temptations (O my God) doth ever more preach Thy praises. My speedy, sudden and perfect conversion doth show sufficiently the power of Thy grace, that neither the flower of my age, nor the fury of youth, nor the pleasure wherein I did live, nor the liberty which I had, nor the company which I haunted, nor the place in which I abode, nor the habitude and long custom of my evil life past, nor yet the austerity of the good life to come, had any force to stay me.

This doth show the extension and protection of Thy right hand, by Thy only conduct without any human persuasion; besides, the sweet streams of tears which came from me abundantly in this my conversion, from what fountain could they proceed but from the unction of Thy Holy Spirit. The bitter sighs, sobs, and groans, from whence came they, but from a compunction which Thou hast exalted in my soul? The sincerity which without partiality I used in searching the true faith and my firm purpose to study, fast, pray, lie upon the hard ground and other austerities which I practised, from whence did they issue, but from an abundance of Thy grace? And to see how it pleased Thee without all these to reveal the truth unto me, this I say, makes me much astonished and to know certainly that *Thou art truly near to those who call upon Thee,* and that whosoever *shall reveal his way to Our Lord, He will do it and will not permit nor give eternal torment to the just.*

And when I consider the excessive consolations manifested to me, the marvellous revelations, extraordinary visions and ravishments, admiring Thy liberality, I know certainly that *there is none like unto Thee among the gods nor according to Thy works,* and that he spoke truly which said: *Awake, thou that sleepest, and arise from the dead, and Christ will illuminate thee.* Thou also, O Lord, didst give me these consolations *in fit time,* to wit, when I was oppressed and overcharged with temptations, so, O Lord, *Thou dost bring to hell and dost bring back again* the efficacy and force of Thy voice in the inward of souls. Thy voice doth express itself in those three callings which I had unto good life, to faith, to religion, resolving to quit bad life, heresy and the world. Thy mercies are infinite in this Thy preservation of my life from my youth among so many perils and dangers. Thy fatherly protection was seen in not permitting me to have conference with that heretic which might have hindered me in my good course. And Thy marvellous providence appeared in the conversion of my other companion and friend, when, as when we being so far distant one from the other, in the country and in the time of vacation we both came to the city the same day. And, which is yet more remarkable, we met at the very hour and instant of this my great illumination, consolation and final resolution. After Thou hadst so well instructed me in Thy faith and inflamed me in Thy love that the few words which I spoke to him did so move his heart that they wrought his conversion.

Wherefore I may say, O Lord, I have heard Thy voice and I have trembled, and therefore in the presence of Thy majesty, I am like a poor mouse seeking to hide myself in some hole; and as a thief which has done ill and hates the light, I fear lest Thy justice should be exercised against my unthankfulness. I fear lest Thou art offended, the saints angered, the angels provoked, men scandalized and all creatures moved much in seeing my ingratitude and my evil life. I fear lest they may cry against me and say: "Behold this wretched ungrateful person, who, not withstanding all those great particular favours and benefits received from his Lord and Master, could not be won to obey Him." It is Thy great mercy that I am not now plunged in the bottomless pit of hell, yet as the son of Thy servant who have put myself under Thy protection, my Lord and my Deliverer, I confess to Thee from my heart and protest before Thy divine majesty that as long as I live I will remember this and never forget those infinite favours which Thou hast done me in my tender youth.

I know that ingratitude, which is the root of all spiritual evil and a wind which dries and burns up all good, yea stops up the fountain of divine mercy, is greatly hateful and displeasing to Thee, and therefore I will humbly beseech Thee that I may never be ungrateful towards Thy clemency and bounty, for as often as this dragon would have swallowed me, Thou hast delivered me from his jaws. When the malign tempter was seizing upon me to carry me to hell, Thou of Thy grace didst restrain him. I did offend Thee and Thou didst defend me; I did not fear Thee and yet Thou didst not cease to preserve me. I went from Thee to my enemy, yet notwithstanding Thou didst hinder him that he did me no extreme violence. Thou hast heaped upon me all these rich favours and I, poor wretch, did not know them, much less acknowledge them. So, O Lord, Thou hast often delivered me from the dreadful devouring teeth of the devil and saved me from the jaws of the lion and, I not witting of it, hast brought me from the very brink of hell mouth; I approach even to the gates of death and Thou hast kept me that I have not entered.

O my Lord, I have likewise been often delivered even from corporal death, even then when I was afflicted with grievous diseases and exposed to many great dangers; both by sea and land, by fire and water, Thou hast oft assisted me by Thy great mercy and goodness, and, O Lord, Thou knowest well that if death had then surprised me I had been perpetually damned. But without doubt Thy unspeakable grace prevented me always, warranting[1] me both from corporal and eternal death.

Many other benefits Thou hast bestowed upon me, but yet I, being altogether blind, did not see them till Thou didst graciously illuminate me. Thou art therefore, O Lord, the life by which I live and the clear brightness which makes me see, the light of my soul, and for this cause I render Thee all possible thanks, although they be poor, small, and no way answerable to Thy benefit; nor such as they should be, but such as my weak frailty can present and offer to Thee. For Thou art my only God which lovest our souls and hatest nothing that Thou hast made, and now hast saved me, being among great sinners, to the end that I may serve for an example to all others, and be witness of Thy great piety and sovereign clemency. I will therefore magnify Thy holy name, that Thou hast delivered me from the pit of hell more than a thousand times. And although I did thrust myself desperately on, yet Thou didst always draw me back, so that if Thou wouldst have entered into judgement and condemnation against me and punish me in rigour according to my faults and merits, Thou hadst justly a thousand and a thousand times condemned me and punished me with eternal death, but Thou wouldst not do it, but out of Thy

---

[1] keeping, preserving

infinite love of souls Thou dost wait till they be converted and do penance.

O infinite Goodness, my soul faints in this Thy great mercy and cannot express it, being so unspeakable. Alas, I was wholly dead, O my sovereign Health, and Thou hast raised me again. My life does depend on Thee and as I do wholly attribute it to Thee I do offer it and give myself wholly to Thee. O my Sanctifier, by whom all things unclean and polluted are sanctified, let me love Thee with all my heart, with all my soul, with all my thoughts, force, powers and all my affections, at all times and moments, that so I may enjoy the fruits of Thy mercy; for were it not that Thou dost continually govern me and guide me, I should be wholly lost. If Thou didst not continually quicken me, I should perish. And as Thou dost at all times confer unto me thy great benefits, Thou dost continually oblige me to praise Thy sovereign majesty. As therefore there is no minute in all my life wherein I do not feel some effect of Thy great goodness, so there ought no time to pass wherein I should not put Thee before mine eyes and love thee with all my force and virtue. But, O Lord, this is not in mine own power, if it proceed not from Thy divine majesty, from whom comes all that is good, as from the Father of lights, with whom there is no change, variety or alteration of things; for it is not in the discretion or will of man to love Thee, if it be not granted him by Thy holy grace. Such a gift comes from Thee, O merciful Lord, from whom come all good things, wherefore command that Thou beest loved and bring about that which thou commandest, and without doubt Thy blessed commandment shall be fulfilled of me, as also Thy most holy will.

★

Of his devotion before he became a Capuchin

THE FOURTEENTH CHAPTER

IT is no marvel if Father Benet showed so great fervour among the Capuchins, since that from the instant of his conversion there was always in him a very particular devotion. He was as a coal all on fire which did kindle others with his glowing heat, but the violence appeared far more after, when he had lived in the observance of so strait[1] a rule. So that it may be truly said of him that the change which he made from a secular life to a religious, was but to give an ample external testimony of the true apostolical life which he would after lead and to bind himself by solemn vows to those actions which he did practise already of his own free will and of a holy affection and merit of life.

He spoke himself in the narration of his conversion, what pleasure he took in visiting churches and beholding their buildings and outward ornament, but his humility forbade him to speak how he passed whole days herein, not knowing how the time went away which was spent so. He signified the unspeakable contentment which he had in hearing the music, how he was so changed thereby that tears trickling down his cheeks, he fell often into thanksgiving to God that He had made him in some manner understand what the joys of heaven should be, since he was so much affected with that sweet harmony here in earth. But humble as he was and hiding diligently the graces which might cause him honour, he did not declare how these pleasures put him into such extasies that he did not remember where he was. At Doway when he made his first retreat and exercised his first devotions, his soul (which knew not as yet in what manner to proceed according to God's holy intention to the attaining of perfection) so gave itself to contemplation that many cannot match him after the long practice of a contemplative life in the cloisters.

It happened then as he was on his knees praying bareheaded, his hands joined, and his heart and eyes lifted up to God, his soul was ravished as the hymns were sung in the church, his body was left as insensible for the time, insomuch that lifting up himself suddenly he went from the place where he was, leaving his hat and gloves behind him, not perceiving it till he came to the church porch, so that he was fain to retire thither where he had prayed to seek his hat and gloves.

What a change was this that a heretic, a young man and a gentleman, being but newly come out of heresy and yet retaining

[1] strict

the other two,[1] should be so devout and so deeply rooted in such acts of devotion? What a change is this to see him frequent churches instead of dances, sermons instead of comedies, sacraments instead of profane company, and to take delight in spiritual songs and hymns instead of youthful, vicious and wanton songs? To turn banqueting and feasting into fasting? To become a friend of solitude? To be retired and recollected, having always God before the eyes of his spirit, to whose will be rendered all his thoughts, affections and actions captive? No man can well consider this unless he confess that the secrets of God are very great and that He did design this blessed father to something extraordinary and of high reach during the rest of his life, seeing that the beginning of his conversion was succoured with so many graces.

These graces growing in him did, as they grew, expel all mundane and earthly affections; for herein it appears if we be enemies of mundanities, and the more we hate the world the more does this quality increase in us, which makes us children of heaven and heirs of so rich an inheritance. This was the cause that this good father, being disquieted with the world, wherein he had taken so much delight, made his first resolution to be a religious man, to which God drew him by divers visions, inspirations, lights of the spirit and kindling of the will; as he reported himself when he was perplexed which of the two religions (the Cordeliers or the Capuchins) did observe perfectly the rule of Saint Francis and did wear his true habit, wherein God inspired him so manifestly that he could not admit any doubt touching this inspiration, as a religious man of this order has related and signed with his own hand, whose name was Peter Edwards,[2] an Irishman of nation, his very familiar and inward friend, to whom he related it one time as they entertained discourse one with another upon the particular benefits toward certain persons.

One day as he was in a deep meditation touching this business and not knowing what to resolve, he prayed and commended this to God with all possible fervour and with all the faculties of his soul, not without many deep groans of his heart and salt tears

---

[1] i.e., he still retained the habits of a young man and a gentleman.
[2] Nothing is known of him, unfortunately. He must have been the source of much of Brousse's detailed information.

falling from his eyes. And there appeared to him an angel most beautiful and glorious, compassed with a great light and a book in his hand, which he opening without speaking one word to him, made a sign to him to read that which was within. He looked upon it and read these words: "O Lord, how difficult and hard is this way which Thou hast showed to me?" The angel turned the leaf and he read the same thing in it and so turning over all the leaves found the same words written. Upon this the angel vanished out of his sight and his soul was left full of consolation and joy, assuring himself that it was God's will that he should be a Capuchin, because their manner of life was more strict and austere than that of the Cordeliers, though they be both the children of blessed Saint Francis and make profession of the same rule. After this, redoubling the fervour of his prayers, he said to God: How good art Thou, and so lay as a man rapt in the contemplation of so great a benefit, which he would not have changed for all the wealth of the world.

After this time he could find no contentment but in their cloisters, making his pilgrimage between the houses of Paris and Meudon, and when he was with them he thought himself in paradise and never rested till they had received him and given him the habit.

How he took the habit of a Capuchin, of his noviceship and his admirable actions during that time

The Fifteenth Chapter

The Capuchins, seeing so great fervour in this young gentleman and a stranger in demanding the habit, did not know what to think of it, for he, not willing to reveal to them the visions and inspirations which he had from God to draw him to religion, told them only that his desire was to forsake the world; that the little experience which he had of the world was sufficient to make him despise it; that he did foresee that in religion he should have more means to keep down the body by mortifications; and he was not ignorant what profit redounds thereby to the soul, if he were tied in the chains of a holy rule. And in the end he knew how great a crown of glory did belong to those that had lived in the holy observance thereof. These considerations overweighed all others; yea, if the whole world had been put into the other scale, this had over-weighed it. But yet for all this he was delayed and put off, that so it might the better appear whether he were truly moved by God's holy spirit or whether some worldly discontentment did not make him to change his life and profession. For among the Capuchins religious are not easily received. Yea, I have known some that have sought five or six years to be received and every year have made journeys of four score or a hundred leagues to make suit to their Provincial Chapter, before that they have been received; and haply[1] they had not so constantly persevered if they had been received at their first request, for as much as we preserve those things with more circumspection which have cost us much pain and travail to get them. But he won them at length to admit him without any more delays. At that time he was but four-and-twenty years of age, which though it be the time when nature is in her greatest violence and seeks most her pleasure, yet then was all his study bent to mortify it and make the flesh obedient to the spirit. The greatest austerities which for the most part are sharp and most sensible to beginners,[2] were his greatest contentment, insomuch that his companion novices were much excited[3] by his devotion and the religious fathers much astonished for to see it.

He was committed to the charge of a father of the same nation,[4] a man of holy life and greatly conversant in mystical theology and in conducting of those which took the way of learning the cross, to the end that he might communicate more freely to him whatsoever he had in his soul and that he might follow his precepts with more resignation. I will not speak here how promptly he put in execution whatsoever his director ordained, though it were contrary to his inclination. Here I will set down how the devil, the enemy of

---

[1] perhaps
[2] to which beginners are most sensitive
[3] stimulated
[4] The novice master at the Rue Saint-Honoré was Fr. Julian of Camerino, a convert Jew, but he was not "of the same nation" as Fr. Benet.

all men in general, but principally of religious, how many gins[1] he laid for him and how he omitted no temptation, neither outward nor inward, to divert him from his holy purpose and to make him forsake the habit, beginning first to terrify him by the rigour of his penances and the violence of his prayers, presaging that he would prevail much to overthrow his kingdom, if he did persevere in religion. Therefore he appeared to him visibly in divers forms, sometimes in the form of a religious man and some other times under the figure of some fearful beast, as his malice and craft made him invent. One while he represented to him the manifold occasions of suffering which occurred in the poverty of Capuchins, and that the time which he might live according to the course of nature was too long to be obliged to such sufferance, whereas after his profession he could not forsake that kind of life but he must be ever reputed an apostate. Sometimes he would make him believe that the way to heaven was so easy and the gate so wide and open, that he might arrive well and assuredly there and yet live in the delights and contentments of the world. He founded his pretext upon the mercy of God, who will not the death of a sinner and has granted heaven to Mary Magdalen and to the good thief; and these be the most dangerous charms wherewith he enchants worldly men and makes them to believe them to their destruction. But this young novice (old in these maxims) by the light of grace resisted valiantly all these batteries, calling to mind Our Saviour's words: *The way to heaven is strait and that which leads to perdition is wide and spacious.* That *it is as hard for a rich man to enter into the kingdom of heaven as a camel to pass through the eye of a needle.* That *a man cannot have his happiness in this world and in the other likewise.* With these and such weapons he did encounter the devil and wielded them so dexterously that he rested always victorious and the devil ashamed to be overcome.

These combats made him humble himself more in his own knowledge. And here it shall not be amiss to give thee, dear reader, an assured rule to know if we be truly out of temptation and that with victory, which is, to see if we are become more humble than before; whereas delight and inward ostentation pro-

[1] snares

ceeding from our own will, does often cause us to attribute so much
to our own forces, that without any relation to God, from whom all
grace proceeds, we think ourselves able to resist it. But this is not
to resist temptation and to carry away the victory, but to fall from
a less evil into a greater, and so the more dangerous because we do
not know it; but when by the grace of a holy reflection we come to
know that our own forces had been too feeble to resist so strong an
enemy, this knowledge brings us to know our infirmity and in
despite of our lifting up ourselves, to humble and cast down ourselves, fearing otherwise lest God might leave us another time all
alone in the battle, whence we are not likely to get out, but with
shameful foil. This good father therefore became still more
humble as the devil did deliver him these assaults, and thereby
showed that he was truly the conqueror. And not contenting himself with this, did practise mortification with more courage and
exercised prayer with more fervour. The visions which he had in
the beginning of his vocation now were more ordinary and fearful
in religion. He had then of all sorts and some so fearful that the
very apprehension troubled him, yea and made him sometimes cry
out for fear.

One time there was represented to him a rough stony way and
full of thorns, which he must pass to enter into a pleasant garden.
The thorns affrighted him but the beauty of the flowers of those
borders and the sweet odours which they sent forth was so great,
that it drew him as it were forcibly, that he passed freely upon
these flint stones and trampled upon the thorns so that the blood
issued, without feeling the wounds which they caused. God would
show him by this vision the difficulties which he was to pass in the
year of his probation, to come to the contentment of his profession
in fastening himself to the Cross of his Saviour, in which he
gathered all the flowers of his affections, the fruits of all sorts of
virtues, which he did savour with unmatchable devotion.

Another time being at mental prayer after midnight (as their
custom is, principally in the winter, to watch and pray when others
provoke God most by the enormity of their sins), having taken his
meditation upon the pains of hell, Our Lord made him see the
diversities of torments and pains which are imposed upon miser-

able souls, the horrible cries of devils and the blasphemies which they yelp forth against their Creator, the stench of those dark dungeons and the despair which tyrannizes over them and many other such like pains which are in this place of malediction. Seeing all this very clearly he sent forth a most terrible cry and astonished all the religious, and he began to rise and run away swiftly. The fathers brought him into his chamber and asked him why he did cry so, but he was so troubled, that he could not answer, but trembled and panted, looking about him continually and came not perfectly to himself till more than two hours after.

These strange accidents made the fathers fear lest there might be illusions of the devil and therefore, to understand them better, they went to the true remedy, which was that they proved him by many and great mortifications, enjoined him extraordinary penances, which he did support with admirable modesty, patience and humility, searching in all occasions contempt of himself and beholding Jesus Christ upon the cross, which are two foundations upon which Saint Francis by divine inspiration established his whole rule. He was almost continually in extasies, that it might be truly said that his soul, united to his body, did live in heaven among the angels. I will not now speak of any other rapt, but that which befell him when he was a novice. For the space of two days he lay speechless and without any function of his senses, as far as could be seen. The fathers, having never seen such strange rapts in any novice, had recourse to the physicians to know what they thought thereof. The physicians, which seldom have recourse to God when they can find any relief in nature, ordained that pigeons new killed should be applied to him and that the blood should distil upon his head, but they gave him no ease in this. Then they pricked his legs and thighs with great pins, and for all this they could discern no motion of sense at all in him. This did so astonish the fathers that they thought to dismiss him as soon as he should begin to be in a little better state. And they had indeed done it if the reverend Father Hierome du Castferet,[1] at that time Guardian of Paris, a man very famous for sanctity and prudence, had not hindered it, who had been General twice, and thrice procurator in

[1] Fr. Jerome of Castelferretti.

the Court of Rome, and for the space of two and thirty years ordered very happily all the important business of religion. This reverend father, well experienced in these cases, was always of opinion that he should not be dismissed. And yet to the end to try farther the solidity of his spirit and his constancy to suffer patiently all things for the love of God, he caused him to be kept shut up in a chamber for the space of forty days, in which time he could not go forth, neither see nor speak to any man, but upon Sundays and feasts when he went to hear Mass; and afterwards he returned to his cell where being voluntarily kept for Jesus Christ's sake, he solaced himself with Christ in extraordinary spiritual rapts.

But to return to our former discourse. After he had been out of himself for two days, he came in the end to himself again, and was so possessed with joy and jubilation that he, seeking to conceal it with all humility, was yet forced to make outward show of it. The reverend Father Benet of Osimo,[1] Provincial, assembling some of the ancient fathers together, sent for him to know in what state he was, commanding him in the virtue of holy obedience to conceal nothing from him, and to tell unto him the naked truth. Whereupon presently, he being abashed and changing his colour, entered into a discourse of two hours long, and treated of many points of perfection which had been revealed to him, with so high conceptions that afterward they never made doubt but that his extasies were true and not to be suspected for illusions. His companions asked him if he felt anything of that which was done to him. He said that he felt it well, but that his spirit was so occupied otherwise that he could not divert it to speak or give any sign of feeling.

Notwithstanding all this, to shut the gate to vanity which creeps in insensibly like a serpent, they did humble him by all sort of inventions. They told him that he was unprofitable and altogether unfit for religion according to the spirit of St. Francis, and that they minded to take the habit from him. At all which speeches he was not a whit troubled, but said that Our Blessed Lady had revealed to him that he should live and die a Capuchin. The father which was director has since declared the circumstances of this revelation, and said that once as he was ungirt, or rather had

[1] Fr. Bernard d'Osimo.

loosed the cord wherewith he was girt, his spirit which was continually elevated entertained itself in meditation upon the perfections of the Blessed Virgin. Then did the Queen of Angels appear unto him very glorious and took his cord and girt him softly, and assured him that he should persevere a child of St. Francis, exhorting him to continue his holy devotions.

All the year of his noviceship was passed in this manner, at the end of which he made humble suit to be professed. And this favour was accorded to him, whereof God has since received the glory, his neighbour edification, and the whole order honour and contentment.

Of his extraordinary fashion of life after his profession

THE SIXTEENTH CHAPTER

THIS good father longed for the day of his profession, which was to him a second spiritual nativity, being first born when he converted himself to the faith of the Church. This day of his profession he celebrated every year with extraordinary affection, renewing his vows with great devotion. From this time he began to live so as if he had done nothing before. He exercised more austerity and more mortification, without any release or remission, even till the hour of his death, which was for the space of five and twenty years; for so long he was in religion. For rules of his actions he proposed no others but Jesus Christ crucified, taking more pleasure to behold Him on the cross and participate in his soul one of His dolours as it pleased Him to communicate it to him, than to consider Him in Cana of Galilee changing water into wine or to see Martha full of care, having the honour to serve Him at table. Hence it came to pass that when he was to treat of spiritual things and of means to attain to perfection, his discourse was so fiery that he was seen all glowing hot, and ever he interlaid somewhat of the Cross, for said he, to suffer and endure for the love of Jesus Christ, O what grace is it, this is the sure way of salvation! No soul ever took it which did not safely arrive, although never so great enemies would stop the passage.

He mounted yet far higher by mystical theology, knowing that our flesh was the more true cross upon the which God was nailed coming into this world, and where He had endured and daily does endure more cruel torments than the cruel Jews inflicted on Him. And for this cause he laboured to render cross for cross, passion for passion, dolour for dolour, flesh for flesh, causing his flesh to suffer in particular (as much as was in his power) the dolours which Our Saviour had suffered in His, both crosses being but one and the same, as they did participate the same nature in their species.

This is very high, yet they shall easily comprehend the same who consider that Jesus Christ having taken our nature and with it all the maims and imperfections excepting sin, it was to it (to use the words of Father Benet) that He was bound by a hypostatical union, upon which He was nailed with great and piercing nails of love, where He was condemned to die by the sovereign and high court. Therefore it is that upon this cross of our flesh that He has endured and does endure daily cruel pains. For when the priest celebrates only for gain, it is then that He is sold by His disciple. When the Holy Sacrament is given to obstinate sinners He is delivered into the hands of Jews. When He is received of an unworthy soul He is traitorously kissed. When we do hinder Him to do His will, He is bound and manacled. When after the communion we spend the time in profane pastimes, He is led shamefully through the streets; He is buffeted by the hardness of our hearts; He is mocked when we pray to Him and think of other things; He is clad as a fool when we despise to follow Him. We bend our knees in scorn when we kneel in the church and do Him not due reverence. We give Him a reed for sceptre when we call Him King and Lord and yet will not obey Him. Besides, those which do disguise themselves do spit in His face; those who paint themselves with vermilion, do cover His face with blood; they which wear strange hair do pull Him by the hair and those which wear them[1] powdered, frizzled, crested and unnaturally dressed, set thorns upon His head.

[1] their hair

Moreover, those who oppress the poor lay the cross upon His shoulders. Those who terrify them with threats do put Him into an agony. They that take away the goods of the Church do strip Our Saviour of His clothes. They who do afflict priests do cruelly scourge Him. He which devises lies against a religious person accuses Him falsely and stains His good name, calls Our Saviour drunkard and friend of publicans. Those who accuse an innocent person bear false witness against Jesus Christ and those which swear profanely, do blaspheme Him. The judges which keep a widow or orphan long in suspense do tie Him to a pillar, and they which send them from one court to another do send Him from Caiphas to Pilate. The judge which for fear of princes or great persons does not justice is another Pilate, and he which against his own conscience does condemn the just cause of the innocent does pronounce sentence against Jesus Christ. They that hinder their servants or others to do good do nail His hands upon the cross, and they that permit them not to go to Mass or to a Catholic sermon do nail His feet to the cross. The soldiers which despitefully treat poor countrymen do handle our Saviour despitefully. Heretics which by their false opinions do afflict the Church, do prepare whips for Him, and the tongue of the minister speaking against the Church is a lance which pierces His side whence the Church comes. And to conclude briefly, they that commit any sins, do put Him cruelly to death, crucifying again in themselves the Son of God, as St. Paul says: *This is the true Cross on which He cried I thirst (O man) for thy salvation, on which He tasted the vinegar and gall of our malice and on which He had His heart and side pierced by our unthankfulness.*

So did Father Benet discover the mystical cross of our humanity, chastising in recompense his own flesh for to make it in some sort like to that of his Master. And whosoever will see some high conceptions upon this matter, let him see the book which he has made, entitled: *The Christian Knight*,[1] and there doubtlessly under the hieroglyphic of a soldier with his arms and that which is needful for corporal war, he teaches every Christian soul which desires to live one day in heaven with Jesus Christ all things which are

[1] *Le Chevalier Chrestien*, Paris, 1609.

necessary in a spiritual warfare and that which it ought to do or avoid, the means to subdue his passions, the art of rooting up vices and planting virtues and, in one word, an abridgement of an active and contemplative life.

This extraordinary manner of meditating the Passion in his own proper flesh, instead of contemplating Him upon Mount Calvary, imprinted in him more lively touches than it would have done by other means. For it is certain that these things do more affect us which touch ourselves than they do when we see them in another. And as an habitude is gotten by actions, imprinting itself more strongly as the actions are violent, so this blessed father did so bend the force of his spirit to God by the meditation of the cruelty of the Passion, that three years before he died he reposed not one hour and a half of four-and-twenty, when he felt not himself drawn by a divinely powerful attraction to a union and transformation into Jesus Christ crucified (according to that which he wrote thereon in his third part of the will of God, in his treatise of the Passion),[1] that it left impressions in him of the pains of Our Saviour; and so violent they were that his body and soul did feel day and night the great and inward dolours caused thereby. He suffered in his body and for that which concerns the inferior powers of the soul, all that can be suffered, but the superior part of reason did take pleasure thereby and received great contentment, which was an infallible argument that such attractions were truly from God and not illusions of Satan.

Notwithstanding that he might not be deceived by an act of profound humility, not trusting in his own knowledge, nor in his own proper sense, he communicated this to one of the fathers (a man eminent in all sorts of sciences both speculative and practical and an excellent preacher), conjuring him most earnestly to tell him whether he were not beguiled in such actions both in regard of the little repose he took, in respect of the weakness of his constitution, as in regard of other occasions, because this divine attraction did seize upon him often before Matins, some times after, and for the most part did hold him all along the whole day, though with less violence by reason of exterior occupation and distractions.

[1] See above, Introduction, p. xxix.

This father, knowing him familiarly for many years and by humility judging of the rest of his actions, assured him that all was from God, protesting afterward to the fathers to whom he made relation of this that he had never heard so high things and so well delivered as he had done in his colloquy with Father Benet for the space of three hours, though he lay at that time sick of his last disease, which ended his life.

In this no doubt he had great occasion to rejoice and to thank God for those graces and favours done unto him which He refuses to many others. But besides these he did suffer violent pains in all parts of his body, in that for the space of twelve years after he entered in religion, he was so oppressed that there was no sort of disease so violent that could put a man to more extreme pain than he endured, with infinite patience, never complaining or murmuring, but always praising God. And for all this he did never relent in his daily mortifications. He did frequent daily the community if he could train[1] himself thither without falling, where it pleased God one time to work a miracle for his health, as I will relate hereafter. In fine, he omitted no actions of his rule nor of his particular devotion if the physician did not command him otherwise strictly for his health and his conscience.

The devil not prevailing in his noviceship against him to bring him again into the world, ceased not to assail him with other temptations afterwards. For the favours of God did serve him as a whetstone to set an edge upon his weapons. He laboured now to make him offend against his vows and for two years' space he continued in the violence of these temptations, bearing the yoke of great afflictions; and his brethren, who could not assist him but with their prayers, did him this charity so much the more willingly, because they judged his state out of danger, so that he might well wish with Job that his faults which he had committed were counterpoised with the dolours and afflictions which he suffered. For in respect of them the others had been lighter than a grain of sand.

[1] drag

Of his learning and how he used it[1]

THE SEVENTEENTH CHAPTER

IF vexation does give understanding, as it is commonly said, then surely was Father Benet endowed with great understanding, having suffered all his life such sorts of afflictions which do exceed human frailty to bear, if it were left only to natural forces; but as there are two sorts of knowledge to raise us to God and to make us despise earthly things, so there are two principal ways to attain it. There is a knowledge of infirmity of nature, with the need that we have of the hand of God, which does support and keep us from falling, as a nurse's hand does hold the little infant whom she guides; and this is caused by afflictions. For there is nothing which does make us return so soon as a snail within his shell, as when God comes to smite the horns of our presumption and arrogance. The other knowledge is that of the secrets of nature, of politic and divine laws, of the mystery of our belief, all which scholastical and mystical divinity does teach us both to assent to those matters of faith and also to know the relation and dependence there is between the creator and creature, as also to discern truth from falsehood and heresy from true doctrine, and to contain us within the Church and to reduce others which are without. And this knowledge comes not from afflictions, but from travail joined with a good temperature of the brain, or from those free graces which God bestows as He sees expedient for our salvation and for His glory.

How excellent Father Benet was in the first sort of knowledge it is already declared, and as yet in the chapters of his patience and mildness will appear more. In the second, which is more profitable to our neighbour, he did also excel. For nature had endowed him with great promptness of wit, and he then confirmed it by his own labour and diligence, that there was almost no sort of art or science wherein he was not well conversant. In his youth, after he had learned his humanities, he gave himself to the study of the common

---

[1] For his theological studies Fr. Benet went to Venice, circa 1588-91.

law, wherein he advanced himself much for the time. After his conversion, when he became a Capuchin, he was put to the studies of philosophy and theology, which he learned with no less facility, for the inward grace which sanctified his soul cleared also his judgement, to pierce into the most obscure difficulties. And will you know what was the book which he held continually in his hands and turned often every day? It was the cross and passion of Our Saviour. The crucifix was his repetitor or repeater,[1] whose lesson he did continually recite. And why did he study so much this lesson? Because he would teach no other doctrine. Those who conversed with him knew this well. And likewise the lancings of his heart in the pulpit accompanied with the compunction and tears of his auditors do show it sufficiently, and an infinite number of souls converted to God by his exhortations, who now being ravished with Mary Magdalen at the feet of the cross, reading this, will witness that I do not speak the hundredth part of that which he merited in this kind.

Besides these sciences he was well seen in the learned tongues, both Greek and Hebrew; in positive divinity and reading of the Fathers; in controversies and cases of conscience, so that it may be said that he had an abridgement of all sciences, there being nothing worthy to be known which the transcendency of his wit made not very familiar unto him. I need not to prove it, for there is no man who does not know it, and a great number of cardinals, archbishops and bishops and other notable persons in the Church, who have admired, cherished and honoured him with their visits and will testify this for a truth. As also for his great travail and success in gaining of souls after he became a preacher. The sublimity of his doctrine has been known and searched after in the cloisters of religions of all sorts, and God only knows the number of religious men and women who, having been comforted by his exhortations and aided by his doctrine, both by word of mouth and writing, have been exalted to the high state of perfection; of whom some now enjoying the recompense do know by effect what a happiness it is for a soul to have no other object in this world but the Cross. And others as yet not released from the thorns of this mortality do

---

[1] Tutor, literally, one who hears over the lesson.

live content and joyful in expectance and hope of the like crown. And who is able to tell how many princes, noblemen, gentlemen, and others of all ranks, qualities and sorts, have found by experience to their own benefit how profitable it is to have good counsel for their consciences against the cumbrances of the world, such as those were which this Father Benet had experimented. His outward carriage and comportment of himself bred devotion in others. For his very countenance and sweet behaviour did teach others piety and devotion. I should never make an end if I would particularize all his actions, his manner of preaching full of fiery zeal, the theological foundation which he gave to his moral precepts, his method of sweetly winning sinners, his manner of treating with secular persons and what preparation he used for his preaching. Among other things it is certain that the fire of charity was so kindled in him, that it made him often forsake his corporal refection to give spiritual. Which he did practise with such a supernatural light, and so quickening, that the streaming of it was sufficient to engrave his name in memory amongst posterity.

One of the greatest losses which we sustain by his death is the want of enjoying certain works which he had begun and left imperfect. In which there were great matters expected touching perfection, since he had already treated it so excellently in his *Rule of the Will of God*,[1] which book is esteemed by spiritual men (who are best able to judge of it) one of the most worthiest and fittest to guide a soul with assurance to the centre of his last rest, and does lead men on more easily, with more love than fear; and it cannot but be such as I say, since he received the argument and knowledge of it from heaven. For during his noviceship in one of his extasies, wherein he continued a long time as a man out of his body that is not seeming to have any sense at all, God by a particular grace and light revealed the subject of it in one instance, with so lively apprehension of it, that some of his friends and novices, being at that time with him, to whom he did communicate them at that present, did testify that he did then discourse more perfectly and more feelingly of this than he has done in his book.

[1] For a discussion of *The Rule of Perfection* see above, Introduction, pp. xxix-xxxi.

And I am well assured that the doctors of the Sorbonne, besides other great eminent persons conversant in mystical theology, do confess that he has taken out the sap of Cedar upon the high mountain of Liban,[1] which is of contemplation.

One of his more particular designs, wherein he employed himself with much fervour and affection, was the conversion of souls infected with heresy. For as we hate more the bitterness of the fruit after we have tasted thereof than if we have only the knowledge of it by the qualities, and we labour more to root up the plants of this bitter fruit wheresoever we find them, so this blessed father, having been formerly infected with heresy and taken in deeply the venom of it, did more perfectly hate it, and therefore did employ the greatest part of that time which he could spare from the exercise of his rule in labouring to this end, not without great profit and benefit to straying souls. For the sweet temper of his conversation, without ever entering into passion (though he were provoked), joined with a great prudence which knew how to make his right advantage as occasion was offered, made him so able to confer with heretics that by the one he won them to conference and by the other he seldom let them depart from him without being wholly converted, or at least troubled and perplexed in their own doctrine.

He did often set before his eyes the pitiful state of the most part of souls in his own country. He detested that error wherewith they were blinded and had great compassion of their misery, and out of charity (which obliges us to love our neighbour) he wished their conversion from the bottom of his soul. Upon this occasion he resolved to go into his country and to labour in that holy harvest of reducing wandering souls and preaching to them the kingdom of God by the way of penance. And no labours (which are great in these kinds), no eminent perils of prisons or death, had any power to divert him from this holy purpose.

[1] Lebanon

*Of his going into England and what happened to him
during three years that he was in prison*[1]

THE EIGHTEENTH CHAPTER

THE love which this good father did bear to the Cross did move him
to a great desire of shedding his blood for the quarrel of his
Master. Wherefore he chose rather to return into his country,
which was in the beginning of the heat of persecution in England,
when racks and tortures were so common that few or none could
escape death by reason of the most bloody laws enacted against
priests. He went from Paris in the month of July in the year 1599,[2]
after he had received the benediction of the most reverend Bishop
of Modena, Legate of the See Apostolic and Nuncio at that time of
our Holy Father Pope Clement the Eighth, and had the obedience
of his superior. He had for his companion Father John Chrisostome, a Scottish priest and preacher, a very zealous and religious
father, whom the incommodities of prisons could not divert from
returning since to his country for the reduction of souls.[3]

The intention of this good Father Chrisostome was to go into
Scotland for the conversion of his father and most of his kindred
which were all heretics and among the most obstinate, four of them
being ministers and preachers. Departing from Paris they went
directly to Havre de Grace, thinking to take shipping there, but
missing of their hope in embarking there, they went from haven to
haven till they came to Calais, where they found a ship ready to
depart, and so went with many gentlemen, Hollanders and other
passengers, most of them being heretics.

[1] Brousse omits all mention of Fr. Benet's part in the exorcism of Marthe
Brossier.
[2] Both the French and English texts read "1589".
[3] Fr. John Chrysostom Campbell, of the house of Argyll. After his first
banishment in 1600 he returned again to the mission and was active around
Stokesley, Yorks. He was arrested and imprisoned circa 1608-11 and released on
the intervention of the French ambassador. Around 1612 he visited the Irish
Capuchin, Fr. Francis Nugent, at Cologne, and came over to Scotland in 1613
with Bl. John Ogilvy, S.J., and Fr. James Moffat, S.J. He was arrested in 1619
and imprisoned in the Tower till his final banishment in 1621. He was still alive
in 1627. (*Études Franciscaines*, x (1903), p. 25; T. Birch, *Court and Times of
Charles I*, London, 1848, vol. i, pp. 482 sq.; *Franciscan Annals*, lix (1935),
pp. 267 sq.)

They had the wind favourable enough to pass, but yet the passage was painful to them. For on the one side the reverend Father Benet was extremely seasick by reason of his tender and delicate constitution; on the other side he was not a little afflicted in mind for his companion who was tormented with a continual fever, which he had contracted by his travail and the great journeys which they had made. For besides that it was in the great heats of summer, the heaviness of their habits did tire them, forasmuch as they wore secular clothes upon their habits, which they had made of some light stuff, that by this disguisement they might avoid danger of being discovered.[1] The morrow after they were embarked, they landed between Sandwich and Dover and going on their way straight towards London, they left their company, telling them that for some occasions they could not take up the same lodging with them, and so staying a little while let the others go before.

How marvellous is God in all His works and how does He oftentimes dispose of our works, when we little think of it! These good fathers had great contentment now in that they had quitted the company of these heretics, that they might the better order their own business, but God disposed otherwise, for the first house which they came to, they thinking that it had been an inn, was a prison. Who can but wonder at this accident! This was doubtlessly God's providence which by a secret inspiration had incited His servants to make choice of this unpleasing and doleful lodging among all other places of the town, to the end they might work the conversion of many prisoners lodged there for divers causes, as they found by their experience afterwards effected.

Scarce were they entered, whilst Father Benet was speaking to the hostess for the relief of his companion, who was grown very weak by his fever, but the serjeants, knowing them to be strangers, came to signify to them from the mayor of the town the law which prohibits any stranger to take up his lodging before he give an account to the mayor of what quality and profession he is. What a beginning is this, I pray you? These good fathers do easily obey

---

[1] For his second visit to England, Fr. John Chrysostom got permission not to wear the habit, but to go in disguise.

and presently follow the serjeants and came to the mayor, who began to interrogate them according to the usual manner when any stranger is brought before him. And he found presently what they were. For besides that they were found with their breviaries (which gave great occasion to suspect them for priests), their aspect full of reverence, the sweetness of their countenances, the gravity of their behaviour, the modesty of their speech, their patience in enduring mocking and railing words poured out of dirty mouths against them, did betray them. And many blasphemies were belched forth against the purity of their religion and against our Holy Father the Pope, whom heretics hold for anti-Christ.

After this they were brought back by sentence of the mayor and attended by the same guard of serjeants unto their first lodging, to wit, to prison, to be kept there until they expected the determination of the Queen of England and her Privy Council. They seeing themselves thus shut up, armed themselves with patience for the time to come and began to deal as effectually as they could for the conversion of those heretics which were in prison with them, there being at that time a great number. This good father, being much occupied in serving and solacing his sick companion, was much afflicted that he had not more time and leisure to confer with them, yet it pleased God so to bless him in this holy work, that in the space of eight days which he was there, he converted some who did him much pleasure and service afterward in many matters of consequence when he was prisoner at London and Wisbech.

After eight days the serjeants were commanded to bring them to a certain castle where the Queen and the Court was, which was but two days distant from thence. It is needless to tell in what manner they were treated in the way and how they were put in fear of death.

Being come to London, they were first brought before the Lord Cobham[1] who received them very courteously and entered into

---

[1] Henry Brooke, eighth Baron Cobham, was Warden of the Cinque Ports, and as such the two prisoners came under his immediate jurisdiction. Cobham was later arrested, in 1603, for his part in the "Main" Plot to place Arabella Stuart on the throne. He was condemned to be executed, but remained in the Tower till his death in 1619 (*DNB*). The French text of Brousse has an important addition here, for it claims that Cobham met Fr. John Chrysostom again when they were both prisoners in the Tower, and that he died a Catholic; but this may have been omitted from the English version because it was not true.

long discourse with Father Benet, insomuch that he seemed to be not a little moved and troubled in mind thereupon. He told him plainly his purpose and likewise gave him to understand that he was a Capuchin and that he had not abandoned his convent for any other end but to come into those parts to procure the salvation of souls which heresy had blinded, and that he was ready to spend his blood even to the last drop in so good a cause. And if the persecutors should exercise all kinds of torments upon his poor body, that he was ready to suffer them, and that neither torments nor death should by God's grace have the least power to alter his intention.

The Holy Ghost, which spoke by the mouth of this blessed father with such words full of zeal and sweetness, made them take root in the heart of this baron, whereupon he looks more earnestly upon the face of Father Benet, considers his comportment and weighs well all the circumstances of this small conference he had with him, and it seemed he was in conscience already well-affected to the Catholic religion.

They were sent afterward to the Queen's house at Nonsuch, where at that time the Queen was, and the Council, and for the second station they were presented to the Chief Secretary of State, Sir Robert Cecil,[1] a man of great credit and authority with the Queen's Majesty, a man most obstinate and stiff in his false religion. He presently began to ask them what they were and whence they came and why they came into the country, now and then interlacing some speeches of mere mockery. Father Benet made him brief and pertinent answers to all his questions with so much gravity and prudence, that all the company which was there had him in admiration for his discreet and modest fashion.

Among other things which the Secretary asked him, this was one: why they came together and one in the company of the other? To whom this good father answered that this was more comformable to the life of Our Blessed Saviour and His apostles, and to put in practice His commandment to His disciples whom He sent *binos et binos*, by two and two, to preach the Gospel. That this was

[1] The texts read "Sir Francis Walsingham" but Walsingham died in 1590. Perhaps the confusion was caused by the misdating of Fr. Benet's mission to 1589 (see above, p. 147).

likewise the practice of the primitive Church and the particular institution of their order, to the end that they might comfort one the other in the way and that one might partake with the necessities of the other. "O," said the Secretary, "it is rather that one may be the witness of the malice and lewdness of the other." Whereupon this good father took occasion to make a speech touch-touching the difference and great contrarity that there is between the children of God and the devil, the children of light and darkness, between the elected and reproved, religious men and heretics, concluding all with this sentence: *Qui male agit odit lucem*, he that does ill hates the light. Briefly, the candour of his proceeding and the freeness of his discourse won so far the affection of the Secretary, that although he was one of the greatest enemies of Catholic religion and one of the greatest persecutors that ever was in England, yet did he show favour to them, for he gave charge that all their cost should be defrayed from the time they were first taken, and commanded the serjeants to restore them all those things which they had taken from them, which they did in part.

The Queen, which could not endure to hear of priests, being advertised of the constancy of this blessed father, of his prudence and discreet behaviour, of his profound learning and his strong defence of the religion he professed, calming her passion in this kind, was desirous to have a sight of him. Whereupon she went to a window where she might see him as he was to go from her Court to be carried to the Tower of London, according to the order of her councillors. In the way the fathers had leisure to confess one to the other, not knowing whether they should have the like hereafter, because they were to be put apart by the sentence of the Council, that so they might be deprived of their mutual consolation and the rather to show their hate to the constitutions of their religion.

The Capuchins of the Province of Paris being advertised of the imprisonment of these two religious men made suit to His Most Christian Majesty[1] that he would interpose himself for their deliverance. For they saw they could not be delivered by any other means. His Majesty condescended to the Capuchins' humble

---

[1] Henri IV, who befriended the Capuchin order, though some of them had been his most violent opponents.

request herein, who hating heresy, because he knew well by experience the poison of it, did bear a particular affection towards Capuchins. His letters were delivered to the Queen to obtain this favourable liberty for them, whereupon Father Chrisostome, being a Scottish man, was enlarged. But Father Benet, being an Englishman and so consequently a vassal of the Queen's, was kept close prisoner still, and so far was he from obtaining liberty, that he was now more afflicted, and by a new sentence sent to the Castle of Wisbech, which is a most unwholesome and uncomfortable prison by reason of the ill air of those parts and the remoteness of the place from all that might yield assistance and comfort, with a great number of other Catholic prisoners, both ecclesiastical and secular persons.[1]

Here is worthy the observation that the very first day that this father was separated from his companion, he putting away all fear forsook the secular habit he wore and openly made his habit appear to the world, practising all the austerities of his rule, as fastings, discipline, and other mortifications, whereby the Catholics received very great comfort and contentment; but the heretics, witnessing their hate and fury against it, did revile him most bitterly for it. Among others one whose name was Wright, the Minister of Dumnington, which came to dispute with him, thought he should put him to great shame for wearing his habit, undertaking boldly to prove that he was prohibited to wear it, both by Scripture and the canons of the Church, but he failed of his proof and indeed he bore away the shame of so bold and false an asseveration.

This Capuchin's habit, unknown in those parts, occasioned much derision and disdain to heretics and comfort to Catholics, insomuch that Father Benet passing by Cambridge (which is one of the famous universities of the realm, for the colleges which are there built long since by Catholic founders for Catholics, though now usurped by heretics, as also the churches with the revenues, contrary to the laws of God and man, and the intention of the founders), passing, I say, by this university, he was led through all their streets as a strange monstrous spectacle. He was followed with odious shouts and cries and all despiteful reproaches they could

[1] See above, Introduction, pp. xxvi-xxvii.

possibly do him. In the meanwhile this blessed father armed himself with extraordinary patience and inwardly rejoiced according to the example of the apostles and martyrs, that he was reputed worthy to suffer such contumelies and outrages for the name of Jesus Christ crucified.

When he was come to Wisbech and shut up with other prisoners he began to exercise afresh the rigours of his rule, and during the eighteen months which he continued there, he brought forth great and notable fruit, both for the consolation of Catholics and conversion of heretics, who could not, maugré their hate to Catholic religion, but admire this strange manner of life. And the fame of it was so generally spread that very many were desirous to see him, some to content only their curiosity and others to hear his discourse and to know the grounds of his doctrine. Among these there were many ministers of the Protestants, who came thinking to convince him, but they departed from him with their own shame. That which did invite and draw them more to confer with him was his extraordinary modesty and sweet fashion of treating with them, which caused (according to the report of those that were fellow prisoners with him) that they chose rather to confer with him than with any other priest, because he did forbear to reprove their impertinences and absurdities with so much eagerness as many others would. Neither would he ever be transported by passion, though provoked to it by the folly and obstinacy of others, knowing well that sweetness and meekness often gains those, when rigour rather hardens, and that it is a usual thing for such obstinate and proud conceited men, to contradict more vehemently when they see their adversary impassioned. Our Blessed Saviour was meekness itself, and the first lesson which He would His disciples should learn of Him, was the practice of this virtue, commanding them above all to be modest and meek as lambs among wolves.

This good father won many souls in this manner, for there passed no day that he had not conference with one or other, and often he spent the whole day in this good work, so that he had scarcely time to say his Office. Other priests wondered much at it, and seeing his so great travail joined with his austerities admonished him to spare himself and told him that his weak body could not subsist with so much labour and so little sustenance. "For," said they, "Father, you are in continual action, always in great occupation of body and spirit, you take little or no rest to repair your strength. This must needs draw on some infirmity to the overthrow of your health." "Yes, rather," said he, "I am better in health for this exercise and was never more healthful and more able in body than I am at this present." And indeed it pleased God to bless him herein extraordinarily in witness of his acceptance of such labours. For as I have said before, for twelve years after his entry among the Capuchins, he was so weak that there was almost no disease whereof he had not his part, being oppressed without any intermission with a great weakness of stomach; which infirmity had now left him, so that he felt hardly any indisposition at all proceeding from his old malady.

Among other conferences which he had with ministers, there was one very remarkable that he had with the pretended Bishop of Ely, who was named Dr. Eaton,[1] who had the fame among them to be a very subtle disputer.

When he came to Wisbech (where this reverend father was prisoner) upon some important affairs of the public assizes, there were some gentlemen of quality in this bishop's company who had formerly known this Father Benet of Canfield in his youth. Among the rest was one knight called Sir John Cuts.[2] They earnestly solicited the Bishop to deal with him and convict him of his error; so that the Bishop undertook it, and having appointed a time, they sent for him to the prison without giving him the least advertisement of this their purpose. He, supposing that it was to be condemned to death for his religion, prepared himself rather to die than to dispute. At the first the Bishop began to interrogate him as if his indictment were now to be made. But he answered him plainly and categorically, not a whit amazed. But presently after a few questions, he entered insensibly into a question concerning the Pope's authority, which is a matter very odious in England. But when the father saw that the Bishop's intention was not to examine

---

[1] Dr. Martin Heton, Bishop of Ely from 1599 till his death in 1609.
[2] Probably Sir John Cutts of Thaxted, noted for his liberality and good-living. (T. Wright, *History and Topography of the County of Essex*, London, 1836, vol. ii, p. 236.)

him as a criminal but to convince him by argument, he defended himself so well and answered the objection of his adversary so pertinently, that many Catholics which were then present thought that it was God's spirit which spoke within him to the dishonour and confusion of the Bishop and his adherents. So did this good father exercise himself with great commendation in defending God's quarrel and daily working the conversion of souls till such time as after he had been kept three years in divers prisons he was then sent back by banishment into France[1] (for so he had his sentence) at the solicitation of His Most Christian Majesty Henry the Fourth of France. But that which occasioned the more speedy execution thereof was another matter which I will here set down.

A certain vicar of the pretended Bishop of Norwich named Master Redman,[2] accompanied with sixty ministers, which came from a synod, came to Framingham Castle,[3] where this father now was, being removed from that of Wisbech, to confer and dispute with the priests which were their prisoners, which were forty in number. And to the end that all might be done with the more glory the governor of the province, who is the Lieutenant of the Shire, was also there, called Sir Wingfield,[4] who gave countenance to this company by his presence.

In the company of these ministers there was one called Wright, who having lived at Geneva and there borne a great name, was greatly esteemed for his learning and sufficiency. This minister entered into conference with Father Benet and with two other priests, but he was so foiled that the Vicar-General, with many others, did change their colour and were ashamed of their champion. And afterwards said among themselves that the faith of the Protestants had received a great blow that day.

But this man being vainglorious was not content with this disgrace, but engaged himself for another day to repair his honour

---

[1] He was banished c 1602-3.

[2] William Redman (d 1602) was in fact Bishop of Norwich.

[3] i.e., Framlingham Castle, Suffolk, whence Fr. Benet and the other priests from Wisbech had been removed, 26 December 1600.

[4] i.e., Sir Anthony Wingfield of Letheringham, Kt. (A. Suckling, *History and Antiquities of the County of Suffolk*, London, 1846, vol. i, p. xlii; Mervyn Edward, seventh Viscount Powerscourt, *Memorials of the Ancient Saxon Family of Wingfield*, London, 1894, p. 30; T. G. Law, *The Archpriest Controversy*, Camden Society, London, 1898, vol. ii, pp. 242-3.)

which he had lost. But to provide for the worst and to recover the honour already lost, there were chosen three of the most able ministers, which were designed for to encounter in a solemn disputation three priests, under promise made by the Protestants that they would obtain warrant from the council for the priests' security in this action, which was otherwise a matter of great danger. Some weeks passed, during which time they treated of the points and circumstances of the disputation whilst the consent of the council was procured. The reverend Father Benet was one of the three priests which were elected for this disputation, as a man well qualified both for learning and for piety. But in the end all came to nothing, for these ministers, becoming wise by the example of the former, after they had well thought upon the business, durst not appear, nor yet could find a more honest excuse than to hasten the banishment of Father Benet and the other priests, which being obtained speedily, they were quit and wholly discharged from this meeting.

Of his return into France

THE NINETEENTH CHAPTER

AFTER that Father Benet had passed three years in prison he was delivered as aforesaid. Whilst he was in prison he made it a cloister for the austerity of his profession, and a pulpit, preaching frequently there the word of God and drawing many souls out of the sink of heresy. The Catholics were glad of his enlargement in regard of their desire that he might return to enjoy the sweet contentments of his cell, but otherwise they were exceeding sorry to be deprived of his conversation, his good instructions and virtuous example.

His brethren, who knew how zealous and strict he was in the observance of his rule, in integrity of life, and great prudence and experience for the direction of souls, made him incontinently[1]

---

[1] immediately

master of the novices. This office he exercised a long time at Orleans and Rouen, giving to everyone such an odour of his holiness of life and of his rare instructions, that many excellent religious men could not speak of him without witnessing singular affection to honour his memory, in recompense of those spiritual benefits which they thought they received from him or by his means.

Among other precepts which he gave to frame a life truly spiritual, that of abnegation was one, as the virtue that does deprive us of all that proceeds from the world or from our own proper interest, to give our souls entirely to God; for as much as He hates hearts that are divided, He seldom imparts His grace to such, because the affection aims at some other object than God alone. At the least wise He never bestows his graces so abundantly as when we are void and quite empty of all other love besides His. Therefore (said Father Benet) there are three sorts of abnegation, one temporal, another corporal, the third spiritual, which do settle, confirm and establish our souls and all her good works, as fastings, disciplines, prayers and mortifications against all the assaults of the enemy. The temporal is against the world, which by a covetous and disordered affection to earthly things seeks to make us strongly affected on her side to all vanity and so to become tributary to her. The corporal is against the flesh, which by fleshly pleasure endeavours with might and main to deprive us of the knowledge of the true and sovereign good, proposing to us the false and masked and covered over with the outward appearance of the true. The spiritual is against the devil, who by pride blinds us and hinders us to reflect upon our own infirmity, stirring us up to take the flight of ambition in soaring on high, to the end we may fall headlong into the flames of hell fire.

The first of these abnegations consists in the renouncing of gold, silver, estates, dignities, inheritances, possessions, a train of servants and the like, and was recommended by Our Saviour Himself in the 14 of S. Luke. For want hereof, Achab, Giezi, Ananias, Judas and many others overthrew themselves most miserably. The second consists in renouncing the actions of all the senses, as seeing, hearing, speaking, tasting, smelling, touching, sleeping, clothing ourselves and the like, which S. Paul does recommend unto us when he says: *Mortify your members which are upon earth.* For want thereof David, Solomon, Herod and infinite others offended God. The third abnegation, extending farther than the others, does deprive us of all sorts of complacency which we may take in our own actions, of all vain and curious thoughts and love of ourselves, and causes us to do all things only for the love of God, seeks His holy will in all things and that which does most especially tend to His greater glory. By the first we have no more to do with the world, nor the world with us. By the second our soul, dwelling as yet in the earthly tabernacle of the body, does lead a life like to angels'. And by the third we are transformed into God, as far as may be, being in the state we are. The first makes us children of heaven, because we do despise the earth. The second does prepare for us a white stole, to go with the virgins, singing and exulting after the Lamb. And the third makes us to taste here the sweetness of those liquors which do inebriate us in blessedness.

This excellent lesson was put in practice by Father Benet before he taught it unto others, which made him so much the more worthy of respect and honour. The contempt of all things made him for to be indifferent and to be all unto all, so that by a wonderful pleasing and shining sweetness of affability, he gained the hearts of his very enemies, even of his religion. So that since his return from England many heretics took occasion upon scruple that they had of their religion, to confer with him, by which means God's holy spirit wrought by him insensibly the conversion of a great number.

It happened one day whilst he was guardian at Rouen, in time of the extremest heats of summer, he not thinking of giving any the least ease unto his body, wore his habit pieced in the self same manner as in winter. The brethren, seeing him work in the garden and to sweat in such great drops as overtook one another, had compassion on him and said: "Father, you spoil yourself, this heavy habit kills you, give us leave to take away these pieces which make it so heavy, they will serve you for another winter." "What?" said he. "You mock me; my habit is as yours is and I find it light enough." "Pardon me," said one of them, "there is a great difference; look well upon it and you shall find it to be so." They had for all this much ado to persuade him. Lo, what mortification this was, not to know in what manner his habit was, as whether it had such pieces upon it, yea or no! Certainly this was the most extraordinary grace of God, which held him always ravished and by the attraction of His love held him always fastened to His cross, so that although he endured very much, yet he thought it to be nothing for as much as the dolours of his Lord and Master were more sensible to him and kept down the feeling of all other exterior pains.

Of his virtues

THE TWENTIETH CHAPTER

IT may seem from the purpose to set down so many excellent virtues wherewith this blessed father was adorned into the narrow compass of one chapter. But not purposing to make any ample discourse of them (which requires a great volume to contain them) I will only point out some few acts of many excellent virtues and by that scantling[1] give the reader occasion to see the true spring and fountain, though it be not deduced into great streams. Who was there that knew him that did not admire in him the greatness of his charity, the light of his faith, the firmness of his hope? Who can speak sufficiently of the ability of his wit, his prudence, and his patience in all sorts of afflictions? His sweetness of conversation, his profound humility, his perfect and prompt obedience, and of his simplicity and modesty in all occasions? Who can worthily express the austerity of his penance, the fruit of his silence, the effects of his preachings, the violence of his labours, the crosses, sufferings, watchings, fastings, mortifications and his disciplines? The reader himself may easily infer most of all these out of our former discourse of this blessed father's life. Therefore I will only here recite some particular actions of each virtue which may move to a true imitation of them.

And first concerning humility, which is as it were the foundation

[1] sample

of all the others, no man ever conversed with him who will not say that he was truly humble. The offices and charges which his piety and rare prudence made him to bear in his order were not accepted of him but when he could in no wise avoid them. And not withstanding these places of superiority, yet he never omitted to stoop to those mean drudgeries which the lay brethren are wont to perform. In so much that when he was Guardian at Rouen, if necessity enforced him to go into the town or do business of the convent or for the comfort of his neighbour, he did ordinarily carry the wallet upon his back and beg from door to door in going and coming. And to give ease to his companion he always would carry the more heavy burden, albeit he were very weak and feeble of nature. Thus he put in practice what we said before of abnegation in the former chapter, affirming often that it was not enough to have the habitual virtue if it were not accompanied with the actual. "We may," said he, "consider abnegation in three manners: as first habitual and resident in our soul; secondly as virtual, for as much as it is joined with an intention of a precedent act; in the third place, as actual for as much as it produces truly acts conformable to her being, which are, a despising of oneself, proceeding from the knowledge of our own weakness. The two first are good, but without the third they languish little by little and in the end do dry and wither quite away. Whereupon great evils do often follow, either in the understanding, by reason of a certain dark cloud which hinders us to know ourselves, or in the will which strives not to get forth out of so dangerous a state." His humility was also seen in hiding diligently those graces which God did show him in an abundant measure. The more he did receive the more was he a true follower of St. Francis, esteeming himself the most imperfect man in the whole world. No man could know his visions but some very few of his most inward and secret friends. One day a brother, seeing him strangely transformed and as it were united with God by contemplation much more straitly[1] than others were, he asked of him somewhat boldly if he had not some extraordinary vision in his extasy. "What," said he, "should I have visions? They are not for such miserable sinners as I am." So much did he humble and

[1] closely

cast down himself in the knowledge of himself and in the nought[1] of his own weakness, as God did raise him up above all others in grace and merit.

As for patience, which is the true sister of humility, he professed it in so high a degree that it seemed almost impossible to attain further in the exercise of this virtue. Affliction did never make him change colour, and that which was very much observed in him whilst he was in England, he had always an extraordinary force and magnanimity of spirit, whereby he was wonderfully fortified in enduring of all torments and guarded by these virtues against the violent assaults of what affliction so ever. During the great rigours of his disease (which were most ordinary and daily, as we have before declared), albeit he was guardian and superior, he was so obedient to the counsel of those that were to counsel him that he never transgressed, yea, he would obey his brother or him that kept him and had a particular charge to serve him, so that oftentimes he found him in the same posture that he had put him and left him the night before without once stirring an arm. So God who is delighted in the sufferances of His friends and does recompense them with increase of charity, made him often taste the fruit thereof by such actions altogether miraculous.

On a time, having had a violent and dangerous sickness for a long time, he began to complain a little of the tediousness of the same, not out of any impatience in enduring the sickness (for he did rather wish to be always so exercised), but because he could not go to the choir and perform other duties of the community. For this I will observe by the way that he was a great enemy of singularity and always thought that most assured and true mark of sanctity in a religious man to be, to see that he does always follow the community without leaving it, unless it be in extreme necessity. And in this Pope Clement the Eighth had a reason to say that he would not have a better argument to canonize a religious man than to be assured that he had always followed that which is ordained by his rule, for as much as singular actions and particularities are never without self-love, which is one of the pestilences of religion. This blessed father therefore, discontented in his mind that he could not

---

[1] nothingness

follow the community, and resigning himself wholly into God's hands, felt in his soul a certain sweetness more than usual and as it were a certain voice which spoke to the ear of his heart, assuring him that he should receive a perfect remedy on the day and feast of their seraphical father St. Francis, so that he would follow the community. The affect showed it afterward, for, the eve of St. Francis being come, he issued forth of the infirmary and goes as well as he can to the refectory with others. They would have given him some other meat, because on this day they fast with bread and water, telling him that he was too weak and sick to fast and that he would thereby increase his sickness. But he forbore to eat otherwise than the rest did, following the inspiration or revelation which he had had, and contented himself only with bread and water. The night following he went to Matins and he was no sooner upon his knees, but lifting up his heart to God to dispose himself to his Office, he felt (which he imparted to some others afterwards) a certain inward cheerfulness and jubilation of heart which cannot be expressed, and he heard as it were a voice full of sweetness, which comforted him and said: "Go and sing confidently, for thou art now wholly cured of thy disease." O how good a thing is it to endure for the love of God!

Presently upon this he recovered his health, and beginning to sing more loud than he was wont before he was sick, the other religious knew right well that God had shown him some particular grace that night. And so recovering more and more, his former voice grew sweeter and stronger. Thus does God repay the travails which we endure threefold beyond the value of them, and makes us to see by infinite effects that patience is one of the most necessary virtues of this life. For indeed the patience was notable that this blessed father did practise with so much resignation, which he did compare to the ark of Noah, which preserved him and his family from the universal flood. His words are these: "The ark of Noah was caulked, to the end that the waters might not enter in. What is this ark floating upon the deluge of mischiefs and tribulations? And what is this pitch wherewith it was caulked, but the fruit of patience which keeps the waters of afflictions from entering into this ark well and closely stopped, to extinguish charity? And for this cause such a soul says: *Aqua multa non potuerunt extinguera charitatem*, 'Many waters could not quench charity'."

Let us pass to other virtues, and without insisting further in his fervour, nor in the observation of his rule, of which we have already treated, I will here recite a strange accident which happened whilst he was Guardian and master of the novices at Rouen. A certain young gentleman was inspired of God to despise the world and to become a Capuchin, who was so at length after many delays and proof of his constancy. His parents (as it falls out commonly) being grieved for this his spiritual advancement, and enemies of this his design, attempted by letters, using therein the mediation of others, to draw him back. But when they saw they could not prevail by this means, they devised another, which they kept very secret under pretext of going to visit him and to be informed of his behaviour and of his new course of life. And after they saw what contentment he found in a religious life, as he accompanied them to the door they drew him by force out of the gates and carried him away with them. The porter hereupon began to cry, and the reverend father being advertised of this lewd action began to run after as a good shepherd does after a wolf which has taken away a lamb out of his fold. But seeing his pursuing to be to no purpose, and that if he should overtake them, he was not able to deliver him forth of their hands, then full of fervour of spirit and of a holy anger, he threatens them with the just judgement of God, saying that He would never leave such an enormous crime as this without some notable and exemplary punishment. A thing very strange and worthy of mark, that at that very time sentence was given from heaven and was very shortly after put into execution, to ratify the true prediction of this good father. For some few months after, this young gentleman, who could not be overcome with any sorts of promises, came back again to take the habit and a little after made his profession. Who told them that from the very time that he was thus taken away, his father began to grow sick, and impairing still in his health, died shortly after. This ought to terrify those which seek to draw all their children by all means from religion. And although many are not so punished in this world, yet ought they to assure themselves that they shall pay for it in another, if they do not satisfy for such heinous crimes by great and extraordinary penances. And principally if such children come to be debauched and lewd and lose their souls by occasion of worldly encumbrances in the way of virtue which leads to heaven. For if religious men have labour enough and much difficulty to save their souls, why should not secular men fear, who have souls of the same mould as they have? I will add another story for proof of this, which happened at the same time and in the same place.

A certain preacher Capuchin, born of one of the best and noblest families of Normandy, bore a singular respect to the piety of Father Benet and he likewise did singularly affect[1] him. One day as they conversed together and discoursed of death and of the state of souls, separated from the mass of corruptible flesh, they made a mutual pact one to the other that whichever should die first should advise the other of his estate, if God of His grace and mercy would permit it. This preacher died first, and two or three days after his burial, as this good father was in prayer in the choir before Matins, where he passed the most part of the night, he appeared unto him in that form and fashion which witnessed a great affliction. After matins he came again and every time he spoke only these words: *Multorum manibus grande levatur onus*: that is to say "A great burden is lightened by many men's hands"; and suddenly he vanished.

This good father, judging of his state by his words, could not forbear to shed tears, and redoubled the fervour of his prayers and for three days' space he caused all the priests to celebrate Mass for him and others to communicate after his intention. Which done this soul appeared no more, giving him thereby to understand that his pains were changed into eternal rest in heaven. This was the entertainment of this blessed father, who occupied himself wholly in prayer and contemplation, by which he was continually united to God his only object. And the virtue of poverty did dispose him the more unto it, which he fostered as his mother. For to pray well it is expedient to think of nothing but of God and this thought cannot be entire and perfect, unless our hearts be void and emptied from the affection of all earthly things. To this end he

---

[1] love

said right well that there were three sorts of poverty necessary for three sorts of prayers; vocal, meditation, and contemplation. The first is a poverty of affection proper to all Christians, which consists in not adhering to earthly things, but following the counsel of St. Paul to use them in possessing them as if we had them not. And those which are endowed with this spirit, say easily to their thoughts when they enter into the church: "Attend me at the gate", as St. Bernard did. The second is the poverty of profession, which belongs only to religious men who by their vow do deprive themselves of all things. And this being more high than the other, does greatly solace a soul and makes it more capable of meditation, lifting it up so much the more in this state, as it has less property or demesnes,[1] either in common or in private.

The third sort of poverty is yet more excellent than these two, which is a poverty of spirit, not as it is ordinarily taken, as that which deprives us of all inordinate affection to riches, but for as much it orders our affections touching spiritual and heavenly things, causing that the soul does not desire them for itself, nor for her particular profit, but only for the glory of God to whom it has given the heart, the thoughts, and all affections. And this stripping the soul perfectly of all spiritual and corporal things, of all desires which tend to her particular interest, is disposed by this manner to contemplation and by continual actions of love and charity kindles itself, yea and consumes itself, to transform itself and become united unto God which is the utmost degree of spiritual life.

Now it is easy to judge how this father was poor in these three kinds of poverties. His profession does sufficiently prove the two first, and his soul fastened to the cross, without intermission tasting the fruits, whereof he has left us the seed in his book *Of the Will of God*, does demonstrate the third. And from this union proceeds charity, yea, perfect charity cannot be without this union; and hence sprang the peace and tranquillity of all his desires within himself; a constant concord with his neighbour; wisdom, which is the first gift of the Holy Ghost, which does penetrate the mysteries of God; and affectionate mercy to comfort his neighbour in his necessity; promptness to God's service; the practice of good works;

---

[1] estates

and the soul, the life, and the merit of all virtues. So that to speak that briefly which I cannot particularize in a whole volume, this blessed father, being united to God, we may truly infer and conclude that passions did never trouble the peace which he did inwardly enjoy. That the salvation of his neighbour was as tender to him as his own. That he thought no time so well spent as when he could co-operate thereto in any manner. That his wisdom did sound the most secret mysteries. That his good works were inestimable and great, his affections great, his virtues great, and therefore his memory and his name ought to be great among men.

Besides these virtues which made him so acceptable in the sight of God, and his admirable actions in the eyes of the world, he had certain other graces or gifts which St. Paul recites as singular benefits of the Holy Ghost to those to whom they are imparted. There was nothing belonging to spiritual beauty whereof he had not some part and portion, and by his piety and zeal which he bore to God's service, he oftentimes did many things which may very well be deemed miraculous.

Being once sent to Les Andelys, there to remain, it happened as he came into the chapel, which is in the entry of the church, he espied that there was no picture upon the altar, whereat he was much moved. For let heretics say what they please out of their foolish malice, images are not only books of ignorant persons, but of more perfect men who find motives in them to devotion, which they would not have otherwise. Whereupon he asked Father Guardian what the cause was that their chapel was not better adorned? He answered him: "Father, we are so poor in this place that we know not how to beautify it or come by those convenient ornaments." Hereupon he willed him to provide some colours with which, although he knew not what belonged to painting, nor ever in his life had handled pencil, he made an image of Our Blessed Lady, in which are represented all the symbols and hieroglyphs which be required to exalt the virtues of the Queen of Heaven. And he so laid and disposed the colours that for the beauty thereof and for the devotion which it does excite in the hearts of those that do behold it, it was changed and put in the place of that image of the high altar where it yet remains to this present.

Of his extasies and rapts and of the graces which
he received in them

THE TWENTY-FIRST CHAPTER

IF I shall speak as it is meet of Father Benet and of his strait union
with Almighty God, of the force, of the perfection and of the
continuation thereof, I should not say that he had extasies or
ravishments, but that his whole life from three-and-twenty years
of age that he became a Capuchin was a continual rapt and perpetual extasy. Whensoever he was seen or wheresoever he was, he
had his spirit always lifted up to God, the sight of the base creature
made him to become engulfed in the knowledge of his Creator.
This was much noted in him that when any man spoke unto him
and asked him any matter, he must repeat the same thing twice
unto him, because his soul being otherwise preoccupied, did not
hear the first time; so that many had not been edified by his conversation, had they not known his great piety. For oftentimes he
spoke so short and so brokenly, as if he had wanted words to
express what he would say.

His extasies were judged for such by those, that being very
conversant in mystical divinity, found them to be truly supernatural. For they could not be soundings[1] as some might imagine,
for as much as a sounding, according to the opinion of Galen, the
prince of philosophers, is an interception of the sense by an
obstruction of the sinews, which takes away the pulse from the
arteries and does wholly deprive us of the use of reason. But so far
was this father from being deprived of knowledge and of the
function of the spirit with that of the sense, that on the contrary
part he was lifted up to God and received great illuminations
touching the illuminative life and assured way of perfection.
Soundings are natural and do follow a sudden failing of all the
forces of the body, which carry away with them those of the spirit,
but extasies are from God, which by a drawing of love attracts
souls to Him to make them taste those sweetnesses which they
could not otherwise.

[1] swoonings

When Father Benet therefore recited[1] those things of so high a nature, after these extasies whereof he now had knowledge before, who can presume to say that this was natural and that they were nothing else but soundings? For they arise from a great emptiness or privation of vital spirits which cannot pass to the place ordained by nature for the functions. But extasies on the contrary part proceed from a repletion or abundance of grace, which makes the soul conversant in heaven, being yet fastened to this mass of earth. So S. Peter in the 10th Chapter of the Acts, falling into extasy of spirit, saw a great sheet which came down from heaven, full of all sorts of unclean creatures, with a voice which said unto him: *Kill and eat.* So S. Paul reports of himself that he was rapt even to the third heaven and there saw things which the sense cannot comprehend. And S. John in the Apocalypse was first rapt in spirit on the Lord's day and saw so many marvellous things, which he recites, concerning the circumstances of the general judgement. So this holy father, being ravished in spirit and receiving the knowledge of that which he could not attain by great labour and painful study of many years, we cannot but judge necessarily that these were graces which he received from God in the sweetness of his extasies.

Whilst he was Guardian at Chartres he fell into a grievous sickness, which most men thought would have been his last. For the violence of the fever was so great that it could not be assuaged by any remedy; and he being but lately recovered from other former diseases, besides his austerities, he was become so weak and lean that he was nothing else but skin and bone, so that it was thought almost impossible that he could resist this brunt.[2] In this case he caused an image of Our Blessed Lady to be brought unto him, being singularly devout unto her, and caused it to be set at his bed's feet, that so he might the better behold it. But he was no sooner entered into contemplation, but that he fell into an extasy for the space of eighteen hours, all which time his senses were deprived of their functions and during this while he had no manner of feeling of his disease. Yea, some did cry in his ear but he did not hear them. His colour for this time was far more vermilion and cheerful than before, being more ruddy where before it was

[1] told of   [2] attack

more pale and wan. To conclude, he was in such a state, that both the physicians and some others who came to see him said there was nothing but his body there and that his soul was united to God in such a manner that they could not express nor well conceive. This then being said is a great argument of his sanctity which they had formerly believed, but that hereafter there was no cause to make the least doubt thereof. Eighteen hours after, he came to himself, seeming to be wakened out of a profound sleep, and presently, very cheerful and well disposed, he raised himself upon his bed as if he never had been sick. God did that in a moment which the physicians could not do in a long time. And who will now be so hardy as to affirm that this was rather a sounding than an extasy?

Another time, the zeal of the glory of God and salvation of souls, particularly of those which were infected with heresy, drew him forth into a village near Orleans, where there were many Huguenots. In all his sermons his first disposition to enter into so holy a work was fervent prayer, that he might lighten their dark understandings and mollify their obstinate and perverse wills. But at this time he was very long and very fervent in his prayer before he went to preach, so that his companion, turning his eye towards him, saw him compassed about with a light and lifted up more than two foot from the ground, absorbed in contemplation of the Divinity, which is the fountain of all learning and of all virtue, and from whom doubtlessly he drew all that which he was afterwards to speak, to conduct and guide the poor abused souls to God. So that it may be more rightly said of him, which Saint Thomas said of Saint Bonaventure: "Let us suffer," says he, "one saint to travail for another." Forasmuch as he did labour but for one which had been formerly a sinner; but Father Benet did labour for Jesus Christ, God and Man also, the fountain of all holiness and the spring of our glory. He was seen divers other times in extasies whilst, staying in the choir after others, he was intentive unto prayer. But I have reported this action more particularly because it was accompanied with the conversion of many who afterwards became devout and fervent Catholics, bearing so much the more true and earnest affection to God's Church as they bore hate and malice to it before.

Of his last sickness and his death

THE TWENTY-SECOND CHAPTER

IN the year of Our Lord One Thousand Six Hundred and Eleven died this blessed father Benet in the convent of the Capuchins of Our Blessed Lady, being at this time the ordinary confessor of the religious women of St. Clare, surnamed the Daughters of the Passion, of whom we have spoken in the life of the blessed Father Angel of Joyeuse, in the chapter of his transporting[1] to Paris. The graces which God did him during his life were augmented in this last passage of his death. His sickness was nothing in a manner but a continual extasy, in which he, being united to God, received great contentment in his soul, and in the superior part thereof, despite the exceeding great dolours of his body, and of the part inferior. His affections always resigned into the hands of God kept his will so occupied in the contemplation of the glory which he was shortly to enjoy, that by reason of a perfect contempt which he had of all earthly consolations, he would hardly be one to speak anything, desiring rather to speak with angels in the inward closet of his heart, than outwardly with men. Whereupon it came to pass that God by a particular grace, which He does not give but to the greatest saints, revealed to him the time, the day, and hour of his death, to the end he might dispose himself with the more fervour for the same and might omit nothing of that which might be most necessary for him in this last passage, whether interior, for charity and compunction, or exterior, for sacraments and prayers. For one of their fathers, an eminent man in this holy religion, visiting him the day after he was sick in bed, and coming to take his leave of him, because he was going to preach in the province of Touraine, asked of him if this should be his last sickness, for the separation of soul and body in yielding the one up to God and the other to the earth? This blessed father, lifting up his eyes to heaven and sending forth a groan to God said: "Yea, without all doubt." And this was also at that very time when discoursing of perfection, he told

[1] being moved

him things which cannot be learned but within the practice of a high contemplation.

Sometimes he was heard to speak within himself with a spirit wholly abstract and retired, but with so soft and low a voice and without any perfect distinct sound of words, that no man could understand what he spoke. In the secret colloquies a man might see as it were a certain light to stream from his face and I know not what kind of serenity, which drove others into admiration of Him who visited him. O, if they could but have heard and comprehended those discourses which his soul had with God privately, if they could have seen the things which he saw and have been made partakers of those mysteries which were revealed to him, how would they have been astonished? For if the outward show was so powerful, how forcible had the truth itself been? But as soon as this father took notice that something was observed in him which might betray his inward perfection, he retired his spirit as much as he could from this contemplation to the knowledge of his own infirmity, or else informed himself of somewhat that was imperfect in himself. Which when a brother of his perceived, who had known him a long time, he began to ask him if he had not some revelation of his future estate or of his life past? To whom he presently returned answer: "What, do you speak to me of revelations, who am the most miserable wretch under the cope of heaven?" And thus showed how much he was offended with such a question, which tended to his own praise and commendation. During his life he was singularly affected to speak of God and of things which help a soul to the pathway of heaven, but in his last sickness this desire had gained a great increase insomuch that he was very desirous to have a religious man still[1] about him, and endowed with the same spirit. For if any man would seem to say that he should by God's grace escape this sickness, he presently showed that such speeches were disgustful[2] to him.

He had a crucifix at his bed's feet, on which he continually fixed his eyes; and by the ordinary feeling of Our Saviour's dolours, whereof he was desirous to be partaker (as we have noted before) he gave free passage unto tears, not able to hold them any longer

[1] constantly   [2] distasteful

by reason of the tenderness of his love, and kissing the cross which he had in his hand, he sent forth many groans, shut his eyes and adored God in his soul, whom this figure did represent unto him and from whom he knew that salvation and all glory that he could hope for had their spring and their beginning. His disease was violent and his strength declining by little and little made men to know that the end of his pilgrimage was at hand.

The night before his death a good religious man who had a great care to serve him and not to forsake him, seeing him very quiet in spirit and of a cheerful countenance as though he had felt no kind of grief, asked him if now he would speak nothing drawing so near to his end, for the comfort of his brethren of whom he had so great care during his life? He made unto him this answer of an affection full of humility and a great abasing of himself: "Alas, miserable sinner that I am, what edification can I give and what good thing can the brethren hope for of me, who am the greatest sinner in the world?" And presently joining his hands and lifting up his eyes and heart to God, he added this versicle of the prophet David: *Pauper sum ego et in laboribus a juventute mea*, "I am poor and have lived in labours from my youth".

The day being come wherein he was to render up his soul to God, he would, like a true Christian warrior, and singularly of the company of St. Francis, arm himself with complete armour for this encounter. The Most Holy Sacrament was brought unto him and presently afterwards extreme unction was ministered unto him. And all the brethren being assembled, could not possibly refrain to weep, not only for the loss of so holy and zealous a man of their religion, but seeing the effects of his profound humility, accusing himself before them all as an ungrateful man, saying that he had never given them good example, and demanding pardon of them with such contrition as cannot be conceived or expressed.

A little while after he had received the sacraments and given thanks unto God for so great a benefit, he asked them saying: "Is not this the day of the Presentation of Our Blessed Lady?" And when it was told him that it was, he began to cry out with a loud voice: "O virgin which ...", and presently stopped, finishing the rest with inward words full of affection, which is more proper and common to holy men than the vocal and exterior. One of the fathers who spoke to him concerning spiritual matters, as they are accustomed to do in such cases, demanded of him if he were not content and glad in his soul that he was so near to his deliverance out of the misery of this life, and now ready to arrive in heaven, there to live eternally, not a dying life as this which we lead, but a quickening life full of glory and felicity, where he should see their seraphical father S. Francis and the soul of the Blessed Father Angel,[1] where he should converse with them and sing with them forever canticles of praises unto God, beholding no more in a glass and through the shadow of faith only, but face to face in an angelical manner? He answered only this: "That is it whereon I now do meditate." He was asked likewise if he would not yet confess again, seeing there is no man so just who does not often fall. To which he replied with the words of the Apostle: "I am guilty to myself of nothing, but yet in this I am not justified." By his short answers he made it appear that he had his spirit well occupied, wherefore he was left a while unto himself in his meditation, having his eyes always beholding and fastened upon the holy crucifix which was standing at his bed's feet.

About half an hour after, he desired them to call for Father Guardian,[2] "for," quoth he, "it is now time." This good father, sick of a violent fever, felt inwardly the greater grief that he could not assist this blessed father at his departure, than he did by the extremity of his disease. For besides that they were both of the same country and had borne one to the other a very particular and fervent affection, from the time that they first met in Flanders, having forsaken their parents and friends, and had both of them the same design and at the same time had both taken the habit together and received great consolation by their mutual conversation. Notwithstanding, hearing that he desired to see him, he went from his chamber, not without much pain, being very sick, and they entertained one the other in spiritual and good discourses. The violence of Father Guardian's fever would not suffer him to stay any longer, so that he was forced to retire himself and to take

[1] Fr. Angel de Joyeuse.
[2] Fr. Archangel Herbert of Pembroke, who had been a novice with him at Paris.

his last farewell of him with his benediction, which he gave him not without many tears.

His Guardian being gone he turned himself to the religious who were present and besought them to pray fervently for him. "For behold," says he, and presently stopped. And as one of the fathers was about to say that they were not worthy to pray for him, but that they were in good hope that he would pray for them, "Ah," said he, "recite some prayers to the honour of the Blessed Virgin and of S. Michael, for as much as there is no spirit so strong but that it may faint." This made them conjecture that he saw something, and that the devil, who during his life could not inveigle him, did now attempt for to wound him. Wherefore, some of the religious praying and one of them reading, he had not read a dozen lines but the blessed father said: "It suffices," which made them presently believe that the temptation was past and the enemy vanquished. For presently he lay very quiet and seemed to be as profoundly occupied in contemplation, as if he had been in one of his extasies, which he had in his best strength. O how ought the wicked to fear death, when such virtuous men are persecuted in such manner! Would to God they would reflect seriously hereon, once at the least in all their lives.

The time drawing on that he was to depart, he turned his eyes upon those that did assist him and asked them what it was o'clock. And it being answered him that it was five o'clock, then said he: "Say no more to me now, but *Jesus, Maria*; now pray ye all for me." Whosoever had seen at that time the poor Capuchins (but rich in heavenly graces) on their knees, their arms spread in form of a Cross, their eyes lifted up to heaven, watering their cheeks with tears, now redoubling the fervour of their prayers and provoking the choirs of angels and all the blessed saints to come and receive this blessed soul, he would doubtlessly have said that one moment in the desert of religion brings more true contentment to a soul than a hundred years in the fair open fields of this miserable world. And to see so many devout souls to pray for a holy soul, who whilst the priest did pronounce without interruption those holy and sacred names of Jesus and Mary, augmenting the fire of his charity and not able to suppress it any longer, broke out into these words with a strange violence: "O wonderful, O incomprehensible abyss of the love of God!"

This said, instantly his spirit failed him all at once, and lifting up his eyes to heaven, he entered as it were into a ravishment where his soul, finding true contentment and the centre of her sweet rest, departed so sweetly that he seemed rather to sleep than to die. And so it was a sweet sleep of peace in the vision of his God, a sleep of glory and fruition of his Creator. Yea, such a sleep it was that every Catholic Christian may desire and say that which Balaam, constrained by the spirit of God, said: *Moriatur anima mea morte justorum.* "Let my soul die the death of the just." So be it.

INDEX

INDEX*

ACARIE, Mme., xxv, xxv *n.*, xxix *n.*

Alençon, Ubald d', xx *n.*

Allison, A. F., vii *n.* 2

Alphonsus, Fr., 60

Angers, siege of, xi

Autobiography (of Benet Canfield), xxii, xxiii, xxiv

BARONIUS, Cardinal, 49

Batarnay, Marie de, mother of Ange de Joyeuse. See under Joyeuse, Marie de

Bellarmine, Cardinal, 49

Birkhead, Fr. George, xxvii *n.*

Bitonto (Bitote), Antonius de, 56, 56 *n.*1

Bolton, Fr. Benedict of, xxiii *n.*

Bourbon, Cardinal Charles de, ix, xiii, 20 *n.*

Bourbon, Henri de, Duke of Montpensier (son-in-law of Ange de Joyeuse), xviii, 5, 53, 58, 59, 69, 69 *n.* 2, 86

Bourbon, Marie de, Mademoiselle de Montpensier (daughter of above), 53, 72

Bouchage, Count of: title of Ange (Henri) de Joyeuse

Bremond, Abbé, xxviii

Brossier, Marthe, xviii, xx, xxv, xxvi, 147 *n.* 1

Brousse, Jacques, vii, vii *n.* 1, viii, xxi, 26 *n.*, 87 *n.*, 131 *n.* 2, 147 *n.* 1 149 *n.*

Bunny, Edward, xxii, 98 *n.* 2

Bunyan, xxiii, xxiv, xxviii, xxx *n.* 3

CAILLERE, J. de, viii

Camerino, Fr. Julian of, 40, 40 *n.*, 133, 133 *n.* 4

Campbell, Fr. John Chrysostom, xxvi, 147, 147 *n.* 3, 148 *n.*, 149 *n.*, 152

Canfield, Benet of (William Fitch). Life, 87–175, *passim*. Other mentions, vii, viii, xviii, xix, xxi
- family of, xxii, 89
- birth, 89
- brought up as Protestant, 87–9
- enters Inns of Court, xxii, 89, 89 *n.* 2
- first vision, 103–5: explanation of this vision, 123–4
- conference with Catholic (over religion), 105–8
- conference with Puritan, 108–10
- spiritual temptations, 110–13
- received into Church, xxiii, 115
- goes to France, xxiii, 117
- enters Capuchin Order, xxiii, 122–4, 132–4
- novitiate, xxv, 133–8
- profession, xxv, 138
- studies in Venice, xxv
- master of novices, xxv, 156–7
- appointed Definitor, xxv
- his extasies, 121, 136–7, 167–9
- his learning, 143–6
- involved in Marthe Brossier case, xxv, xxvi
- goes to England, xxv, xxvi, 147–8
- arrested in England, xxvi, 148–9
- imprisonment, xxvi–xxvii, 149–56
- banished to France, xxvii, 155, 155 *n.* 1, 156
- dies, xxvii, 170–5
- See also under his writings: *Autobiography, Chevalier Chrestien, Rule of Perfection, Of the Will of God*

* Note: responsibility for the compilation of this index rests with the publishers.

Capuchins, vii *n*. I, ix, x, xi, xvi,
xviii, xx, 20, 20 *n*., 21, 22, 38, 44,
45, 55, 63, 84, 122, 123, 124, 131,
132, 133, 134, 151, 151 *n*., 154, 174
Caraman, P., S.J., xxii *n*. 2
Castelferretti, Fr. Jerome of (Hierome
du Castferet), 136, 136 *n*.
Cecil, Robert, xxvi, 150, 151
Challoner, R., xxiii *n*.
Charke, William, 92, 92 *n*.
Chevalier Chrestien, Le, xxvii, 140,
140 *n*.
Clarisses, *see* Daughters of the Passion
Clement VIII, Pope, xv, xvi, xvii, 49,
51-2, 57, 57 *n*., 147
Cloud of Unknowing, The, xxx, xxx *n*. I
Cobham, Baron Henry, xxvi, 149,
149 *n*.
Condé, xi
Cordeliers, 13, 122-4, 131, 132
Coutras, Battle of, xii, 8, 10, 37
Cowper, J. M., xxx *n*. 2
Cressy, Dom Serenius, xxx *n*. 6
Crowley, Robert, xxx, xxx *n*. 2
Cruppi, Jean, xxxii
Cuthbert, Fr., O.F.M. Cap., xxxii
Cutts (Cuts), Sir John, 154, 154 *n*. 2

Daughters of the Passion (Clarisses),
xxi, 83, 170
Dalrymple, Sir David, xi *n*. I
Darbyshire, Fr. Robert, xxiii, xxvi,
115, 115 *n*. 2
Dominicans, xx
Dreux, Fr. Pierre Besson de, 123, 123
n. 2
Duplessis-Mornay, xviii *n*. 2
Dupuis, Fr. Archange, xviii, xviii *n*. 2,
xix, 54, 54 *n*., 56, 58, 58 *n*. 2, 61,
61 *n*.
Duval, Dr. André, xviii–xix

Edict of Nantes, xix
Edwards, Peter, viii, 131, 131 *n*. 2
Elizabeth I, 149, 150, 151, 152
Epernon, Duke of, xi, 17, 59, 84–85
exclaustration (of Ange de Joyeuse),
xv, 51-2

Fitch, Anne (mother of Benet Canfield), xxii
Fitch, William (name of Benet Canfield in the world), xxii, 89
Fitch, William (father of Benet Canfield, xxii
Fitzherbert, Fr. Francis, xxiii *n*.
Folembray, Treaty of, xvii
Framlingham Castle, xxvii, 155, 155
n. 3
Francis, St., 20, 21, 31, 32, 45, 55, 56,
65, 68, 75, 76, 122, 123, 131, 132,
136, 137, 160, 162, 172, 173
Furley, Benjamin, xxx, xxx *n*. 6,
xxxi *n*.

Gatehouse (prison), xxii, xxiii, xxvi
General Chapter (attended by Ange
de Joyeuse), xx, 69–73
Gerard, John, S.J., xxii, xxii *n*. 2
Gondi, Cardinal de, xvi, 83
Gonzague, Fr. Louis de, O.F.M.
Cap., xxxii, 12 *n*. I
Guise, Cardinal of, xiii
Guise, Henri de, xii, xiii
Guise, Duchess of; see Joyeuse,
Henriette-Catherine de
Guise, Duke of (son-in-law of Ange
de Joyeuse), 5
Guyon, Jean, xi, 15

Hamilton, John, xi
Hendriks, L., 115 *n*. 2
Henri III, ix, x, xi, xii, xiii, xxi, 4, 5,
8, 16, 17, 21, 24, 26, 33, 34, 35, 38, 53
Henri IV (Henri of Navarre), xiii,
xvi, xvii, xviii, xix, xx, xxi, xxvii,
8, 9, 51, 53, 57, 59, 69, 84, 123 *n*. 2,
151, 151 *n*., 155
Heton (Eaton), Dr. Martin, Bishop
of Ely, 154, 154 *n*. I, 155
Hilton, Walter, xxx *n*. 6
Hooker, Richard, xxiv
Hosque, Fr. Robert de la, 12, 14
Huguenots, ix, x, xiii, xviii *n*. 2, xix, xx,
xxi, xxvii, 46, 169
Huxley, Aldous, viii, xxviii

IGNACE, Fr., S.J., 55

JANSENISTS, vii *n.* 1
Jesuits, xx, xxvii *n.*, 9, 55
Jones, Rufus M., xxx *n.* 5
Joyeuse, Ange de, Life, *passim.*
  General mentions, vii–xxi, xxv,
    xxvi, 170, 173
  – birth of, x, 11
  – father of, x, xiii, xvi, 5, 8
  – mother of, x, 5, 6, 7, 8, 36, 52
  – brothers of; see Joyeuse, Anne de,
    Antoine-Scipio de, Claude de,
    François de
  – early education of, 11
  – enters College of Navarre, x, xi, 15
  – goes to Court, xi
  – appointed Grand Master of the
    Royal Wardrobe, xi, 16
  – marries, xi, 17
  – married life, 17–20, 21, 22
  – takes Angers, xi
  – appointed Governor of Touraine,
    Maine and Perche, xi
  – birth of daughter, xi
  – death of wife, xi, 22
  – enters Capuchin Order, xi, 26,
    29–31
  – his "Farewell" on entering reli-
    gion, 26–9
  – novitiate, xii, 33–40
  – profession, xii, 41–5
  – sent to Italy, xiii, 44, 44 *n.*
  – ordained, xiii, 44 *n.*
  – appointed Guardian at Toulouse,
    46
  – leaves cloister on public appeal,
    xiii–xiv, 47–51
  – appointed Governor of Languedoc,
    xiv–xv, 51–3
  – exclaustration, xv, 51–2
  – joins Order of Malta, xv, 52
  – negotiates truce, xvii
  – breaks truce, xvii
  – reconciled to Henri IV, xvii
  – created Marshal of France, xvii, 53
  – marriage of daughter, xviii, 53
  – re-enters Capuchins, xviii, 53–60

  – involved in Marthe Brossier case,
    xviii–xix, xx
  – as preacher, xxi, 64–9
  – methods of study, 62, 63, 66
  – elected Provincial, xx, 69, 69 *n.* 2
  – elected General Definitor, 69
  – journey to Rome, 69–70
  – attends General Chapter, 70–2
  – returns from Rome, 73–5
  – last illness, 75–81
  – death, 81–2
  – transference of body to Paris, 82–5
  – funeral, 85
  – epitaph, 85–6
Joyeuse, Anne de (brother of Ange),
  Baron d'Arques, x, xi, xii, 4, 8, 37
  – Antoine-Scipio de (brother of
    Ange), x, xii, xiii, xiv, xvi, 10, 46
  – Catherine de (wife of Ange), xi,
    17–20, 21, 22
  – Claude de (brother of Ange), x,
    xii, 10, 37
  – François (Cardinal) de (brother of
    Ange), x, xi, xiii, xiv, xv, xv *n.*,
    xvi, xvii, 9, 44 *n.*, 47, 50, 82, 84
  – Henriette-Catherine de (daughter:
    became, first, Duchess of Mont-
    pensier, and later the Duchess of
    Guise), xi, xviii, 4–5, 9, 22, 26,
    58, 59, 77, 82, 83, 84, 85, 86
  – Marie de (born Marie de Batarnay,
    mother of Ange), x, 5–8, 36, 52
  – William de (father of Ange), x,
    xiii, xvi, 5, 8
Juliana of Norwich, xxx *n.* 6

LANGLAND, xxviii, xxx
Languedoc, x, xiii, xvi, xvii, 5, 10, 51
Lavalette, Catherine de, wife of Henri
  (Ange) de Joyeuse. See Joyeuse,
  Catherine de
Law, T. G., xxvii, 155 *n.* 4
League, the, ix, xii, xiii, xvi, xvii, xx.
  See Wars of the League
Lorraine, Cardinal of, 20, 20 *n.*

MALTA, Order of, xv, xvi, xviii, 52, 54

Maran, William of, xv
Martin (tutor to Ange de Joyeuse), 11
Mayenne, Duke of, xv, xv *n.*, xvi
Médicis, Catherine de, ix
– Marie de, xx
Memoirs of Missionary Priests, xxiii *n.*
Moffat, Fr. James, S.J., 147 *n.* 3
Montmorency, Marshal de, 11, 51, 51 *n.*
Montpensier: *see* Bourbon, Henri de, Duke of Montpensier: and Bourbon, Marie de, Mademoiselle de Montpensier

NAVARRE, College of, x–xi, 15
Navarre, Henri of; *see* Henri IV
Newgate, 115
Nugent, Fr. Francis, 147 *n.* 3

OF the Will of God, 165
Ogilvy, Bl. John, S.J., 147 *n.* 3
Optatus van Veghel, Fr.; *see* Veghel
Osimo, Bernard d' (Capuchin Provincial), ix, xiii, 30, 30 *n.*, 33, 41, 34, 137, 137 *n.*
Owst, G. R., xxx *n.* 3

PARIS, Fr. Agathange de, xiv, xv *n.* 1, xxxii
– Godefroy de, xxxii, 20 *n.*
– Honoré de, xxv
– Léonard de, xxv
Parlement (of Paris), xviii, xix, xx
Parsons, Fr. Robert, S.J., xxii, xxx *n.* 6, 98 *n.* 2
Passau, Treaty of, xix *n.*
Pembroke, Fr. Archangel of, xxiii *n.*, xxv, 77, 77 *n.*, 173, 173 *n.* 2
Poiret, Pierre, xxxi *n.*
Polizzi, Fr. Jerome of (Father Policius), 58, 58 *n.* 1
Powerscourt, Lord, 155 *n.* 4
Puritans, xxiv, xxv, xxx, 87, 92 *n.*, 108–110

QUAKERS, xxx, xxx *n.* 5, xxxi

RANDALL, Giles, xxx, xxx *n.* 5, xxxi *n.*
Real Presence, xxiii, xxiv, 109–110
Rebelliau, A., xxviii *n.* 1
Redman, William, 155, 155 *n.* 2
Recusants, viii, xxvi, xxvii
Reel, Fr. Cassian J., O.F.M. Cap., xxxii
Renold, P., xxvii
Reusch, F. H., xxviii *n.* 2
Rookwood, Robert, vii, vii *n.* 2, viii
Rue S. Honoré, Capuchins of, xii, xviii, xix, xxiii, xxv, 20, 59, 83
Rule of Perfection, xxv, xxvii, xxviii, xxix–xxx, xxx *n.* 6, xxxi *n.*, 90 *n.* 1 (*Reigle de Perfection*), 145, 145 *n.*

SAVOY, Grand Duke of, 74, 75, 80, 82, 83
Screwtape Letters, The, xxviii
Seraphin, Fr., xviii
Sheppard, L. C., xxv *n.*, xxxii
Sillery, Fr. Brûlard de, xix, xx
– Nicolas Brûlard de, xx
Sixtus V, Pope, xiii, 123, 123 *n.* 1
Sorbo, Fr. Jerome of (General of Capuchins), 56, 56 *n.* 2, 57, 58, 64
Sorbonne, xix, 146
Sourdis, Madeleine de, Abbess, xxvii
Suckling, A., 155 *n.* 4

TERRASSE, Sieur de la, 57 *n.*
Tierney, M. A., xxvii *n.*
Toulouse, x, xiii, xiv, xv, xvi, xvii, 13, 14, 46, 49, 52, 54, 56
Tower of London, xxvi, 147 *n.* 3, 149 *n.*, 151

VAISSIERE, P. de la, xxxii
Valois, Marguerite de, xx
Veghel, Fr. Optatus van, O.F.M. Cap., xxii *n.* 1, xxxii, 123 *n.* 2
Ventadour, General, xvii
Vic, de, xvii
Villemur, Battle of, xiii, 10, 46

WALTON, Christopher, xxxi *n.*
Watkin, E. I., xxx *n.* 4
Wars of the League, viii, ix
Weston, Fr. William, S.J., 107, 107 *n.*

Wingfield, Sir Anthony, 155, 155 *n.* 4
Wisbech Castle, xxvi, xxvii, 149, 152, 153, 154, 155, 155 *n.* 3
Wiseman, Jane, xxii